P9-CAN-072

BART SIMPSON'S TREEHOUSE OF HORROR
SPINE-TINGLING
SPOOKTACULAR

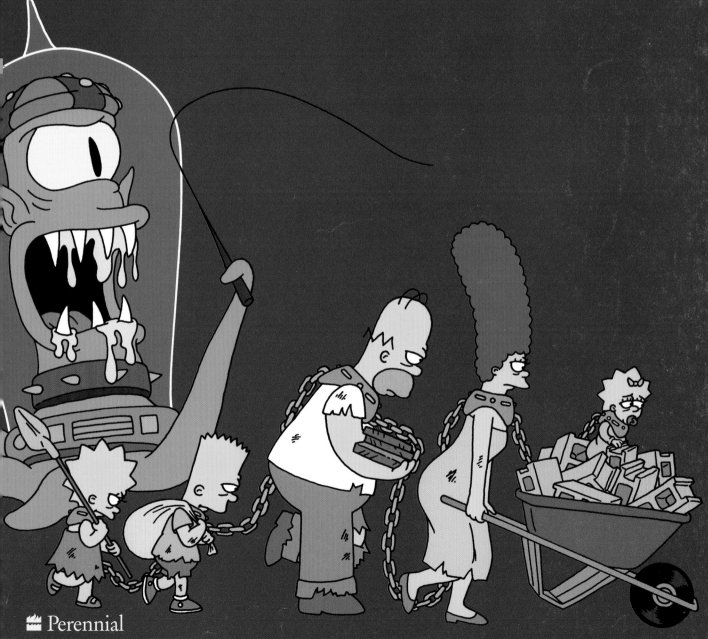

Perennial

An Imprint of HarperCollinsPublishers

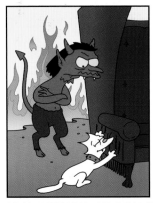

IN LOVING MEMORY OF SNOWBALL I:
YOU ALWAYS MADE OUR FURNITURE LOOK LIKE HELL.

THE SIMPSONS™, created by Matt Groening, is the copyrighted and trademarked property of
Twentieth Century Fox Film Corporation. Used with permission. All rights reserved.

BART SIMPSON'S TREEHOUSE OF HORROR SPINE-TINGLING SPOOKTACULAR.
Copyright © 1998, 1999, 2000, 2001 by Bongo Entertainment, Inc. and Matt Groening Productions, Inc. All rights reserved.
Printed in the United States of America. No part of this book may be used or reproduced in any manner whatsoever without
written permission except in the case of brief quotations embodied in critical articles and reviews.
For information address HarperCollins Publishers Inc.,
10 East 53rd Street, New York, NY 10022.

HarperCollins books may be purchased for educational, business, or sales promotional use.
For information please write: Special Markets Department, HarperCollins Publishers Inc.,
10 East 53rd Street, New York, NY 10022.

First Edition

ISBN 0-06-093714-9

01 02 03 04 05 RRD 10 9 8 7 6 5 4 3 2 1

Publisher
Matt Groening

Creative Director
Bill Morrison

Managing Editor
Terry Delegeane

Art Director
Nathan Kane

Director of Operations
Robert Zaugh

Production Manager
Christopher Ungar

Production/Design
Karen Bates, Arturo Villanueva

Production Assistance
Chia-Hsien Jason Ho, Mike Rote

Editorial Assistance
Eric Rogers, Sherri Smith

Legal Guardian
Susan A. Grode

Contributing Writers
Neil Alsip, Sergio Aragones, Chuck Dixon, Peter Kuper, Batton Lash, Bill Morrison, Scott Shaw!, Doug TenNapel, Jill Thompson

Contributing Artists
Sergio Aragones, Karen Bates, Tim Bavington, Jeannine Black, Geof Darrow, Dan DeCarlo, Chia-Hsien Jason Ho,
Nathan Kane, Peter Kuper, Christianna Lang, Batton Lash, Oscar González Loyo, Istvan Majoros, Scott McRae,
Bill Morrison, Robert Oliver, Phil Ortiz, Julius Preite, Chris Roman, Michael Rote, Horacio Sandoval, Robert Allen Smith,
Steve Steere, Jr., Doug TenNapel, Christopher Ungar, Arturo Villanueva

HarperCollins Editors
Susan Weinberg, Kate Travers

Special thanks to:
Pete Benson, Serban Cristescu, Claudia De La Roca, N. Vyolet Diaz, Evan Dwin,
Deanna MacLellan, Mili Smythe, and Ursula Wendel

TABLE OF CONTENTS

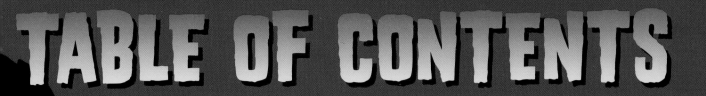

APPLAUSE
RIGELIAN
MARINATION UNIT 7000™

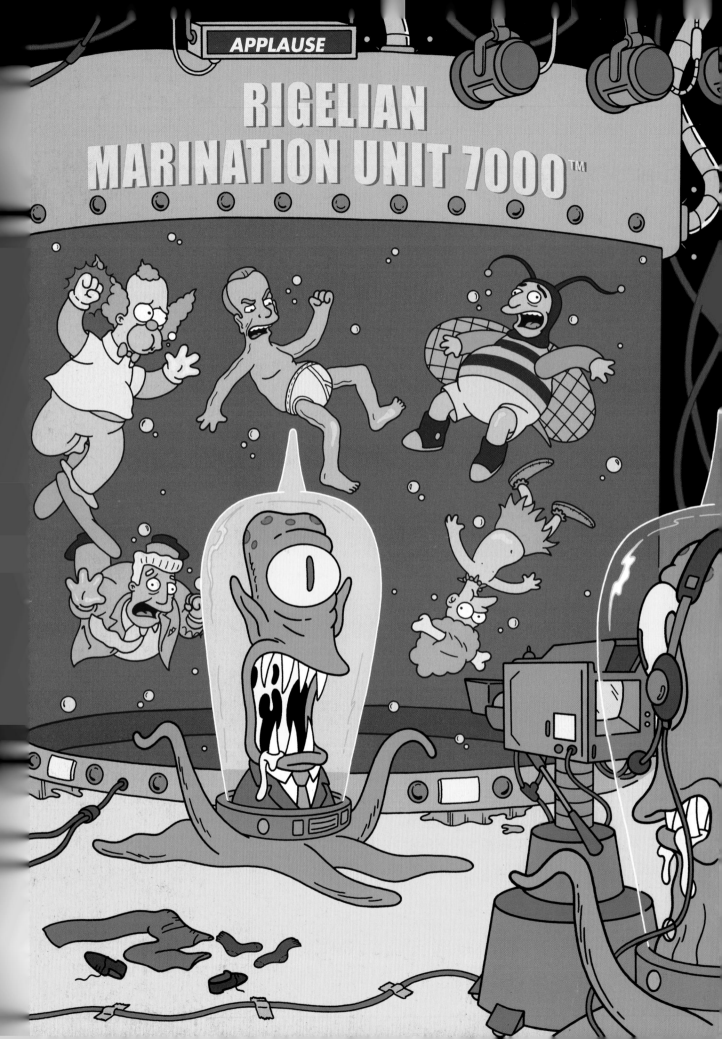

GREETINGS, FELLOW EARTHLINGS!

I am the one you call "Rupert Murdoch," supreme commander of the FOX television device delivery system, and this is my sister, Kodos... Murdoch. We thank you for your purchase and, needless to say, our pleasure glands are vibrating. But we also understand you have made a horrible error. For what you have purchased is NOT a television device. It is called a "non-television device"... or "book." I understand your confusion. Both are shiny, non-stick, and provide insufficient defense against a Rigelian Brain Torpedo. But here the similarity ends! Books are tiny, voiceless, paper-cut dispensers that strain the eyeballs. And you know what they say about strained eyeballs... NOT TASTY! Perhaps your soft cerebral cortex needs more convincing...

Commence anecdote. I recall my youth back on my home planet of... "Australia." It was the fifth celebration of my hatching and I asked my male parental unit for the gift I most desired, a book. My male parental unit looked at me with a serious look in his eye and said, "Who let you out of the sulfur mines?" Anecdote complete.

Now you understand why we do not want you to read this book. But why do we want you to watch television? Is it just because your television device is the only way to send a hypnosis ray strong enough to turn your human central nervous system to a savory jelly? Yes. DISREGARD THE LAST STATEMENT!

I shall announce, "Hooray for television and its edu-infotainment!" For it is television that asks the difficult questions such as "Who squeezed the Charmin?," "Where is the Beef?" and "Who can turn the world on with her smile?"* And television is most important for the growth of human juveniles. As the popular saying explains: "Give a human a book and he will read for a day. But give a human a television device, and he will NEVER READ AGAIN!"

This is why you should have purchased a television device. But fear not! Kodos and I have scattered throughout this book several human advertisements, or "mind traps", to remind you of what wonderful brain-jellying programs await when you finally give in to the all-powerful talking screen.

So read this book if you must. And, hopefully, it will cause you to laugh, for your Earth-saying is true, "Laughter is the best medicine... since any other medicine taints the meat."

END COMMUNICATION,

The One Known as Rupert Murdoch

*The answer, of course, is Smiletor, the plasma beast from Galliron Sector 3. FEAR HER!

A GUIDED TOUR OF MARGE'S HALLOWEEN HAIR!

SO YOU WANT TO SEE WHAT I KEEP IN MY HAIR DURING HALLOWEEN? OKAY, BUT WIPE YOUR FEET!
"REFLECTIVE TAPE: TO BE SAFELY VISIBLE TO CARS AND LOW-FLYING PLANES."
"101 POLITICALLY CORRECT, NON-VIOLENT, MILDLY DISCOMFORTING GHOST STORIES."
101 POLITICALLY CORRECT
"SUGAR-FREE CANDY: FOR THE CHILDREN WHO ARE...HRRMMM... SURPRISINGLY STOUT."
I Can't Believe It's Not Candy!
"BART'S 'LI'L GENERAL DEMOLITIONS KIT': HE'LL GET THIS BACK AFTER THE HOLIDAYS."
LI'L GENER DEMOLITION
"STEREO SYSTEM: SCARY MUSIC FOR THEM, CELINE DION FOR ME."
"ANTACIDS: FOR WHEN LISA EATS TOO MUCH CANDY...OR HOMER EATS THE EGGS OFF THE FRONT OF OUR HOUSE."
"SPARE PANTS FOR BART: IN CASE I CATCH HIM TRYING TO GO TRICK OR TREATING AS THE 'NAKED PIRATE' AGAIN."
$50
"EASTER CANDY: OKAY, IT'S BEEN THERE A WHILE, BUT THE KIDS STILL HAVEN'T FOUND IT."
"BAIL MONEY: IN CASE HOMER DECIDES TO GO AS THE 'NAKED PIRATE'."
"HUMAN HAND!!!!!: (OF MY SON AS HE TRIES TO FIND THE EASTER CANDY.)"
"CRYSTAL BALL: FOR KEEPING TRACK OF KIDS. THANKS TO THE GOOD PEOPLE AT RADIO SHACK."
"LEPRECHAUN: I KNOW IT'S THE WRONG HOLIDAY, BUT LET'S FACE IT, THEY'RE EVERYWHERE!"
"GRAMPA'S TEETH IN BOBBING APPLE: THAT WAS AN AWKWARD MOMENT FOR EVERYONE."
"ASSORTED HALLOWEEN PACIFIERS FOR MAGGIE: HRRMMM...SHE SEEMS TO LIKE THE HUMAN SKULL THE BEST."
"EYE OF NEWT: JUST THE EYE. LET'S NOT GO CRAZY!"
"BAT-B-GONE: YOU THINK IT'S TOUGH HAVING DANDRUFF, TRY HAVING BATS!"
BAT -B- GONE
"JACQUES' BOWLING GLOVE: BUT REALLY, I'M OVER HIM."
Jacques

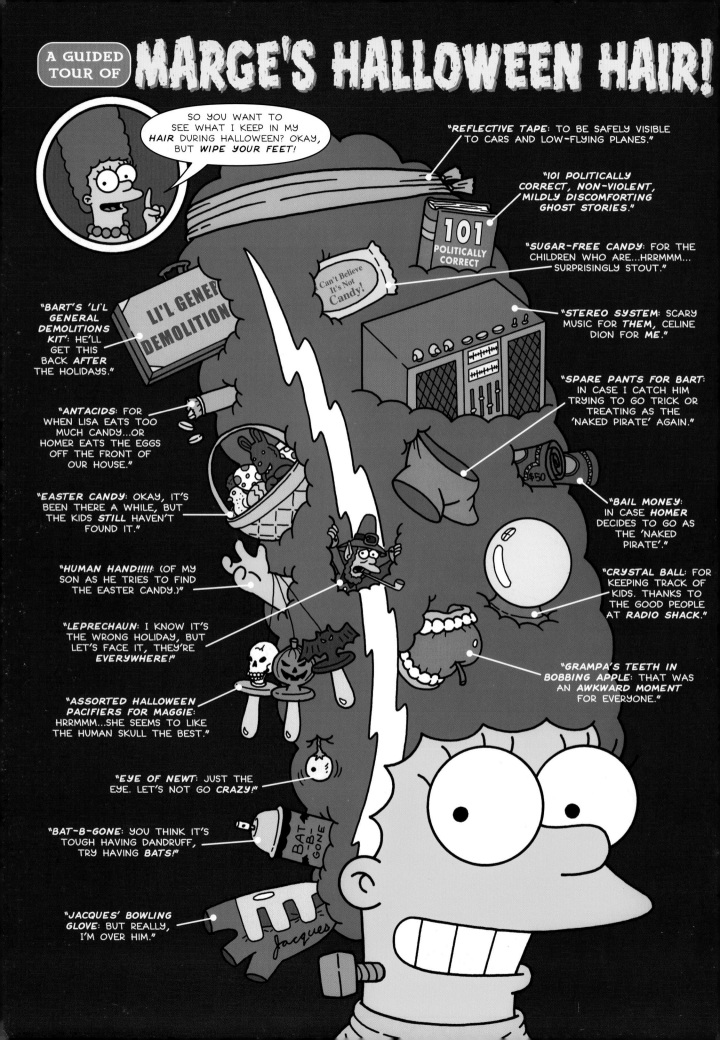

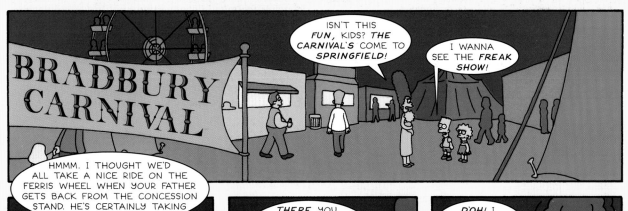

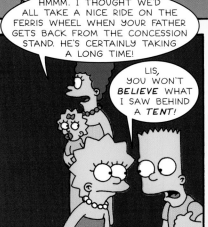

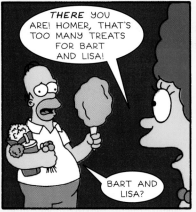

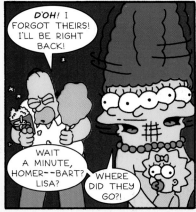

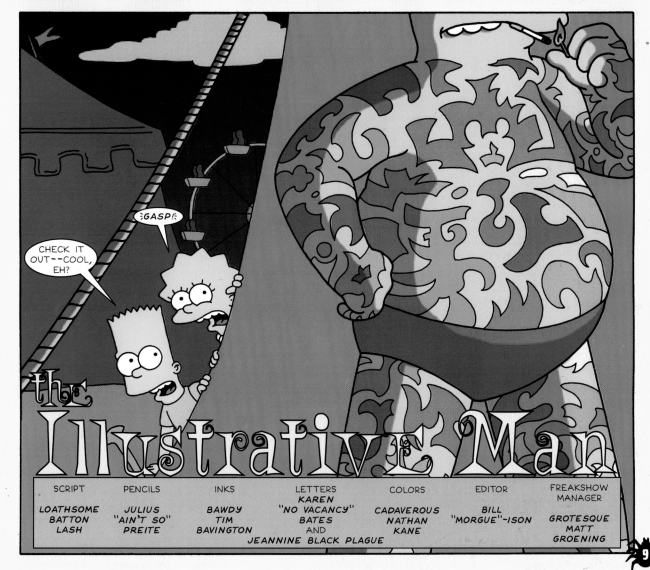

the Illustrative Man

SCRIPT	PENCILS	INKS	LETTERS	COLORS	EDITOR	FREAKSHOW MANAGER
LOATHSOME BATTON LASH	JULIUS "AIN'T SO" PREITE	BAWDY TIM BAVINGTON	KAREN "NO VACANCY" BATES AND JEANNINE BLACK PLAGUE	CADAVEROUS NATHAN KANE	BILL "MORGUE"-ISON	GROTESQUE MATT GROENING

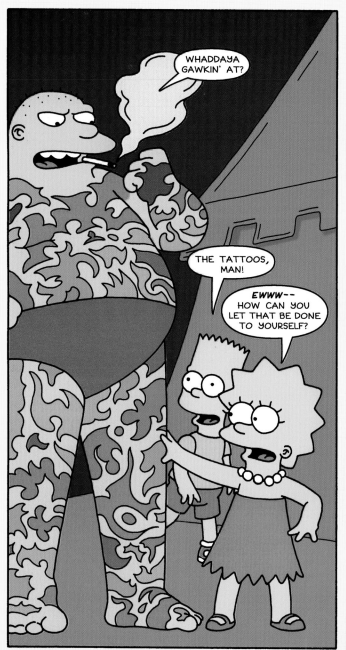

WHADDAYA GAWKIN' AT?

THE TATTOOS, MAN!

EWWW-- HOW CAN YOU LET THAT BE DONE TO YOURSELF?

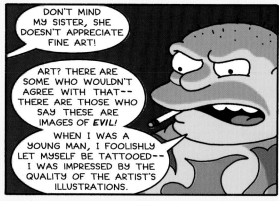

DON'T MIND MY SISTER, SHE DOESN'T APPRECIATE FINE ART!

ART? THERE ARE SOME WHO WOULDN'T AGREE WITH THAT-- THERE ARE THOSE WHO SAY THESE ARE IMAGES OF *EVIL!* WHEN I WAS A YOUNG MAN, I FOOLISHLY LET MYSELF BE TATTOOED-- I WAS IMPRESSED BY THE QUALITY OF THE ARTIST'S ILLUSTRATIONS.

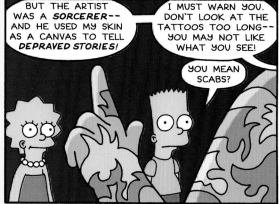

BUT THE ARTIST WAS A *SORCERER*-- AND HE USED MY SKIN AS A CANVAS TO TELL *DEPRAVED STORIES!*

I MUST WARN YOU. DON'T LOOK AT THE TATTOOS TOO LONG-- YOU MAY NOT LIKE WHAT YOU SEE!

YOU MEAN SCABS?

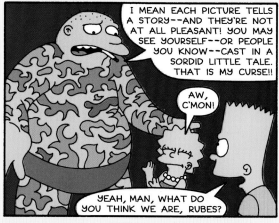

I MEAN EACH PICTURE TELLS A STORY--AND THEY'RE NOT AT ALL PLEASANT! YOU MAY SEE YOURSELF--OR PEOPLE YOU KNOW--CAST IN A SORDID LITTLE TALE. THAT IS MY CURSE!!

AW, C'MON!

YEAH, MAN, WHAT DO YOU THINK WE ARE, RUBES?

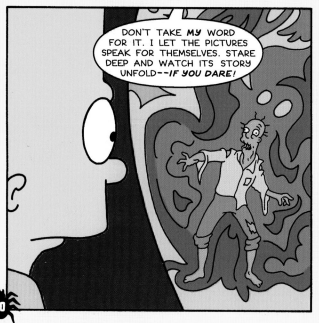

DON'T TAKE *MY* WORD FOR IT. I LET THE PICTURES SPEAK FOR THEMSELVES. STARE DEEP AND WATCH ITS STORY UNFOLD--*IF YOU DARE!*

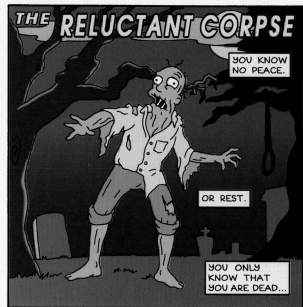

THE RELUCTANT CORPSE

YOU KNOW NO PEACE.

OR REST.

YOU ONLY KNOW THAT YOU ARE DEAD...

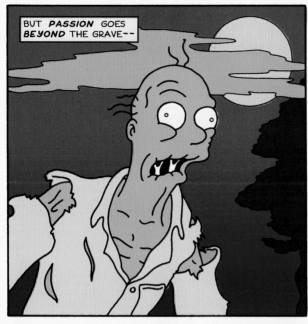

BUT *PASSION* GOES *BEYOND* THE GRAVE--

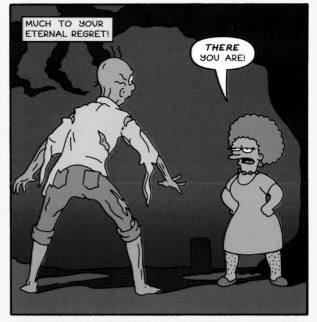

MUCH TO YOUR ETERNAL REGRET!

THERE YOU ARE!

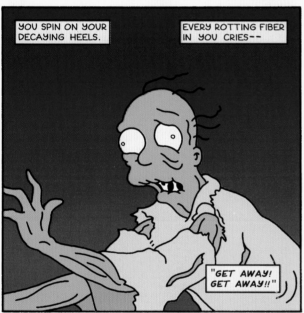

YOU SPIN ON YOUR DECAYING HEELS.

EVERY ROTTING FIBER IN YOU CRIES--

"*GET AWAY!* *GET AWAY!!*"

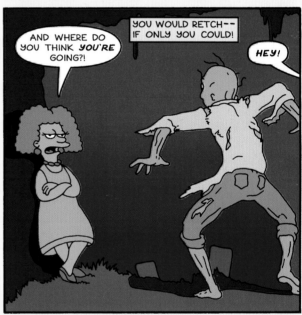

AND WHERE DO YOU THINK *YOU'RE* GOING?!

YOU WOULD RETCH-- IF ONLY YOU COULD!

HEY!

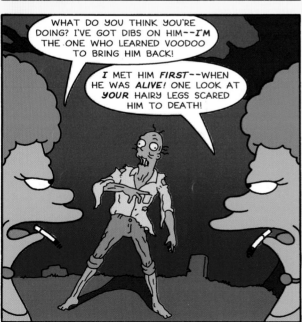

WHAT DO YOU THINK YOU'RE DOING? I'VE GOT DIBS ON HIM--*I'M* THE ONE WHO LEARNED VOODOO TO BRING HIM BACK!

I MET HIM *FIRST*--WHEN HE WAS *ALIVE!* ONE LOOK AT *YOUR* HAIRY LEGS SCARED HIM TO DEATH!

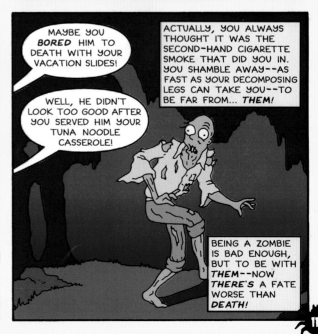

MAYBE YOU *BORED* HIM TO DEATH WITH YOUR VACATION SLIDES!

WELL, HE DIDN'T LOOK TOO GOOD AFTER YOU SERVED HIM YOUR TUNA NOODLE CASSEROLE!

ACTUALLY, YOU ALWAYS THOUGHT IT WAS THE SECOND-HAND CIGARETTE SMOKE THAT DID YOU IN. YOU SHAMBLE AWAY--AS FAST AS YOUR DECOMPOSING LEGS CAN TAKE YOU--TO BE FAR FROM... *THEM!*

BEING A ZOMBIE IS BAD ENOUGH, BUT TO BE WITH *THEM*--NOW *THERE'S* A FATE WORSE THAN *DEATH!*

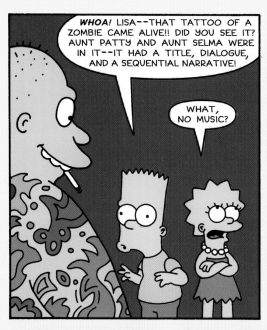

WHOA! LISA--THAT TATTOO OF A ZOMBIE CAME ALIVE!! DID YOU SEE IT? AUNT PATTY AND AUNT SELMA WERE IN IT--IT HAD A TITLE, DIALOGUE, AND A SEQUENTIAL NARRATIVE!

WHAT, NO MUSIC?

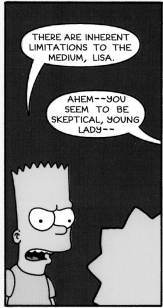

THERE ARE INHERENT LIMITATIONS TO THE MEDIUM, LISA.

AHEM--YOU SEEM TO BE SKEPTICAL, YOUNG LADY--

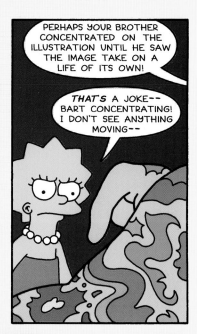

PERHAPS YOUR BROTHER CONCENTRATED ON THE ILLUSTRATION UNTIL HE SAW THE IMAGE TAKE ON A LIFE OF ITS OWN!

THAT'S A JOKE-- BART CONCENTRATING! I DON'T SEE ANYTHING MOVING--

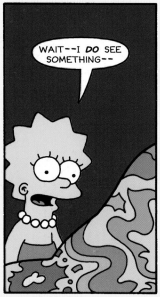

WAIT--I DO SEE SOMETHING--

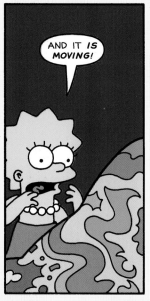

AND IT IS MOVING!

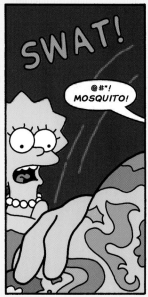

SWAT!

@#*! MOSQUITO!

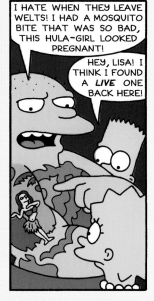

I HATE WHEN THEY LEAVE WELTS! I HAD A MOSQUITO BITE THAT WAS SO BAD, THIS HULA-GIRL LOOKED PREGNANT!

HEY, LISA! I THINK I FOUND A LIVE ONE BACK HERE!

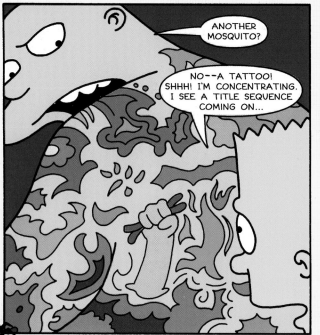

ANOTHER MOSQUITO?

NO--A TATTOO! SHHH! I'M CONCENTRATING. I SEE A TITLE SEQUENCE COMING ON...

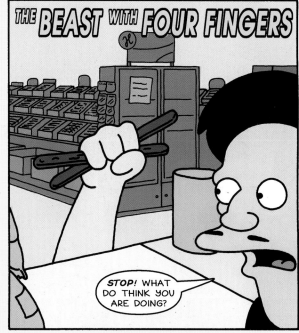

THE BEAST WITH FOUR FINGERS

STOP! WHAT DO THINK YOU ARE DOING?

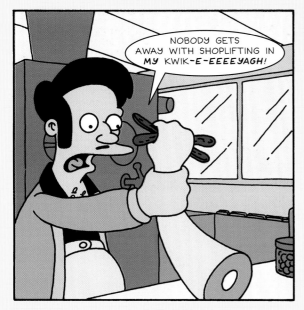

NOBODY GETS AWAY WITH SHOPLIFTING IN *MY KWIK-E-EEEEYAGH!*

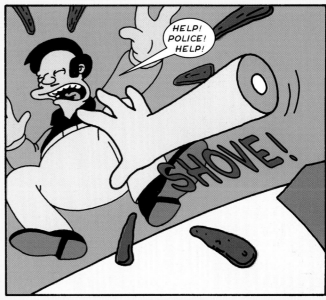

HELP! POLICE! HELP!

SHOVE!

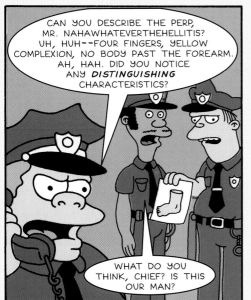

CAN YOU DESCRIBE THE PERP, MR. NAHAWHATEVERTHEHELLITIS? UH, HUH--FOUR FINGERS, YELLOW COMPLEXION, NO BODY PAST THE FOREARM. AH, HAH. DID YOU NOTICE ANY *DISTINGUISHING* CHARACTERISTICS?

WHAT DO YOU THINK, CHIEF? IS THIS OUR MAN?

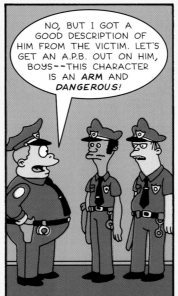

NO, BUT I GOT A GOOD DESCRIPTION OF HIM FROM THE VICTIM. LET'S GET AN A.P.B. OUT ON HIM, BOYS--THIS CHARACTER IS AN *ARM* AND *DANGEROUS!*

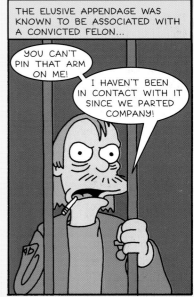

THE ELUSIVE APPENDAGE WAS KNOWN TO BE ASSOCIATED WITH A CONVICTED FELON...

YOU CAN'T PIN THAT ARM ON ME!

I HAVEN'T BEEN IN CONTACT WITH IT SINCE WE PARTED COMPANY!

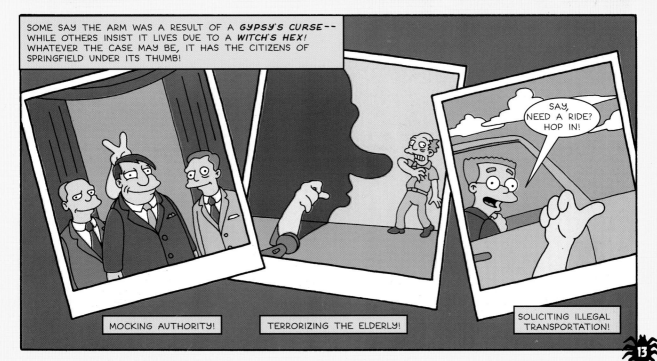

SOME SAY THE ARM WAS A RESULT OF A *GYPSY'S CURSE*-- WHILE OTHERS INSIST IT LIVES DUE TO A *WITCH'S HEX!* WHATEVER THE CASE MAY BE, IT HAS THE CITIZENS OF SPRINGFIELD UNDER ITS THUMB!

SAY, NEED A RIDE? HOP IN!

MOCKING AUTHORITY!

TERRORIZING THE ELDERLY!

SOLICITING ILLEGAL TRANSPORTATION!

SPRINGFIELD WAS UP IN ARMS--WHAT IS THE SOUND OF ONE HAND *LOOTING* WHILE THE CITY SLEEPS?
I SAW THE ROBBERY! IT SLAPPED ME SILLY AND FLED-- BUT NOT BEFORE I PULLED OFF ITS DISGUISE! I'D KNOW IT *ANYWHERE!*
DO I GET A *REWARD?*
FINALLY, THERE WAS A BREAK IN THE CASE. A JILTED MANICURIST PHONED IN WITH A TIP, AND A SUSPECT WAS BROUGHT IN FOR QUESTIONING. BUT--
CAN YOU IDENTIFY ANY OF THESE INDIVIDUALS AS THE ONE YOU SAW BREAKING INTO THE JEWELRY SHOP?
IT WAS SO DARK-- I'M NOT SURE NOW-- I DON'T WANT TO SEND SOMEONE INNOCENT TO JAIL...
DO I STILL GET A *REWARD?*
SO, DUE TO A TECHNICALITY, THE SUSPECT WAS RELEASED. NATURALLY, THE MEDIA HAD A FIELD DAY--
...HOW MUCH LONGER WILL THE POLICE LET THIS CULPRIT GET THE UPPER HAND? THIS REPORTER IS KEEPING *HIS* FINGERS CROSSED THAT HE DOESN'T CROSS *THOSE* FINGERS.
COMING UP NEXT, KRUSTY THE CLOWN ASSAULTS HIS HEAD WRITER FOR USING TOO MANY PUNS IN HIS SCRIPTS. STAY TUNED.
BUT EVEN THE MOST CALLUSED CRIMINAL WILL SLIP UP EVENTUALLY--UNEXPECTEDLY!--WHEN LAYING LOW...
EXCUSE ME, PAL...
MOE'S
...I *TOLD* YOU TO STOP SNAPPING TO THE MUSIC! IT'S *ANNOYING!*
IF YOU WERE ALL MAN, YOU'D SING OFF-KEY LIKE EVERYONE ELSE!
SNAP! SNAP!
YOU'RE GIVING ME HALF THE PEACE SIGN?! WHY YOU--!

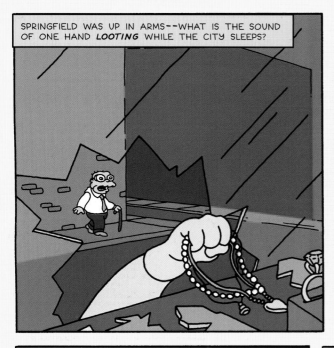

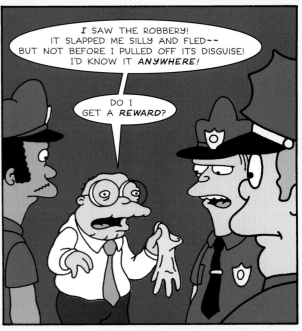

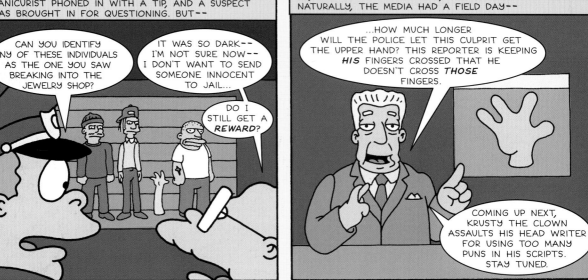

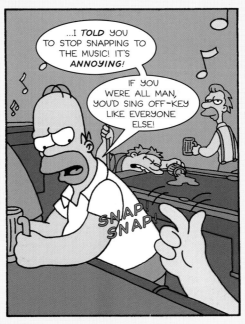

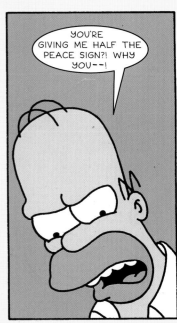

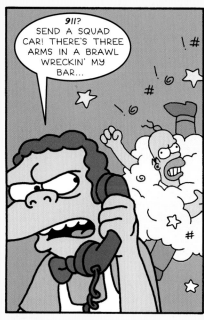

911? SEND A SQUAD CAR! THERE'S THREE ARMS IN A BRAWL WRECKIN' MY BAR...

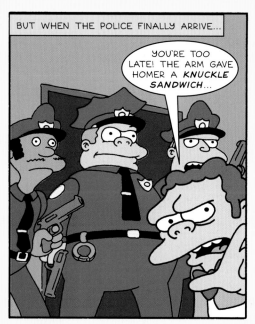

BUT WHEN THE POLICE FINALLY ARRIVE...

YOU'RE TOO LATE! THE ARM GAVE HOMER A *KNUCKLE SANDWICH*...

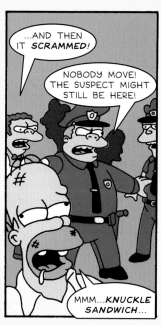

...AND THEN IT *SCRAMMED!*

NOBODY MOVE! THE SUSPECT MIGHT STILL BE HERE!

MMM...*KNUCKLE SANDWICH*...

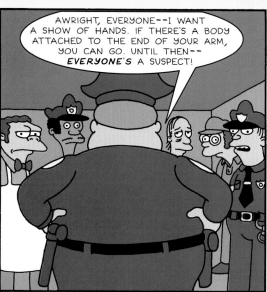

AWRIGHT, EVERYONE--I WANT A SHOW OF HANDS. IF THERE'S A BODY ATTACHED TO THE END OF YOUR ARM, YOU CAN GO. UNTIL THEN-- *EVERYONE'S* A SUSPECT!

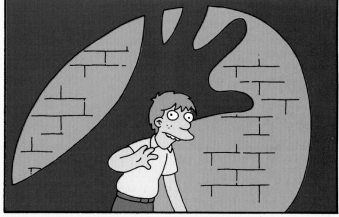

ALAS, THE HAND IS QUICKER THAN THE EYE--THE FUGITIVE *DID* ESCAPE AND IS CURRENTLY STILL AT LARGE! IF BY CHANCE, YOU ARE WALKING DOWN A DARKENED STREET LATE AT NIGHT AND SOMEONE BECKONS YOU TO A HIGH FOUR *BEWARE!* YOU JUST MAY BE PUTTING YOUR LIFE IN ITS HAND! *BEWARE!*

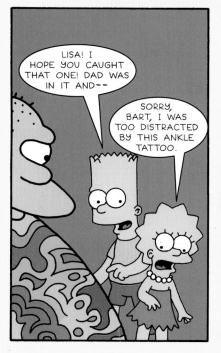

LISA! I HOPE YOU CAUGHT THAT ONE! DAD WAS IN IT AND--

SORRY, BART, I WAS TOO DISTRACTED BY THIS ANKLE TATTOO.

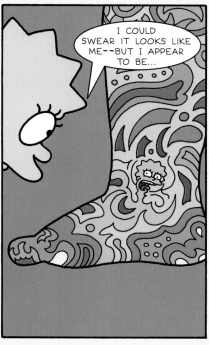

I COULD SWEAR IT LOOKS LIKE ME--BUT I APPEAR TO BE...

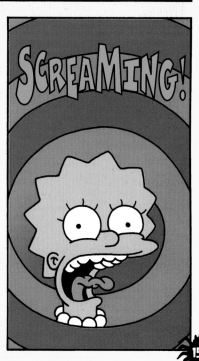

SCREAMING!

YOU FEEL LIKE SCREAMING, LISA SIMPSON, BUT YOU DON'T. NOT AT THE FAIR-WEATHER FRIENDS WHO MOCK YOU BEHIND YOUR BACK...

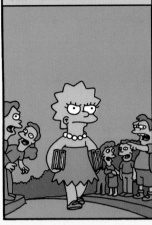

OR THE PHILISTINES YOU'RE SURROUNDED BY WHO CANNOT UNDERSTAND YOUR ART...

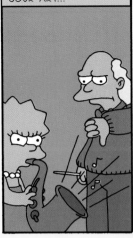

NOR DO YOU SCREAM AT THE EMBARRASSMENT YOU FIND IN YOUR OWN HOME...

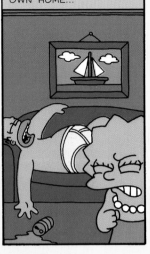

YOU FEEL LIKE SCREAMING, LISA SIMPSON, BUT YOU DON'T--BECAUSE YOU'RE ABOVE IT ALL!

YOU'VE GOT *THAT* RIGHT!

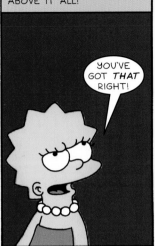

BUT SOMETIMES, LISA SIMPSON, EVEN THE MOST IRON-WILLED TEMPERAMENT CAN ONLY ENDURE SO MUCH--UNTIL IT FINALLY SNAPS!

...DUE TO CONGRESS PULLING FUNDS, *NPR* WILL NO LONGER BE HEARD! STAY TUNED FOR *THE BIRCH BARLOW SHOW*...

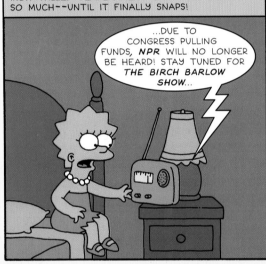

YAAAAAAAH!

LISA! WHAT *WAS* IT? WHAT DID YOU *SEE*?

MAYBE HER WORST NIGHTMARE...

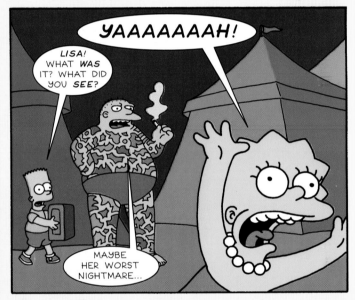

TOO BAD I MISSED IT! I'D BE CURIOUS TO SEE WHAT HER WORST NIGHTMARE IS. IT'S PROBABLY SOMETHING STUPID, LIKE NPR GOING OFF THE AIR!

NOW, LESSEE-- ARE THERE SOME TATTOOS UP HERE THAT MIGHT SPIN A YARN? *HEY*! DO YOU KNOW *GROUNDSKEEPER WILLIE*?

WHY, NO, I DON'T!

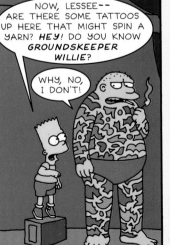

ARE YOU SURE? THIS TATTOO SURE *LOOKS* LIKE HIM. HMMM... AND WHAT'S HE CARRYING?

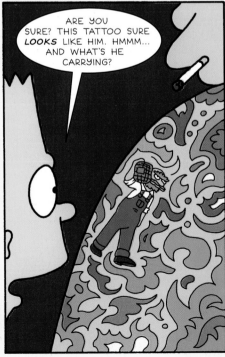

BASKET BAWL

BART! HERE COMES GROUNDSKEEPER WILLIE AGAIN!

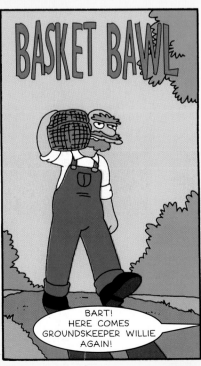

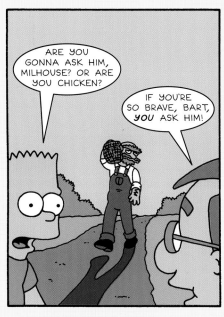

ARE YOU GONNA ASK HIM, MILHOUSE? OR ARE YOU CHICKEN?

IF YOU'RE SO BRAVE, BART, *YOU* ASK HIM!

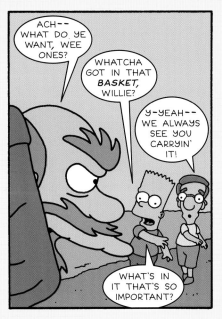

ACH-- WHAT DO YE WANT, WEE ONES?

WHATCHA GOT IN THAT *BASKET*, WILLIE?

Y-YEAH-- WE ALWAYS SEE YOU CARRYIN' IT!

WHAT'S IN IT THAT'S SO IMPORTANT?

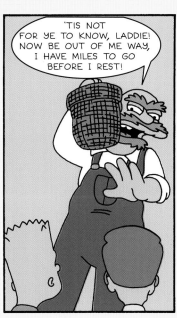

'TIS NOT FOR YE TO KNOW, LADDIE! NOW BE OUT OF ME WAY, I HAVE MILES TO GO BEFORE I REST!

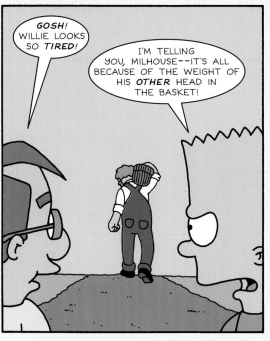

GOSH! WILLIE LOOKS SO *TIRED!*

I'M TELLING YOU, MILHOUSE--IT'S ALL BECAUSE OF THE WEIGHT OF HIS *OTHER* HEAD IN THE BASKET!

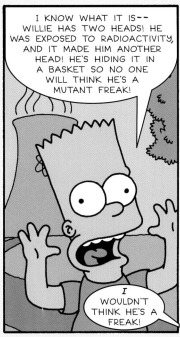

I KNOW WHAT IT IS-- WILLIE HAS TWO HEADS! HE WAS EXPOSED TO RADIOACTIVITY, AND IT MADE HIM ANOTHER HEAD! HE'S HIDING IT IN A BASKET SO NO ONE WILL THINK HE'S A MUTANT FREAK!

I WOULDN'T THINK HE'S A FREAK!

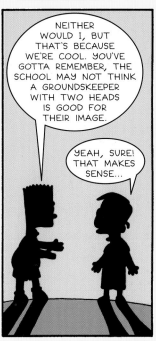

NEITHER WOULD I, BUT THAT'S BECAUSE WE'RE COOL. YOU'VE GOTTA REMEMBER, THE SCHOOL MAY NOT THINK A GROUNDSKEEPER WITH TWO HEADS IS GOOD FOR THEIR IMAGE.

YEAH, SURE! THAT MAKES SENSE...

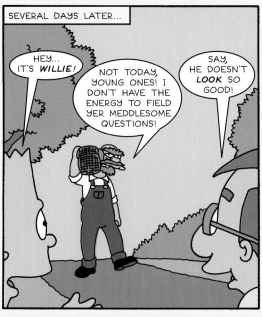

SEVERAL DAYS LATER...

HEY... IT'S *WILLIE!*

NOT TODAY, YOUNG ONES! I DON'T HAVE THE ENERGY TO FIELD YER MEDDLESOME QUESTIONS!

SAY, HE DOESN'T *LOOK* SO GOOD!

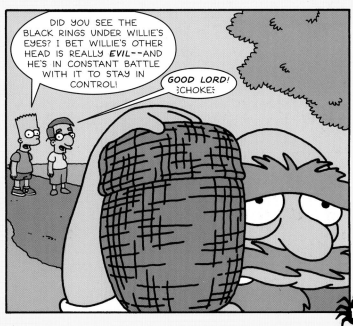

DID YOU SEE THE BLACK RINGS UNDER WILLIE'S EYES? I BET WILLIE'S OTHER HEAD IS REALLY *EVIL*--AND HE'S IN CONSTANT BATTLE WITH IT TO STAY IN CONTROL!

GOOD LORD! ⋛CHOKE⋛

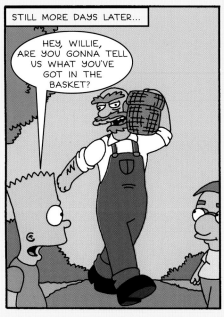

STILL MORE DAYS LATER...

HEY, WILLIE, ARE YOU GONNA TELL US WHAT YOU'VE GOT IN THE BASKET?

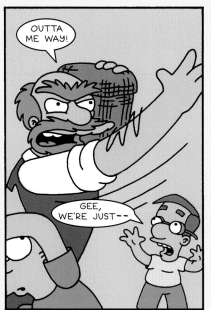

OUTTA ME WAY!

GEE, WE'RE JUST--

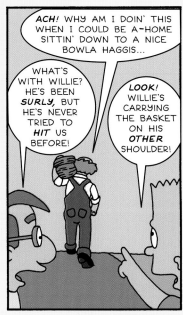

ACH! WHY AM I DOIN' THIS WHEN I COULD BE A-HOME SITTIN' DOWN TO A NICE BOWLA HAGGIS...

WHAT'S WITH WILLIE? HE'S BEEN *SURLY*, BUT HE'S NEVER TRIED TO *HIT* US BEFORE!

LOOK! WILLIE'S CARRYING THE BASKET ON HIS *OTHER* SHOULDER!

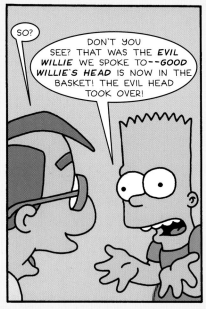

SO?

DON'T YOU SEE? THAT WAS THE *EVIL WILLIE* WE SPOKE TO--*GOOD WILLIE'S HEAD* IS NOW IN THE BASKET! THE EVIL HEAD TOOK OVER!

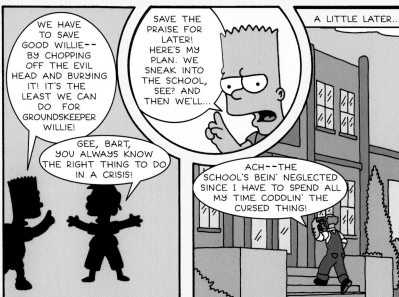

WE HAVE TO SAVE GOOD WILLIE-- BY CHOPPING OFF THE EVIL HEAD AND BURYING IT! IT'S THE LEAST WE CAN DO FOR GROUNDSKEEPER WILLIE!

GEE, BART, YOU ALWAYS KNOW THE RIGHT THING TO DO IN A CRISIS!

SAVE THE PRAISE FOR LATER! HERE'S MY PLAN. WE SNEAK INTO THE SCHOOL, SEE? AND THEN WE'LL...

A LITTLE LATER...

ACH--THE SCHOOL'S BEIN' NEGLECTED SINCE I HAVE TO SPEND ALL MY TIME CODDLIN' THE CURSED THING!

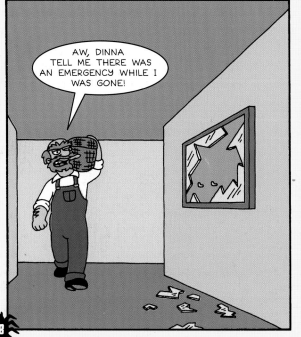

AW, DINNA TELL ME THERE WAS AN EMERGENCY WHILE I WAS GONE!

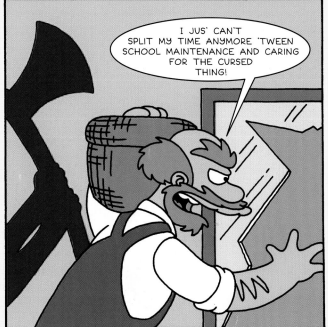

I JUS' CAN'T SPLIT MY TIME ANYMORE 'TWEEN SCHOOL MAINTENANCE AND CARING FOR THE CURSED THING!

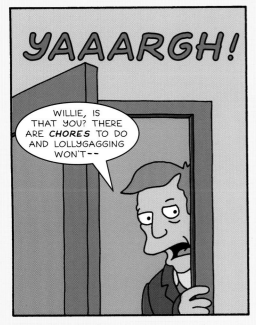

YAAARGH!

WILLIE, IS THAT YOU? THERE ARE **CHORES** TO DO AND LOLLYGAGGING WON'T--

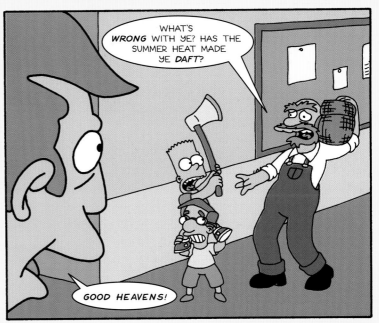

WHAT'S **WRONG** WITH YE? HAS THE SUMMER HEAT MADE YE **DAFT**?

GOOD HEAVENS!

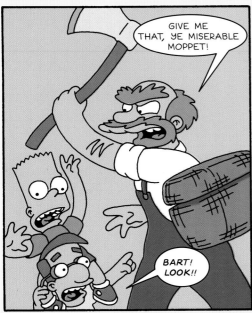

GIVE ME THAT, YE MISERABLE MOPPET!

BART! LOOK!!

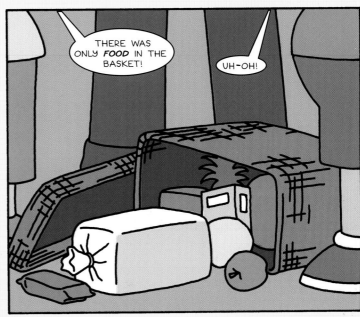

THERE WAS ONLY **FOOD** IN THE BASKET!

UH-OH!

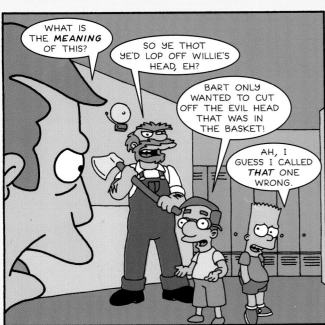

WHAT IS THE **MEANING** OF THIS?

SO YE THOT YE'D LOP OFF WILLIE'S HEAD, EH?

BART ONLY WANTED TO CUT OFF THE EVIL HEAD THAT WAS IN THE BASKET!

AH, I GUESS I CALLED **THAT** ONE WRONG.

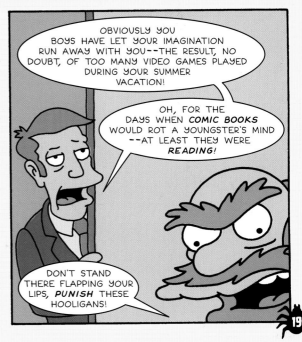

OBVIOUSLY YOU BOYS HAVE LET YOUR IMAGINATION RUN AWAY WITH YOU--THE RESULT, NO DOUBT, OF TOO MANY VIDEO GAMES PLAYED DURING YOUR SUMMER VACATION!

OH, FOR THE DAYS WHEN **COMIC BOOKS** WOULD ROT A YOUNGSTER'S MIND --AT LEAST THEY WERE **READING**!

DON'T STAND THERE FLAPPING YOUR LIPS, **PUNISH** THESE HOOLIGANS!

19

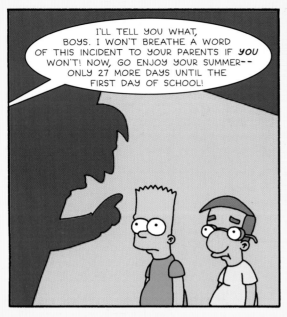

I'LL TELL YOU WHAT, BOYS. I WON'T BREATHE A WORD OF THIS INCIDENT TO YOUR PARENTS IF *YOU* WON'T! NOW, GO ENJOY YOUR SUMMER-- ONLY 27 MORE DAYS UNTIL THE FIRST DAY OF SCHOOL!

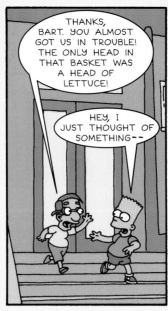

THANKS, BART. YOU ALMOST GOT US IN TROUBLE! THE ONLY HEAD IN THAT BASKET WAS A HEAD OF LETTUCE!

HEY, I JUST THOUGHT OF SOMETHING--

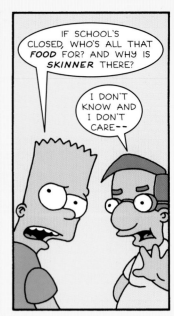

IF SCHOOL'S CLOSED, WHO'S ALL THAT *FOOD* FOR? AND WHY IS *SKINNER* THERE?

I DON'T KNOW AND I DON'T CARE--

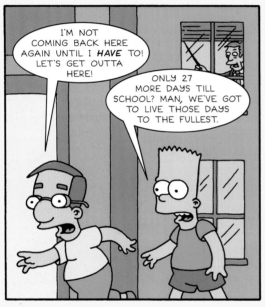

I'M NOT COMING BACK HERE AGAIN UNTIL I *HAVE* TO! LET'S GET OUTTA HERE!

ONLY 27 MORE DAYS TILL SCHOOL? MAN, WE'VE GOT TO LIVE THOSE DAYS TO THE FULLEST.

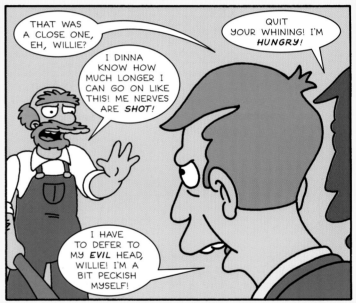

THAT WAS A CLOSE ONE, EH, WILLIE?

QUIT YOUR WHINING! I'M *HUNGRY*!

I DINNA KNOW HOW MUCH LONGER I CAN GO ON LIKE THIS! ME NERVES ARE *SHOT*!

I HAVE TO DEFER TO MY *EVIL* HEAD, WILLIE! I'M A BIT PECKISH MYSELF!

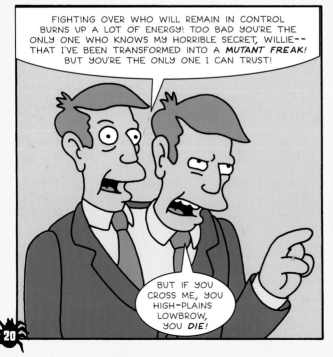

FIGHTING OVER WHO WILL REMAIN IN CONTROL BURNS UP A LOT OF ENERGY! TOO BAD YOU'RE THE ONLY ONE WHO KNOWS MY HORRIBLE SECRET, WILLIE-- THAT I'VE BEEN TRANSFORMED INTO A *MUTANT FREAK*! BUT YOU'RE THE ONLY ONE I CAN TRUST!

BUT IF YOU CROSS ME, YOU HIGH-PLAINS LOWBROW, YOU *DIE*!

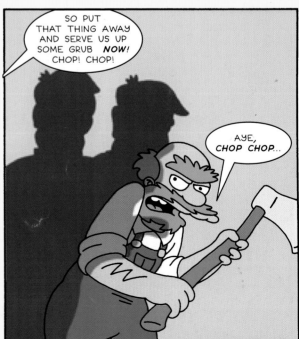

SO PUT THAT THING AWAY AND SERVE US UP SOME GRUB *NOW*! CHOP! CHOP!

AYE, *CHOP CHOP*...

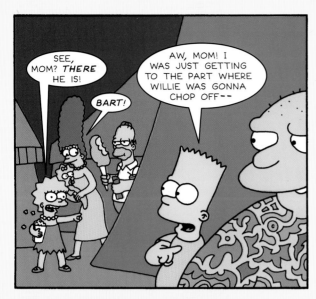

SEE, MOM? *THERE* HE IS!

BART!

AW, MOM! I WAS JUST GETTING TO THE PART WHERE WILLIE WAS GONNA CHOP OFF--

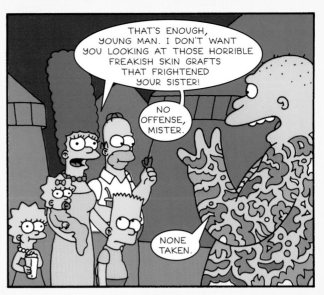

THAT'S ENOUGH, YOUNG MAN. I DON'T WANT YOU LOOKING AT THOSE HORRIBLE FREAKISH SKIN GRAFTS THAT FRIGHTENED YOUR SISTER!

NO OFFENSE, MISTER.

NONE TAKEN.

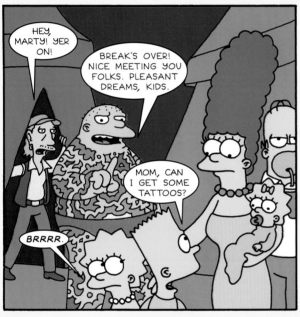

HEY, MARTY! YER ON!

BREAK'S OVER! NICE MEETING YOU FOLKS. PLEASANT DREAMS, KIDS.

MOM, CAN I GET SOME TATTOOS?

BRRRR.

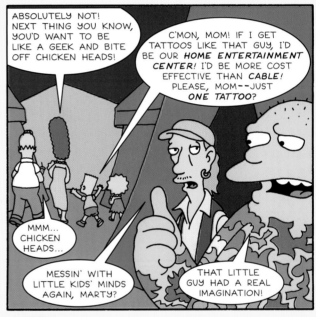

ABSOLUTELY NOT! NEXT THING YOU KNOW, YOU'D WANT TO BE LIKE A GEEK AND BITE OFF CHICKEN HEADS!

C'MON, MOM! IF I GET TATTOOS LIKE THAT GUY, I'D BE OUR *HOME ENTERTAINMENT CENTER!* I'D BE MORE COST EFFECTIVE THAN *CABLE!* PLEASE, MOM--JUST *ONE TATTOO?*

MMM... CHICKEN HEADS...

MESSIN' WITH LITTLE KIDS' MINDS AGAIN, MARTY?

THAT LITTLE GUY HAD A REAL IMAGINATION!

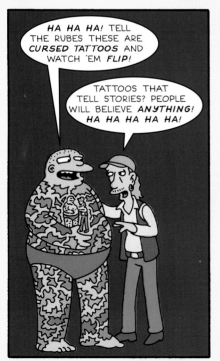

HA HA HA! TELL THE RUBES THESE ARE *CURSED TATTOOS* AND WATCH 'EM *FLIP!*

TATTOOS THAT TELL STORIES? PEOPLE WILL BELIEVE *ANYTHING!* *HA HA HA HA HA!*

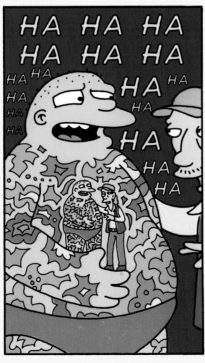

HA HA HA HA HA HA HA HA HA HA HA HA HA HA

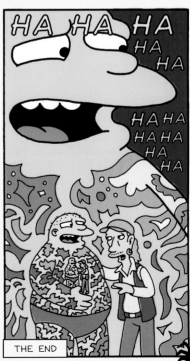

HA HA HA HA HA HA HA HA HA HA HA HA

THE END

SO YOU WANNA KNOW WHERE HALLOWEEN COMES FROM?
WELL, YOU'VE COME TO THE RIGHT PLACE, 'CAUSE IF THERE'S ONE THING I CAN B.S. ABOUT, IT'S...
THE HISTORY OF HALLOWEEN!!
HALLOWEEN ACTUALLY STARTED BACK IN STONE AGE TIMES WHEN A GUY NAMED OG SAW SOME DINOSAURS PLAYING THE FIRST GAME OF "BOBBING FOR CAVEMEN."
THAT LOOK LIKE FUN! OG NEXT! OG NEXT!
OG WASN'T EXACTLY THE SMARTEST BONE IN THE PILE.
ROME, 100 BC: ALTHOUGH THE "TREATS" WERE STILL A FEW YEARS OFF, LEAVE IT TO THE BARBARIANS TO COME UP WITH THE "TRICKS."
IF I COME OUT AND FIND A FLAMING BAG OF ANYTHING OTHER THAN BUFFALO WINGS, I WILL NOT BE AMUSED!
SPAIN, 1483: THE SPANISH INQUISITION GAVE US THE FIRST PERSON TO GET SICK FROM EATING TOO MUCH HALLOWEEN CANDY.
THIS IS A LITTLE SOMETHING I CALL "FUN SIZE!"
OH DEAR, AND ME ALLERGIC TO NOUGAT.
CHINA, 1275: HALLOWEEN WAS BROUGHT TO THE CHINESE AS A GIFT FROM THAT MARCO POLO GUY. ALTHOUGH THEY DIDN'T ALWAYS "GET" IT...
THANKS FOR THE PUMPKIN SHOES, MARKY!
LOOKIN' SHARP, HOMER ZHANG!
IDIOT.
SALEM, 1640: HALLOWEEN GOT OFF TO A ROCKY START IN AMERICA...
HRRRMMM...
RELAX! YA GOTTA LEARN TO START SMOKING SOMEWHERE.

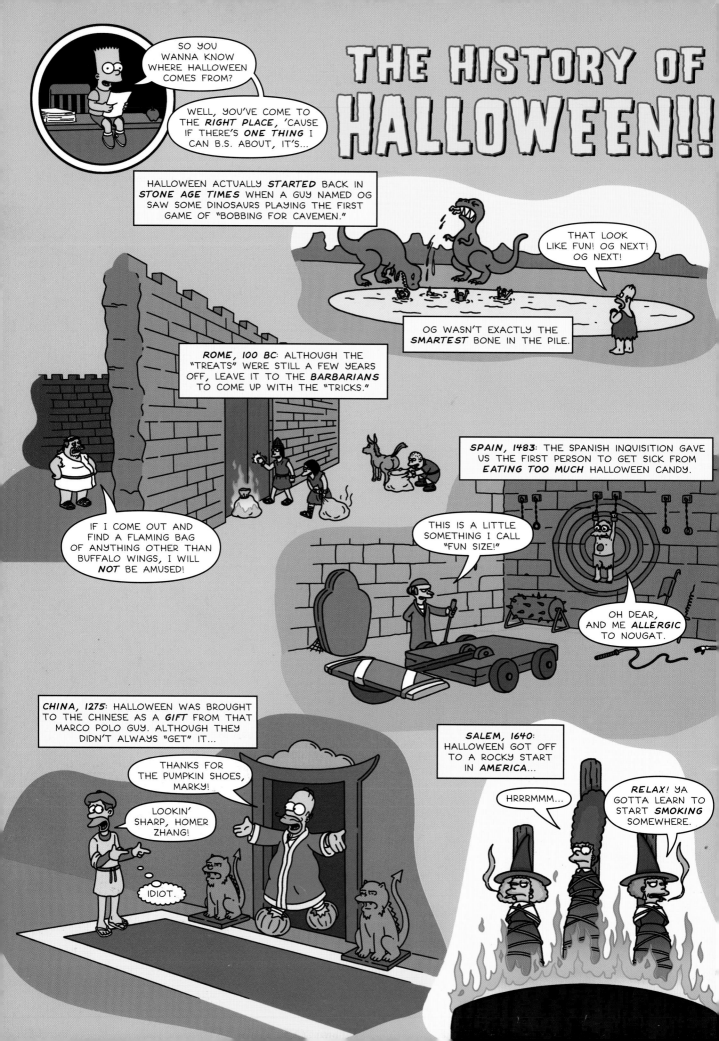

CARIBBEAN, 1789: WERE YOU MOCKED FOR GOING AS LAST YEAR'S POKEMON CHARACTER? WELL, EARLY COSTUME-WEARERS FACED JUST A LITTLE BIT MORE DANGER...
ARRGH!! I ONLY BE DRESSED AS A PIRATE!
WORLD WAR II, 1945: EVERYTHING CHANGED WITH THE WAR, AND HALLOWEEN WAS NO DIFFERENT.
ISN'T TODAY HALLOWEEN?
IN HONOR OF OUR BOYS OVERSEAS, IT'S NOW "VICTORY DAY!"
WHAT ABOUT THE PUMPKINS?
VICTORY GOURDS!
CANDY?
VICTORY CLUMPS!
AND PRINCIPAL WIENERS?
PRINCIPAL VICTORY WIEN-- HEY!
PPY VICTORY DAY!
SAN FRANCISCO, 1967: THE SIXTIES WERE A SIMPLER TIME...
BRAAAAAP!
MIAMI, 1984: THE EIGHTIES TAUGHT US THAT THE MORE THINGS CHANGE, THE MORE THEY STAY THE SAME.
ARGH!! I ONLY BE DRESSED AS A DRUG RUNNER!
AND OF COURSE THE FUTURE WILL BE FILLED WITH NOTHING BUT ALCOHOLIC ROBOTS AND PIZZA DELIVERY GUYS WHO--
BART!
HEY, IT CAN'T ALL BE TRUE!

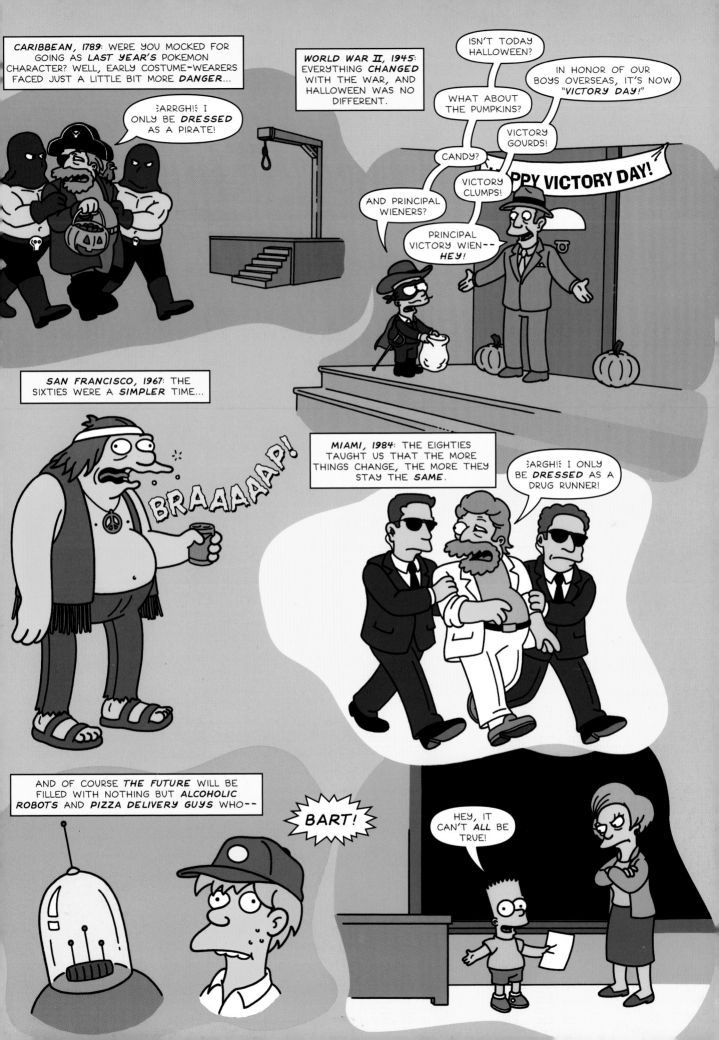

BART AND LISA'S GU

WHAT IF...THAT SMELL IN THE BATHROOM COMES WITH A CREATURE ATTACHED!
WHAT IF...YOU'RE NOT ALLOWED TO
MOVIES BECAUSE THEY'RE REALLY
THAT AIN'T GOOD.
WHAT IF...CATS ARE PLOTTING THEIR REVENGE?
WHAT IF...
NEVER HIT
BRA!
WHAT IF... EVERYTIME YOUR
"I LOVE YOU," SHE REALLY
TO SELL YOU TO A MEXICAN
AH, FINALLY SOMETHING TO WRESTLE THE MONKEY!

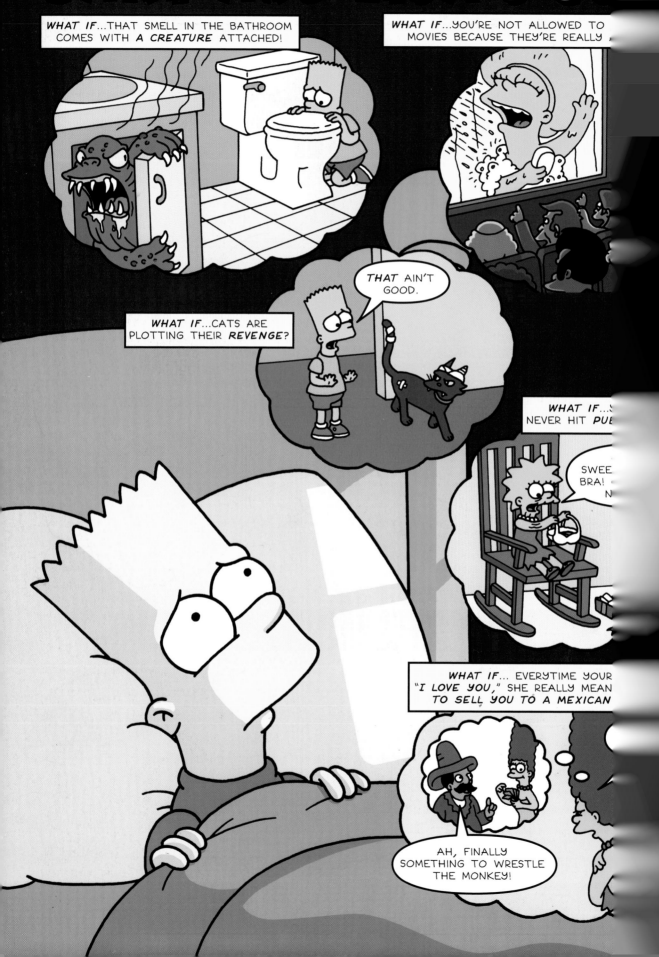

TO CHILDHOOD FEARS!

WHAT IF...WHEN GRANDMA KISSES YOU SHE IS ACTUALLY TRYING TO SUCK OUT SOME OF YOUR LIFE FORCE?
LET ME KISS SOME OF THAT SWEET SUPPLE NECK...
WHAT IF...YOU WAKE UP IN THE MORNING AND THE ONLY CANDY LEFT IN THE WORLD IS PEANUT BRITTLE!
THEY'VE NEVER BEEN BEFORE, BUT WHAT IF...THIS TIME THE NEW ROLL OF TOILET PAPER IS POISONOUS?
WHAT IF...YOU HIT PUBERTY, AND IT JUST WON'T STOP?
LITTLE HELP HERE!
AAAAAHHH!!!
AND WHAT IF...YOUR DAD REALLY IS YOUR DAD!!

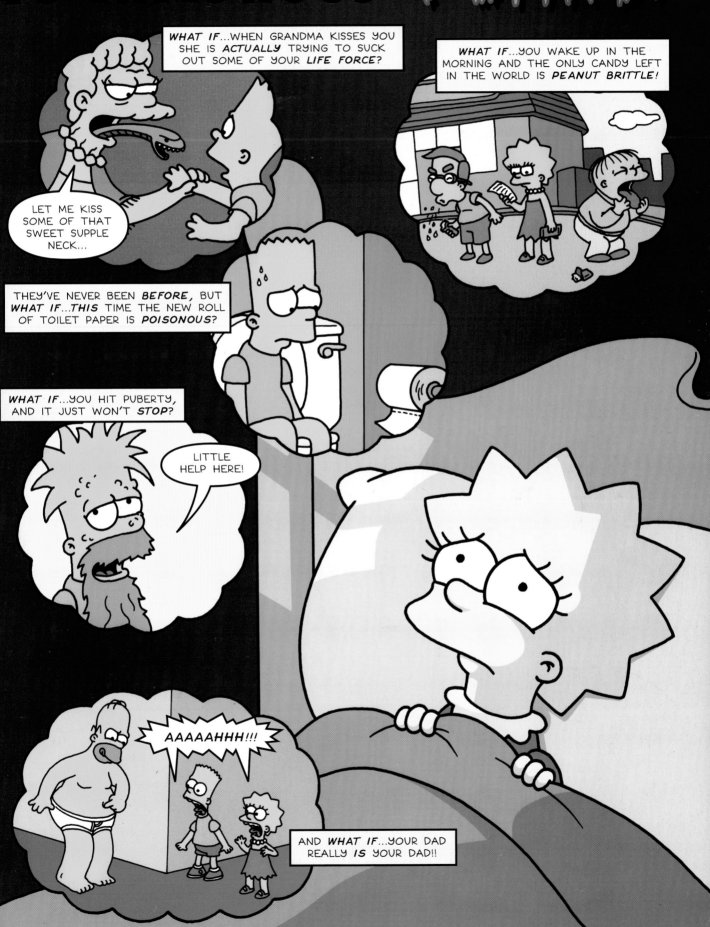

Like to watch underdressed humans parade about in a leech swamp? Wish you could betray your friends and get paid for it? Then set the coordinates on your anesthesia box to...

Kang and Kodos' Survival-Oriented Escapade!

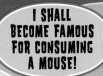

I SHALL BECOME FAMOUS FOR CONSUMING A MOUSE!

NO, I SHALL BECOME FAMOUS FOR CONSUMING A MOUSE!

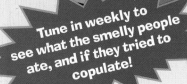
Tune in weekly to see what the smelly people ate, and if they tried to copulate!

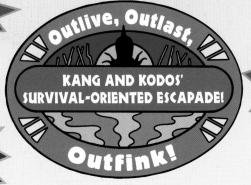
Outlive, Outlast,
KANG AND KODOS'
SURVIVAL-ORIENTED ESCAPADE!
Outfink!

Every episode is like your presidential elections, except they only vote for *one* human's demise instead of a whole country's!

This week: Kangy gets so hungry, he is forced to eat one of the well-fed cameramen!

You'll meet such participants as:

KANGY
AGE: Youth-orientedly young!
OCCUPATION: Attractive young gadabout!
MARITAL STATUS: Ripe!
REASON FOR PLAYING: I respect mean-spirited democracy.

KODOS
AGE: Chesty!
OCCUPATION: Distractress.
REASON FOR PLAYING: The extreme starvation increases my chances of participating in a beer commercial.

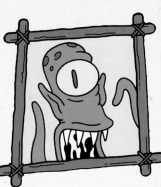

Kang and Kodos' Survival-Oriented Escapade!
Mondays on CBS!

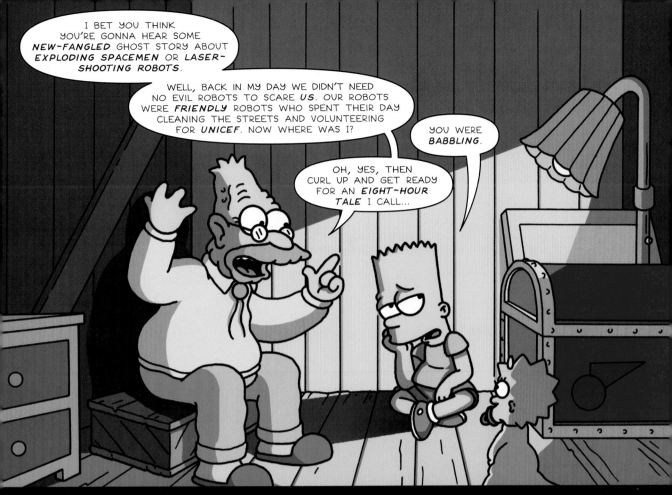

"THE PROSPECTOR'S REVENGE"

 MY STORY TAKES PLACE A LONG TIME AGO BACK WHEN I WAS A YOUNG MAN EAGER TO MAKE MY FORTUNE. HAVING ALREADY LEARNED THERE WAS NO MONEY TO BE HAD AS A SAILOR...AND EVEN LESS AS A COMMUNIST SYMPATHIZER, I DECIDED TO BECOME AN ARIZONA PROSPECTOR AND SEARCH FOR THE FABLED "LOST DUTCHMAN'S MINE," A MINE SO RICH YOU BARELY HAD TO SCRATCH THE SURFACE TO FIND ALL THE GOLD A MAN COULD CARRY. OF COURSE, SCRATCH A LITTLE DEEPER AND YOU'D FIND *DEEEEAAAATTTTH!!!!!* DID YOU HEAR THAT?

YEAH, IT'S WHAT I'M PRAYING FOR.

WELL, THE DUTCHMAN HIMSELF WAS A PROSPECTOR BY THE NAME OF LARS VANDERBEEK. OF COURSE, BACK THEN PEOPLE WERE SCARED OF THE DUTCH, BELIEVING THEY HAD WOODEN FEET (WHICH THEY DON'T), AND THAT THEY TRAVELED IN GIANT FLYING WINDMILLS (WHICH THEY DO). BUT OL' ANDY WOULD SHOW THEM WHAT WAS WHAT. HE SEARCHED FOR GOLD DAY

NUGGET HEAVIER THAN A BARN FULL OF PREGNANT LADIES. WHICH WAS HOW THEY WEIGHED THINGS AT THE TIME. YOU'D SAY "I'D LIKE A PREGNANT LADY'S WORTH OF CHEESE." AND THEY'D SAY "YOU CAN'T EAT THAT MUCH CHEESE!" AND YOU'D SAY-- GRAMPA! GRAB THE REINS, BUDDY. WELL, VANDERBEEK SWORE HE'D COME BACK WITH NUGGETS TWICE THE SIZE, BUT THAT NIGHT, ON HIS WAY BACK INTO THE MINE, HE WAS KILLED IN A HOOORRIBLE CAVE-IN. SOME SAY IT WAS AN EARTHQUAKE, SOME SAY IT WAS THE MOUNTAIN GOD'S REVENGE, AND SOME SAY THE ROOF OF A MINE IS A STUPID PLACE TO HOLD A SENIOR SOCK-HOP. EITHER WAY, WITH HIS LAST DYING WORDS, HE SWORE A TERRIBLE FATE TO ANYONE WHO TRIED TO TAKE THE GOLD, A FATE HE WOULD DELIVER FROM BEYOND THE *GRAAAAAAVE!* NEXT TIME LET'S RUIN MY OTHER EAR. YEARS PASSED AND NO ONE DARED ENTER THE EVIL DUTCHMAN'S MINE, ITS WHEREABOUTS ALL BUT FORGOTTEN BUT NOT BY PLUCKY YOUNG ABE SIMPSON (THAT'S ME!). I HAD PURCHASED A MAP FROM A LOCAL SEAMSTRESS AND WOULD HAVE BEEN ON MY WAY TO THE GOLD, BUT I HAD NO MULE. AND FINDING A MULE WAS NO EASY TASK YOU'VE HEARD OF A "ONE-HORSE TOWN"? WELL, THIS WAS A "ONE-*MULE*" TOWN...WITH OVER A THOUSAND HORSES. BUT THERE WAS ONE MULE AND T BELONGED TO A CRAFTY YOUNG CHINAMAN BY THE NAME OF MONTY BURNS. UM, GRAMPA... "CHING CHANG MONTY" WE CALLED HIM, AND HE WAS BAAAAD NEWS. ALTHOUGH HE LENT ME THE MULE, HE PLANNED TO FOLLOW ME, HIT ME OVER THE HEAD WITH A SHOVEL, AND KEEP THE GOLD FOR HIMSELF! SO THERE WE WERE...AT THE MOUTH OF THE DUTCHMAN'S CAVE, THE WIND HOWLING LIKE THE DEVIL IN A DIXIE CUP! I HAD AN EERIE FEELIN N MY BONES. SLOOOOOWLY WE STEPPED TOWARDS THE GIANT MOUND OF GOLD...ONE FOOT THEN THE NEXT, THEN ANOTHER FOOT, THEN...ONE MORE FOOT...THEN TWO FEET...THEN JUST A KNEE, THEN--HEY! WHERE YA GOIN'? AWAY FROM THIS STORY! NOT GOOD ENOUGH FER YA, EH?! IT'S A BUNCH OF CRAZY STUFF! AND EXACTLY WHICH PART DID MR. YOUNG BRITCHES THINK WAS SO "CRAZY?" I DUNNO...SOMEWHERE BETWEEN THE PREGNANT WOMEN AND BURNS BEING CHINESE. CONSARN IT! YOU KIDS TODAY THINK YOU'RE SOOO SMART! WELL, I DIDN'T SEE YOU LIVING THROUGH THE DEPRESSION BACK THEN WE DIDN'T HAVE NO MICROWAVE DINNERS. WE ATE WHATEVER THERE WAS AND BEGGED FOR JUST ONE BITE MORE. WHY, WE'D GET IN KNIFE FIGHTS OVER A TATER TOT! AND WHO TOOK ON THE NAZIS? WHO STORMED NORMANDY AND GAVE HITLER THE OL' KALAMAZOO HICKEY? WAS T KIDS TODAY? 'A COURSE NOT! IT WAS OLD PEOPLE! OLD PEOPLE WHO CARE ABOUT YOU! AND YOU KNOW WHAT? WE'D DO IT AGAIN IN A MINUTE, ALL TO GIVE YOU KIDS A LIFE OF COMFORT AND SAFETY...A LIFE WE OLD FOLKS NEVER HAD. GEE, GRAMPA, I'M SORRY. GO AHEAD. TELL ME WHAT HAPPENED TO CHING CHANG MONTY. I ALREADY TOLD YOU, HE GOT EATEN BY THE DRAGON! THE DRAGON? WHAT DRAGON? SO THERE WAS NO DRAGON. THEN WHY'D YA BRING IT UP?! THAT'S THE WORST STORY YOU'VE EVER TOLD! BUT GRAMPA-- NUTS TO THIS! I'M GOING TO THE SQUIRREL PARK!

Huh?!
AS HOMER SIMPSON AWOKE ONE MORNING AFTER ***DISTURBING DREAMS***, HE FOUND HIMSELF TRANSFORMED IN HIS BED INTO...
Marge, I just had the *weirdest* dream that I turned into a...
METAMORPH SIMPSONZ
D'OH!!
Art and Story
PETER "KAFKAESQUE" KUPER
Letters
CHRIS "THE CREATURE" UNGAR
Colors
NASTY NATHAN KANE
Edits
BILL "DIAL M. FOR" MORRISON
Grublisher
SPLAT GROENING

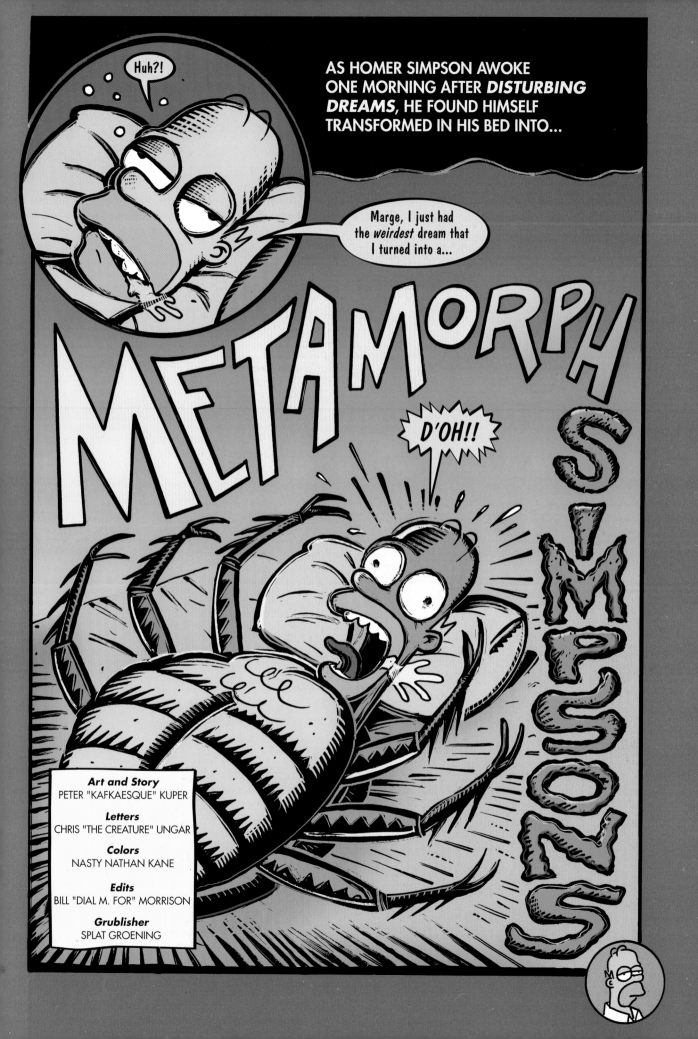

That boy's *overslept* as long as I can remember!
Which reminds me, what was I trying to recall?
Please, Grampa. This is the *first time* he's been late for work *all week...*
It's Monday...
...and since that *minor leak* in the radioactive containment area, his work has been most *unsatisfactory!*
Homie, come on out, that *nice* Mr. Smithers is here...
... and he's offered to drive you to work...
B-be right there!
Yuck Darn *bug breath...*
Mr. Simpson, on behalf of Mr. Burns and the entire nuclear power industry, I must *insist* that you open this door *immediately!*
EEK!
P.U.! Bug-breath!
HOMIE!
Sorry to be running late, I think I must have a little bug...
Burns Industries takes no *responsibility* for your condition and *disavows* any knowledge of your *existence.*
Also, *you're fired!*
Oh!
Boy, how many times did I tell you not to eat insects?

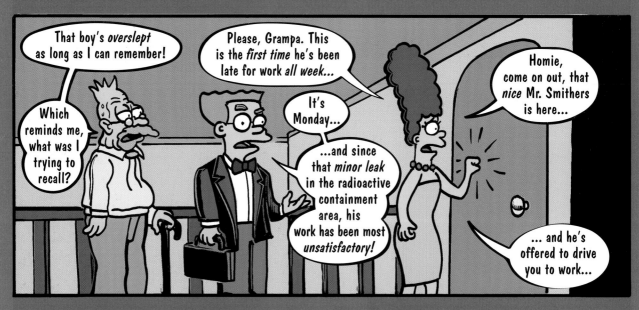

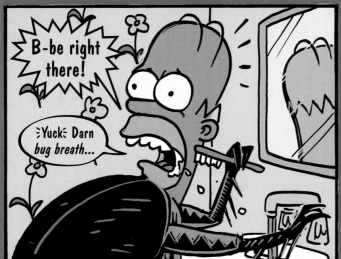

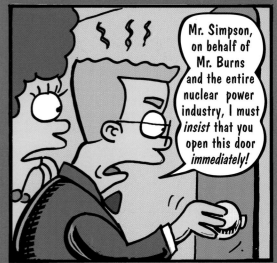

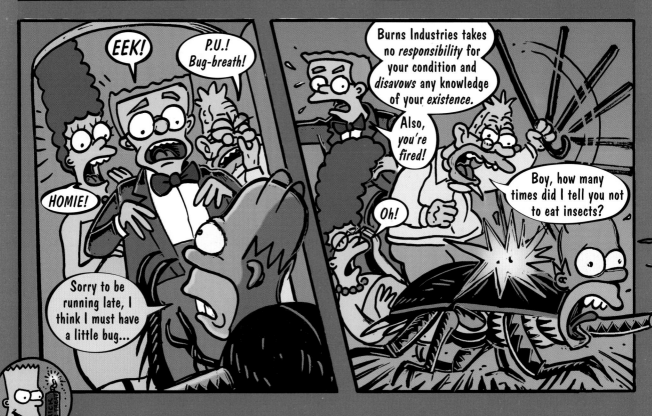

Sheesh, they act like they've never seen a *half-man/half-insect* before!
It's not like I flipped the car a fifth time or anything...
...or released toxic waste in the river accidentally *again*...
...or started *another* forest fire with Johnny Cash...
Hey this bug thing has it's *perks*...
WOO-HOO!! Look at me! I'm hanging from the...
D'OH!
CRASH
KNOCK KNOCK
Dad? It's Lisa and Bart. May we come in?

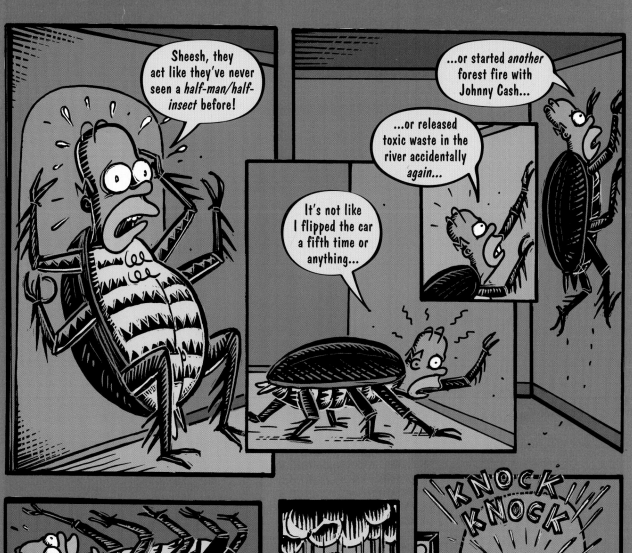

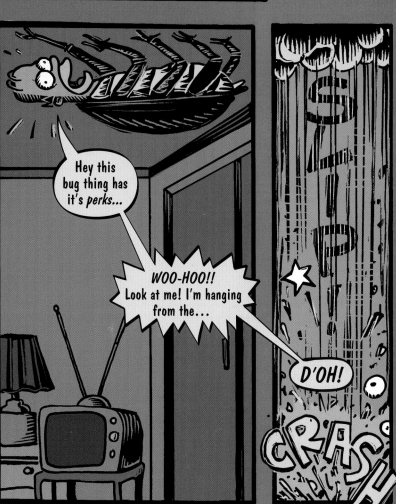

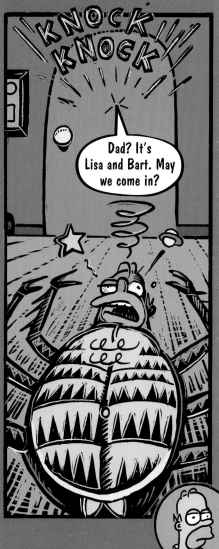

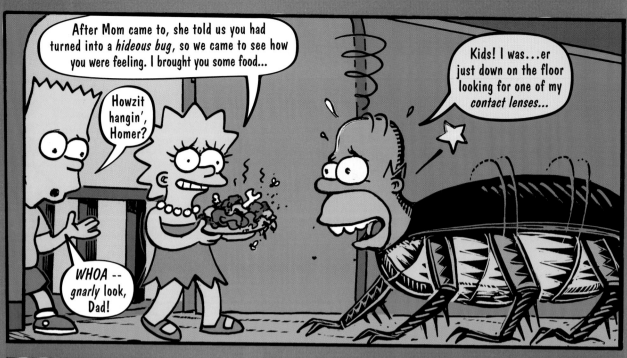

After Mom came to, she told us you had turned into a *hideous bug*, so we came to see how you were feeling. I brought you some food...

Howzit hangin', Homer?

Kids! I was...er just down on the floor looking for one of my *contact lenses*...

WHOA -- gnarly look, Dad!

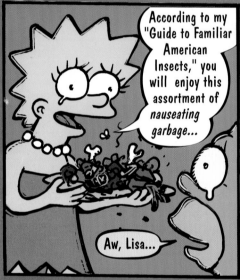

According to my "Guide to Familiar American Insects," you will enjoy this assortment of *nauseating garbage*...

Aw, Lisa...

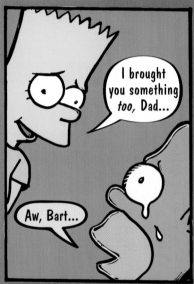

I brought you something *too*, Dad...

Aw, Bart...

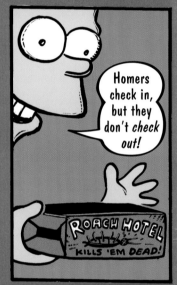

Homers check in, but they don't *check* out!

ROACH HOTEL
KILLS 'EM DEAD!

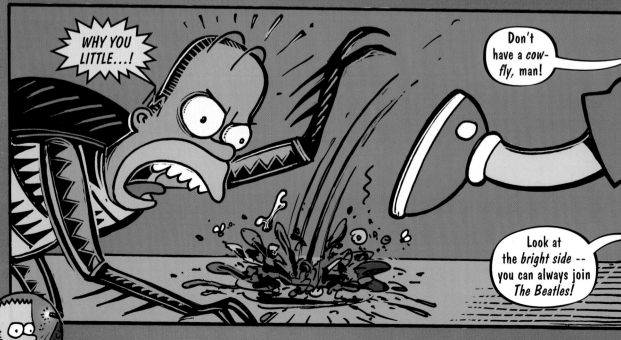

WHY YOU LITTLE...!

Don't have a *cow-fly*, man!

Look at the *bright side* -- you can always join *The Beatles!*

Ahh, I can't blame him...
I am a *repulsive, vile,* and *disgusting...*
sniff
sniff Say, what's that *smell?*

Speaking of repulsive, vile, and disgusting...
Mmm... there's nothing quite like *moldy, week-old Spam!*

SPAM AGAIN?
Now that your father has turned into a giant beetle, we'll have to tighten our belts...
Bart, please, you'll wake Grampa.
I'll take grapes over Spam any day!
You know, Bart, we should be thankful for what we've got.
During the Great Depression, people like the Joad Family described in John Steinbeck's "Grapes of Wrath" would have rejoiced to have Spam!
Z

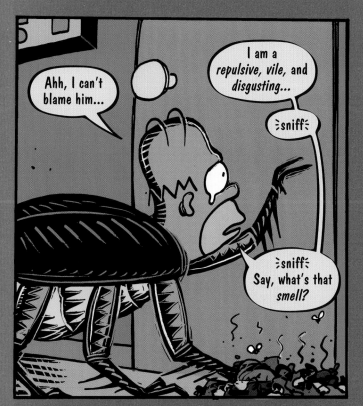

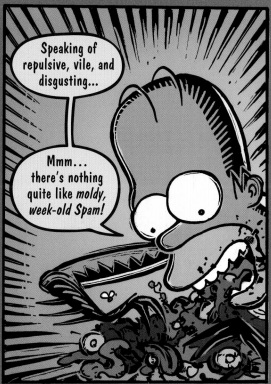

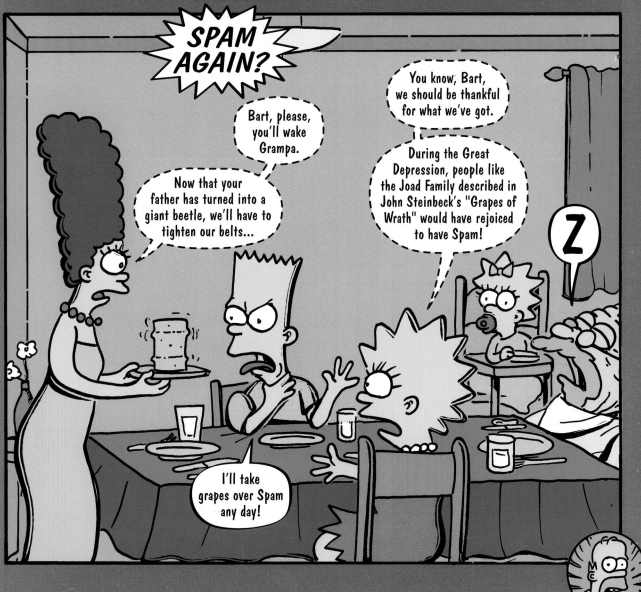

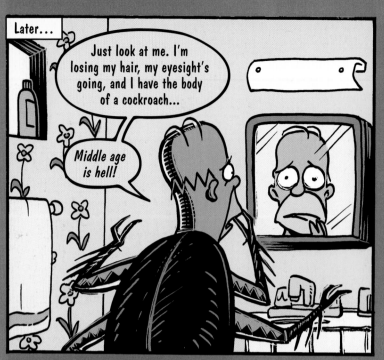

Later...

Just look at me. I'm losing my hair, my eyesight's going, and I have the body of a cockroach...

Middle age is hell!

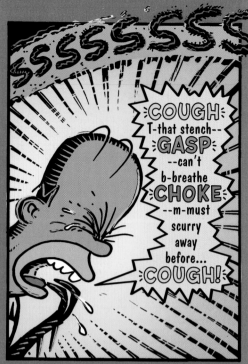

SSSSSSSS

≶COUGH≷ T-that stench-- ≶GASP≷ --can't b-breathe ≶CHOKE≷ --m-must scurry away before... ≶COUGH!≷

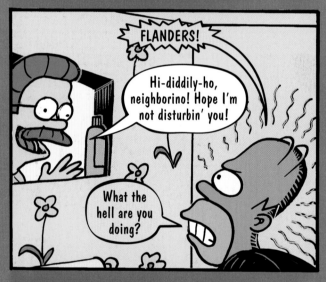

FLANDERS!

Hi-diddily-ho, neighborino! Hope I'm not disturbin' you!

What the hell are you doing?

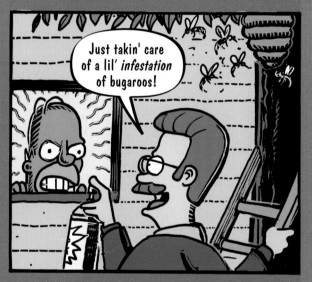

Just takin' care of a lil' infestation of bugaroos!

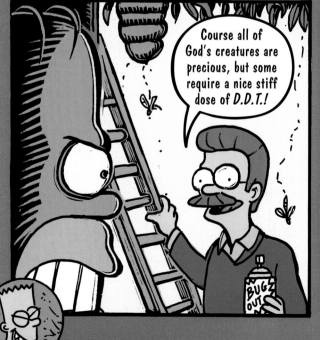

Course all of God's creatures are precious, but some require a nice stiff dose of D.D.T.!

BUGZ OUT

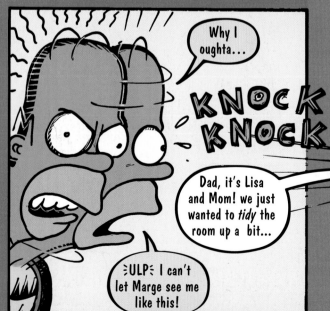

Why I oughta...

KNOCK KNOCK

Dad, it's Lisa and Mom! we just wanted to tidy the room up a bit...

≶ULP≷ I can't let Marge see me like this!

Lisa, are you sure this is such a *good idea?*
I've done this before. You know Dad would never have kept the room this clean himself!
And don't worry about seeing him, he always *hides* when I come in.
Dad, Mom and I are going to get some of the furniture out of your way.
Now that your father's an insect, I don't suppose he's watching...
NOT THE TV!
EEK!
Dad, now look what you've done! You made Mom *faint* again!
But Lisa... she touched the TV!
Marge, Lisa-- wait, I didn't mean to...

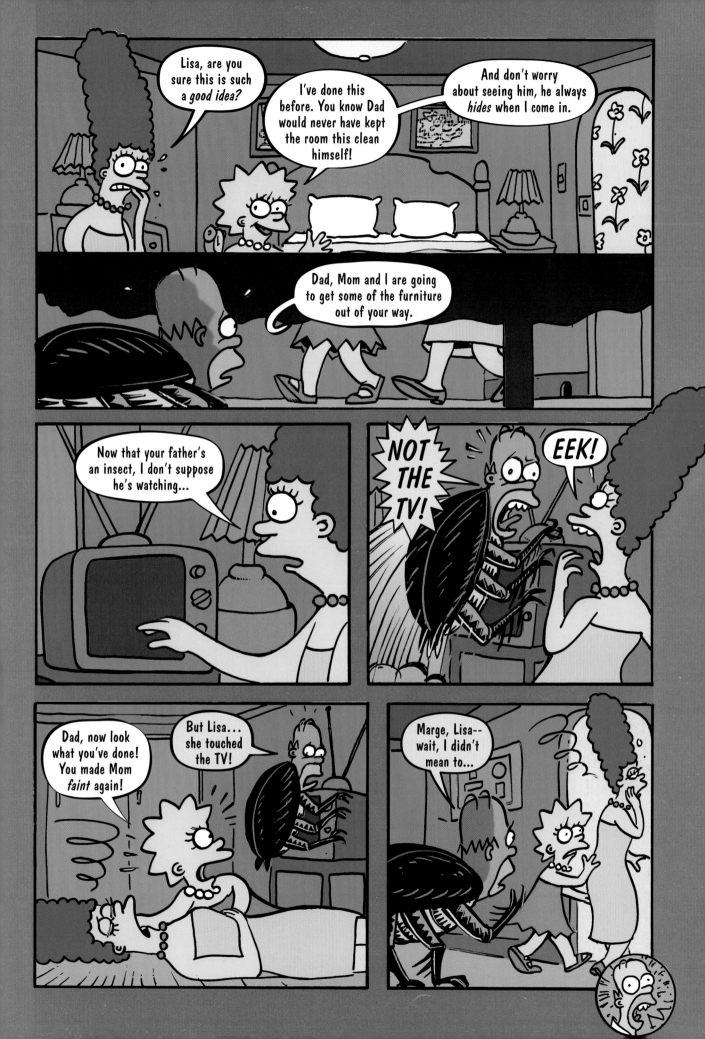

Marge, sweetheart, I'm sorry I *upset* you...
Lisa, Daddy's sorry. I want to help --
?
Well, well, looky what we have here...
Hey, Homer, what's the 'J' stand for?
Junebug?
Patty! Selma! W-what a *pleasant* surprise!
Homer J. Simpson as usual, *lowering* to our expectations...
Or is it for *'Jumpy'*?
EEYOW!
STOP!! All you may see is a loathsome, lowly, disgusting pest, but to me he's the man I call *Dad!*
Thanks, Lisa!
P.U., bug breath!

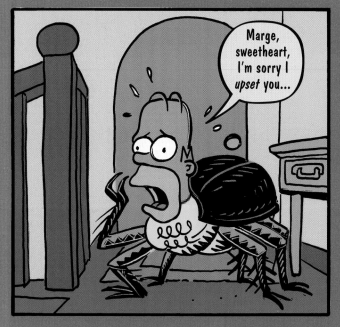

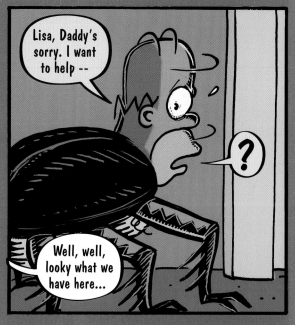

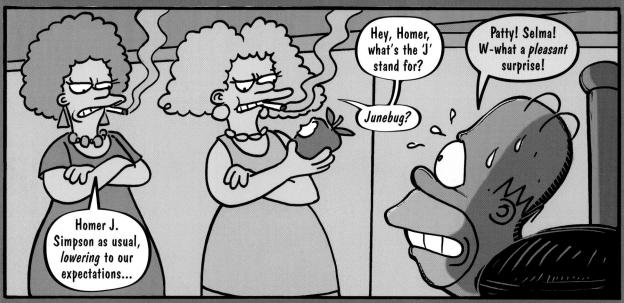

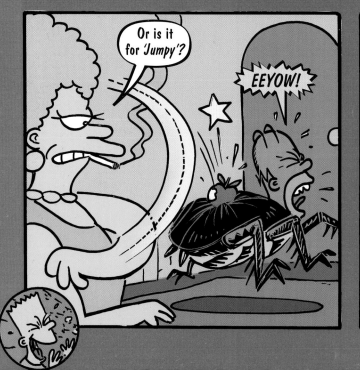

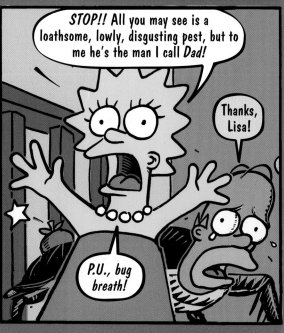

Ouch! If anybody wants me I'll be hanging from the bedroom ceiling...
Even if my family can't stand me, I still have friends I can depend on to cheer me up...
CLICK!
ITCHY & SCRATCHY in
"BUGGIN' OUT"
Acme STINGIN' WASPS
STING!
STING!
STING!
WASP KILLER
WASP KILLER
DANGER
FLAMMABLE
FOOM!
Acme Maggots

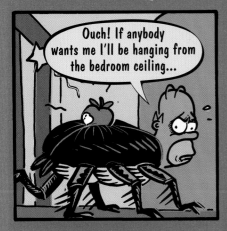

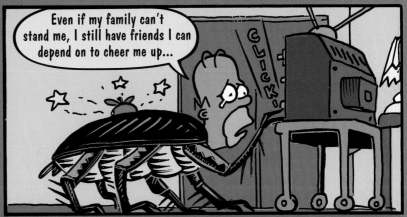

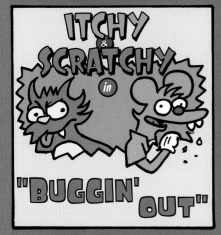

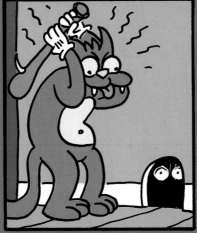

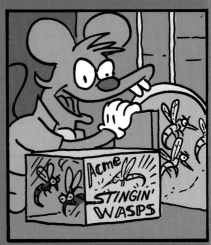

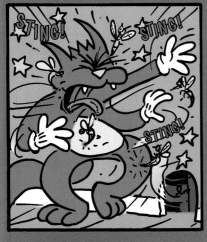

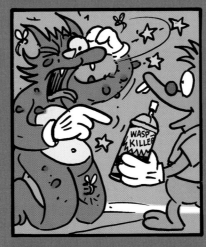

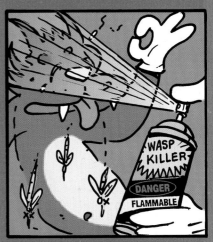

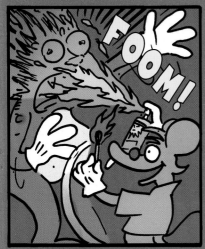

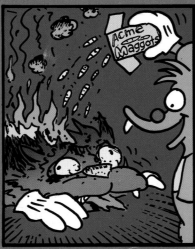

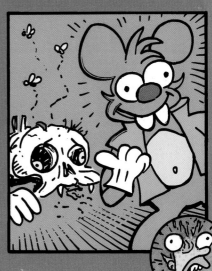

One month later...
BURP
Can I get another helping of Spam?
Lisa, can you give me a hand in the kitchen?
GRRR!
Do you like beer?
Z
While you're up, can you get me another brewski?
Yes, Mom.
I know having *tenants* is hard on you kids, but with your father out of work it's the *only thing* I could do...
... speaking of which, how is *he* doing?
All I know is that his breath has gotten *worse.*
Hey, kid, know any good tricks?
I can give you the wedgie of your life.
Tanks! Say, girlie, don't you play the saxophone?
Well, yes...
Give it a *honk* for us!
sniff

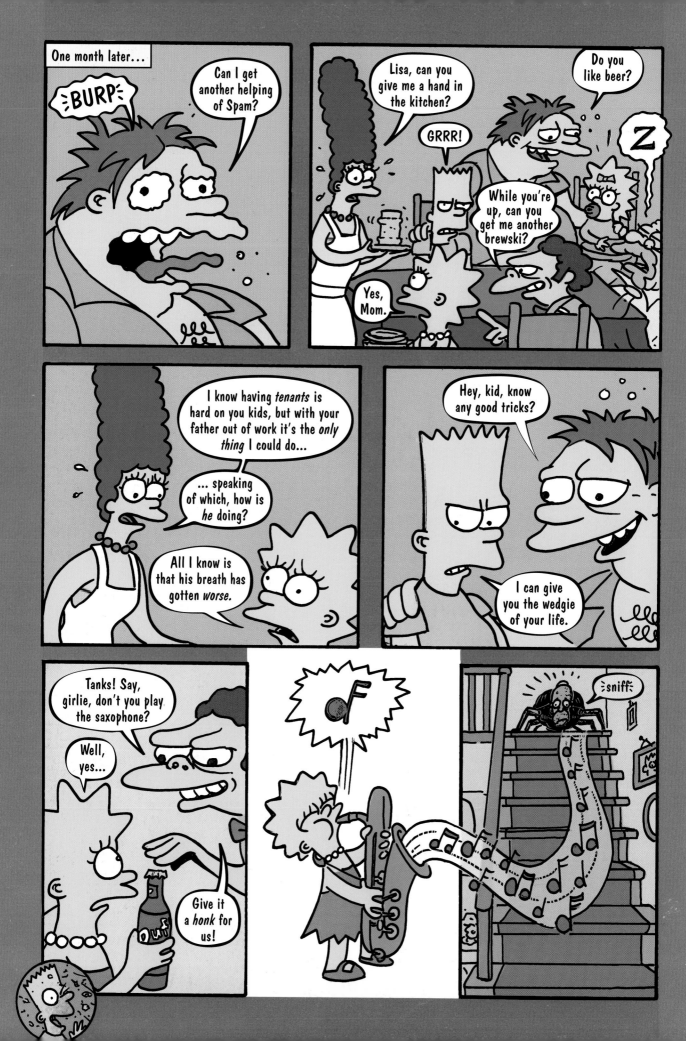

Boy, what a *beautiful movement...*
...and speaking of which, hold that note...
...I gotta go to the...
What the hell?
Now, Barney, let me *explain...*
...the bathroom's the first door on the right.
If I wanted *giant cockroaches* with *horrible breath,* I'd have kept my apartment!
Come on, Moe, let's blow this *bug stand.*
Jeez, Homer, test drive a *breath mint!*
GANG WAY!
Huh?

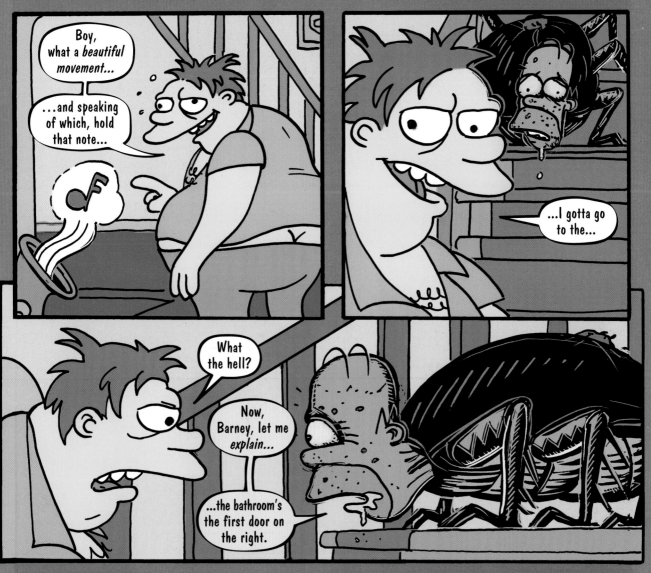

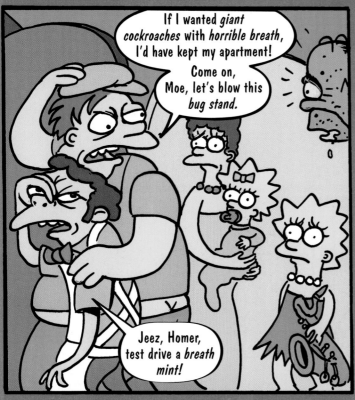

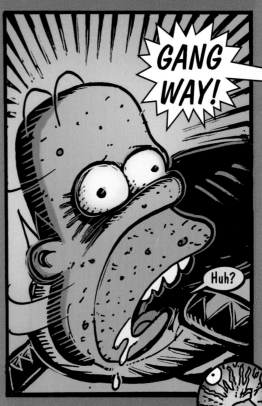

CRUNCH
Whoopsy Daisy!
DAD! He's not *moving!* He's not *breathing!*
You mean...
Homer is *no more...*
No more will I faint at the sight of him...
No more will I feel his fingers around my neck...
No more will I smell his bug breath...
YIPPIE!!

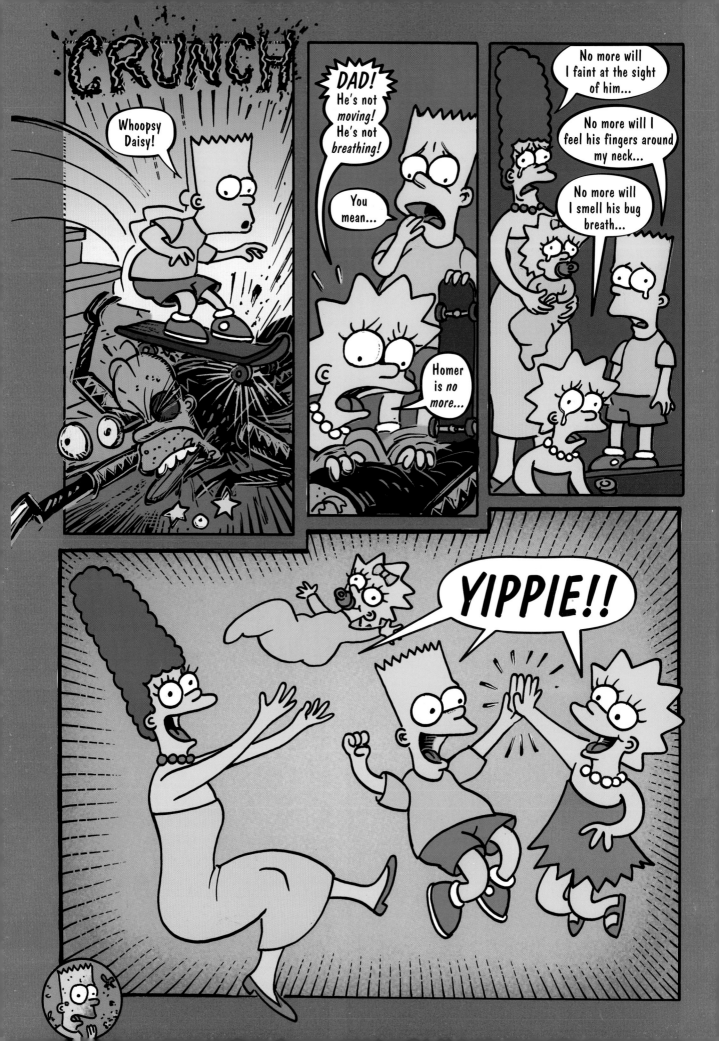

YEEAAH!!
What th-- WHEW! It was *only* a dream!
I've got to lay off that rarebit Cheez-Whiz...
Mmm...rarebit Cheez-Whiz...
Boy, if I were a *Czech writer* living in the 1920s, that would have made a great *short story*...
HEY, MARGE, KIDS, you'll never believe the dream I just had...

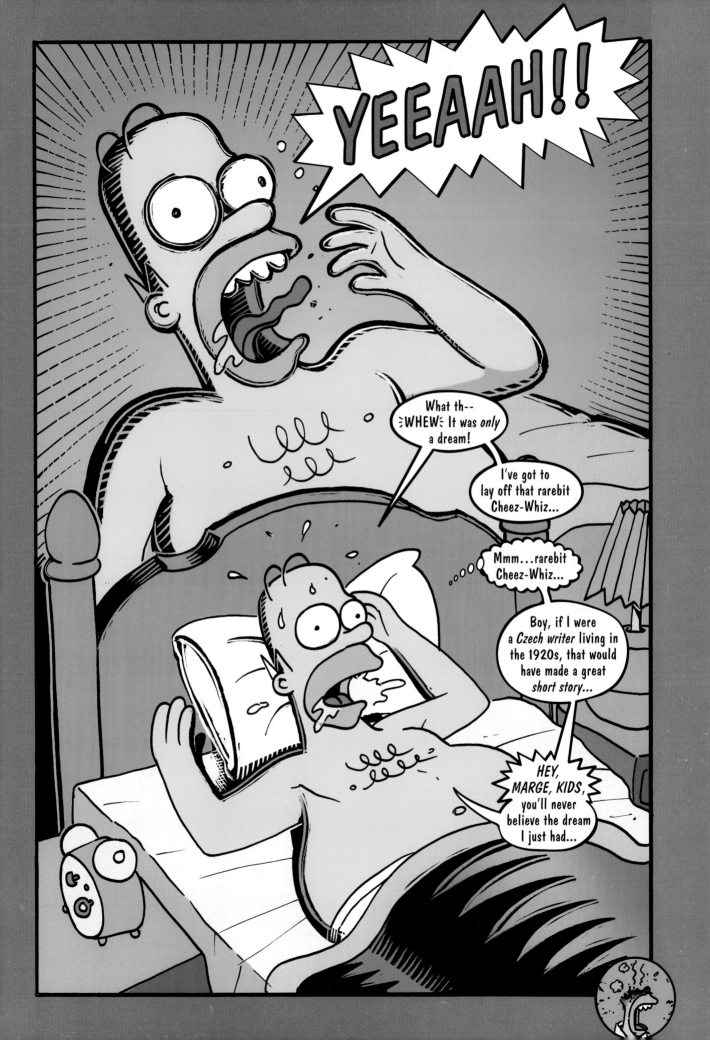

What was it about, Homie?
D'OH!
Z
I must insist that you read this...
Charlotte's Web
E. B. WHITE
Something buggin' you, Homer?
KONEC

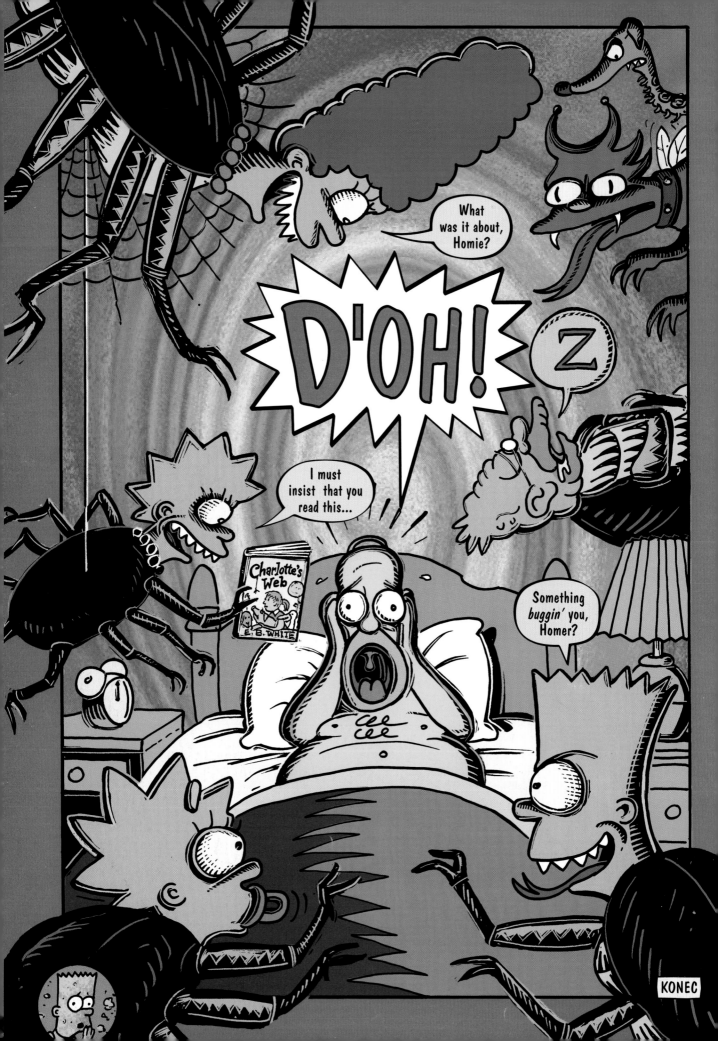

GREETINGS, EARTHLINGS! WE INTERRUPT YOUR HYPNO-VIEWING FOR ANOTHER COMMUNICATION FROM RUPERT AND KODOS MURDOCH.
WE ASSUME THE SPOOKIFYING TALES IN THIS ENTERTAINMENT VEHICLE HAVE HAD YOU SCREAMING AT THE TOP OF YOUR LUNGS WITH JOY. WE ALSO ASSUME YOU ARE NOW IN NEED OF SOMETHING CALMING, SOMETHING TO DRAIN YOUR ANXIETY BELLOWS AND INFLATE YOUR RELAXATION NODULES.
THUS ON THE FOLLOWING TWO PAGES WE OFFER A PLEASANT GLIMPSE INTO YOUR EARTHLING FUTURE. THE WORK WAS PRODUCED BY GEOF DARROW AND NATHAN KANE, TWO TALENTED HUMANS WHO HAVE COMPLETED THEIR USEFULNESS AS ARTISTS, BUT HAVE BEGUN THEIR USEFULNESS AS QUICHE FILLING.
SO SIT BACK AND ENJOY THE SOOTHING SIGHTS WE HAVE TITLED...
"RIGEL 7, SPRINGFIELD 0."

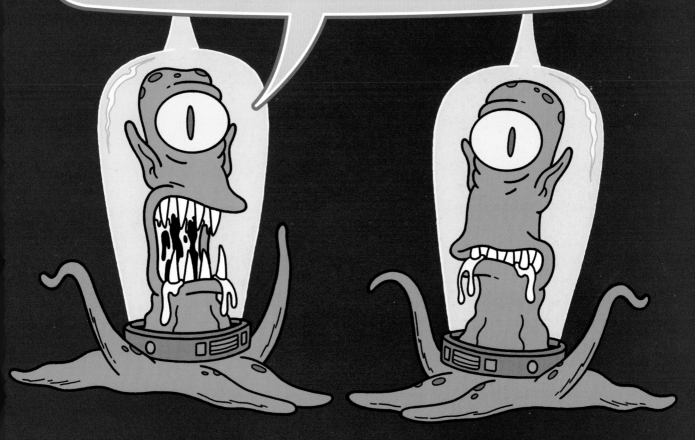

KRUSTY
SHOWCASE
Can't Stop the Music
the Musical
MAYOR
Security
OPEN 22 HRS
CHIEF Wiggum
SAYS
"SUPPORT YOUR
NEIGHBORHOOD WATCH"
GROENING DARROW

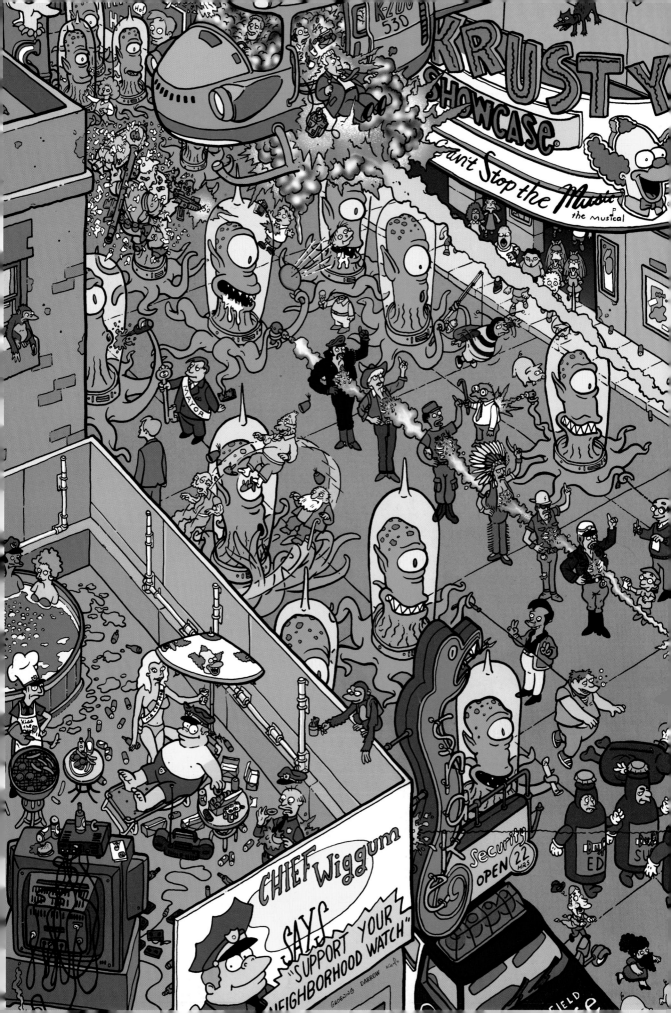

ANDROIDS Dungeon
CLOSED
ORGANS for SALE
YIELD
RIGEL IS #1
Doc TOMPERS
ALIENS with LADIES Drink Free
MOE'S
Tuesdays!!! Free Cocktail NAPKINS
is NEAR
Burns' Mr. SMITHEREEN 2
Duff

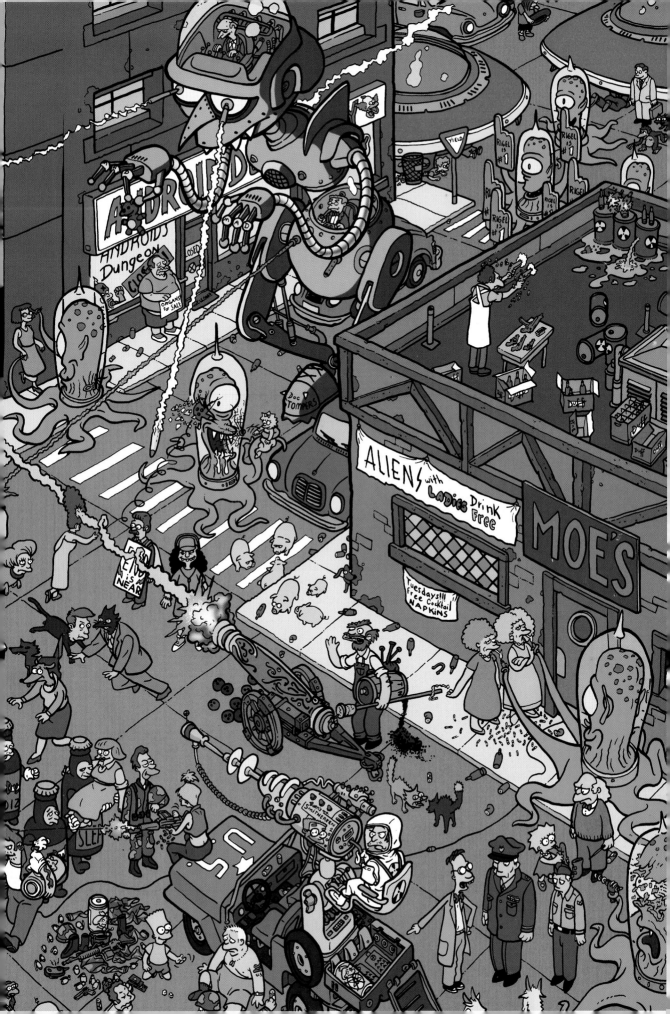

AHH, HALLOWEEN! THE NIGHT OF THE BULLY! IF YOU'VE EVER WONDERED WHY, JUST FOLLOW...
NELSON MUNTZ'S
Trail of TRICKS!
IT'S LIKE GETTING YOUR PH.D. IN CRUD-OLOGY!
7:04-THE HALLOWEEN FUN BEGINS...
JUST WHERE DO YOU THINK YOU'RE GOING?
LITTLE OL' ME? SAME PLACE I GO EVERY HALLOWEEN...TO THE FLANDERS TO BOB FOR APPLES.
LIKELY STORY! BETTER NOT BE UP TO ANY FUNNY BUSINESS, MUNTZ...
...'CAUSE I GOT MY EYE ON YOU.
POLICE
7:15-NELSON DECIDES ON A COSTUME.
HMMM...WHAT TO BE THIS YEAR...
PLEASE DON'T LET HIM PICK EIGHTEENTH-CENTURY BRITISH DANDY!
7:16-PICKS EIGHTEENTH-CENTURY BRITISH DANDY.
THIS FINE KENSINGTON LACE FEELS LIKE WHISPERS ON MY SKIN. I WONDER IF IT COMES IN A VEST?
8:34-ENTERS ZOO. TRIES TO FEED CAT TO GORILLA.
VEGETARIAN?! GEEZ, DO I HAVE TO FEED EVERY-THING TO THE SNAKES?!
8:42-USES DRYER TO SEPARATE CANDY FROM CHILD.
IT'S EASIER THAN A FULL BODY CAVITY SEARCH!*
DISCLAIMER
*THE PRODUCERS OF THIS BOOK IN COOPERATION WITH THEIR SPONSOR, THE AMERICAN ASSOCIATION OF LAUNDROMATS, WOULD LIKE TO REMIND YOU IT IS NEITHER SAFE NOR WISE TO RIDE IN A DRYER. ALTHOUGH IT MAY LOOK LIKE FUN ("HOORAY! I GET TO TUMBLE LIKE A SOCK!"), IT CAN RESULT IN PAINFUL BRUISING, BURNING, ORGAN DAMAGE, AND EVEN SEVERING OF FINGERS AND/OR THUMBS. THAT'S RIGHT, SMART GUY, IMAGINE WHAT IT'S LIKE TO BE THUMBLESS IN TODAY'S SOCIETY! FORCED TO BEG FOR NICKELS ON THE STREETS, ENDURING CRUEL NICKNAMES LIKE "STUMPS," "FINGERS," AND "LITTLE SALLY PAW PAW!" IT'S BEEN A LIVING NIGHTMARE! SO LEAVE THE DRYERS ALONE. BESIDES, FOR REAL FUN YOU CAN'T BEAT RIDING DOWN THE STAIRS IN A SHOPPING CART.**
DISCLAIMER #2
**THE AMERICAN ASSOCIATION OF SHOPPING CARTS WOULD LIKE TO TELL THE AMERICAN ASSOCIATION OF LAUNDROMATS TO SHUT THE HELL UP.
GLUE
8:51-POURS INDUSTRIAL GLUE IN CLOCK.
CRUD, I'M BORED. THERE MUST BE SOMETHING ELSE TO DO...
SPRINGFIELD TOWN HALL

7:28–DROPS PUMPKINS FROM TOO GREAT A HEIGHT.
I HOPE *THAT* LOOKED COOL.
7:45–CHECKS IN ON HIS STOLEN CANDY-SORTING SWEATSHOP.
NO, DUMMY! YOU'VE MIXED THE GOOD 'N' PLENTYS WITH THE MIKE 'N' IKES! I'M NOT EATING NO ***MIKE 'N' PLENTYS!***
GBS
IT CERTAINLY IS.
7:58–UNSUCCESSFUL IN EFFORTS TO HOTWIRE CRANE. GIVES UP GRAND PLANS TO "SWING SOME STUFF."
GOOD EVENING.
LOOKING GOOD.
HELLO.
8:07–CHANCE MEETING OF THE "WEDGIE BRIGADE."
8:21–FINDS PRISTINE FIRST EDITION COPY OF PROUST'S "REMEMBRANCE OF THINGS PAST" IN DUMPSTER.
8:22–BURNS IT.
9:00
WHO'D A GUESSED I'D ***ACTUALLY*** END UP BOBBING FOR APPLES LIKE I SAID I WOULD?
AND LOOK, I ***GOT*** ONE!

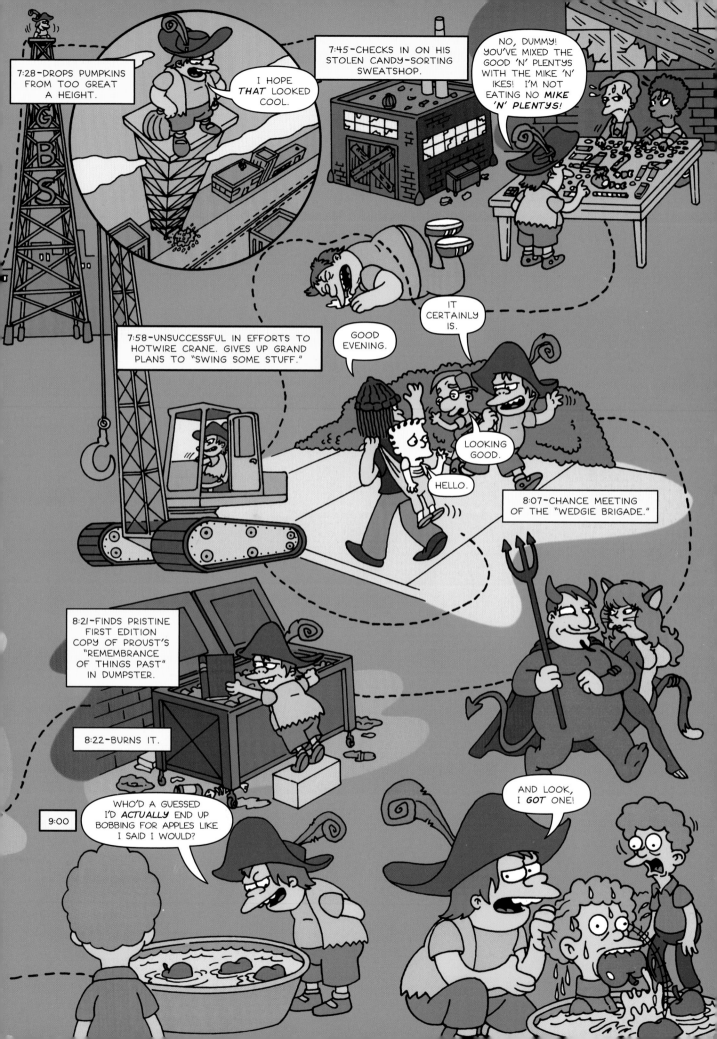

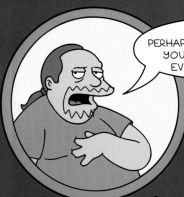

HERE, DEAR READER, IS PERHAPS THE MOST *IMPORTANT* THING YOUR *PEDESTRIAN MIND* WILL EVER ATTEMPT TO *ABSORB*.

A SERIES OF PUT-DOWNS, ZINGERS, IF YOU WILL, TO *VERBALLY SKEWER* EVEN THE MOST VICIOUS ALIEN, OR SHE-BEAST.

COMIC BOOK GUY'S
101
PUTDOWNS
FOR THE
SUPERNATURAL

ZOMBIE

WITCH

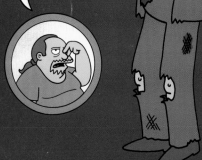

I HAVEN'T SMELLED SO MUCH *ROTTING FLESH* SINCE I SAUNA-ED WITH *ADAM WEST*!

BUBBLE BUBBLE, TOIL AND TROUBLE, I'VE SEEN *TEAMSTERS* WITH LESS STUBBLE!

WEREWOLF

THE MUMMY

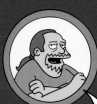

RUN ALONG THERE, *SCRAPPY DOO*!

WELL, IF IT ISN'T THE GREAT PHARAOH, *KING STINK-UNCOMMON*! YES, YOU'RE NEVER *TOO OLD* FOR MY BITING SARCASM!

GHOST TRAIN

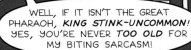

ALL ABOARD THE LAST TRAIN TO *DORKSVILLE*!

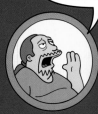

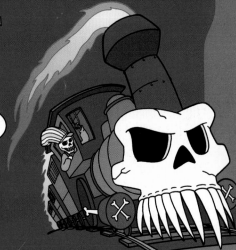

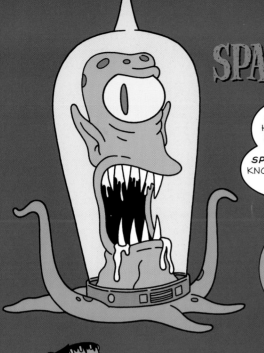

SPACE ALIEN

JACK PALANCE CALLED. HE WANTS HIS SKIN BACK. OR... YOU REMIND ME OF THE ALIEN IN THAT *SPIELBERG MOVIE*. YOU KNOW, *OPRAH WINFREY*. LOOK OUT! PAPA'S ON A ROLL!

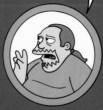

GHOST INDIAN

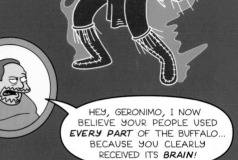

HEY, GERONIMO, I NOW BELIEVE YOUR PEOPLE USED *EVERY PART* OF THE BUFFALO... BECAUSE YOU CLEARLY RECEIVED ITS *BRAIN!*

FRANKENSTEIN'S MONSTER

LOOK, FRANKENBERRY, IF I WANTED TO SEE A BUNCH OF PARTS SEWN TOGETHER, I'D *DOWNLOAD* A PICTURE OF *CHER!*

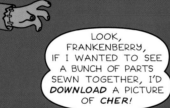

VAMPIRE

AH YES, THE EVIL THAT DARE NOT SPEAK ITS NAME. WELL, I'VE GOT A NAME FOR YOU... *SIR SUCKS-A-LOT!*

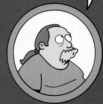

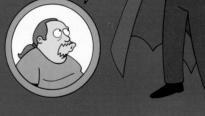

MUTANT FLY CREATURE

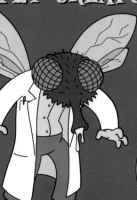

GIANT PEOPLE-EATING IRIS OF THE PLANET THAR-TAC

YOU THINK *YOU'RE DISGUSTING?* PLEASE! I'VE SEEN A *FIRST-GRADER* EAT A *HO-HO!*

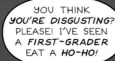

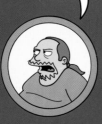

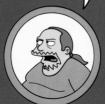

ALAS, IT WOULD APPEAR THE LAST JIBE HAS *TOLLED* FOR ME.

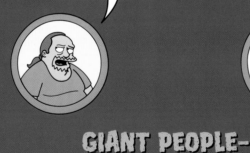

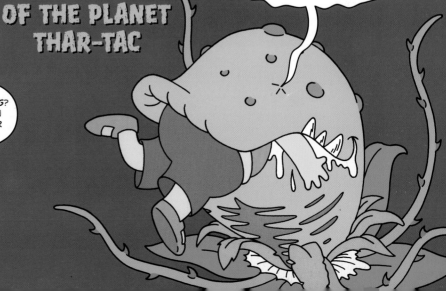

HOMER'S FAVORITE

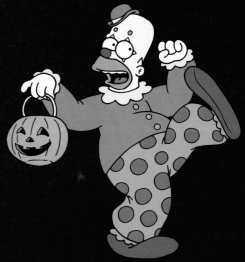

"AS WITH *ALL* HOLIDAY CAROLS, THEY'RE BETTER SUNG WHEN *DRUNK!*"

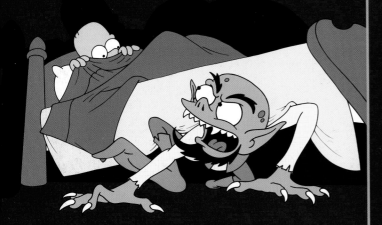

I'M DREAMING OF A GREEN GOBLIN

(SUNG TO THE TUNE OF "I'M DREAMING OF A WHITE CHRISTMAS")

I'M DREAMING OF A GREEN GOBLIN,
JUST LIKE THE ONE BENEATH MY BED.
WILL IT BREAK MY TOES-IES
OR BITE MY NOSEY
AND USE A SPOON TO EAT THE CONTENTS
   OF MY HEAD?

I'M STILL DREAMING OF A GREEN GOBLIN,
BUT NOW MY HEART IS FILLED WITH JOY.
I PLAN TO MAKE A DASH FOR THE
   DOOOOOOR,
ONCE I'VE GOT IT FEASTING ON THE BOY!

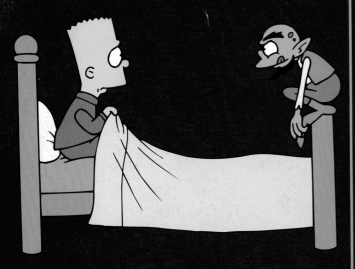

TRICK OR TREAT!
(FATTY NEEDS SOME FOOD!)

(SUNG TO THE TUNE OF "JINGLE BELLS")

DASHING THROUGH THE STREETS,
HE BANGS ON EVERY DOOR,
DRESSED UP LIKE A CLOWN
EVEN THOUGH HE'S THIRTY-FOUR...

HE'S TOLD TO GO AWAY,
BUT HE REALLY NEEDS A FIX,
HE WOULD SELL HIS GRANDMA FOR
A MEASLY PIXIE STICK, OH...

TRICK OR TREAT! TRICK OR TREAT!
FATTY NEEDS SOME FOOD!
HE DON'T CARE IF HE'S BOSTON BEANED
OR MERELY CHARLESTON CHEWED, OH...

TRICK OR TREAT! TRICK OR TREAT!
THIS REALLY IS THE WORST.
WHEN YOU'RE A BALDING TRICK OR TREATER
AND IT'S NOON DECEMBER FIRST!

OH, HOLY CRAP!

(SUNG TO THE TUNE OF "O HOLY NIGHT")

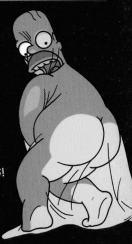

OH, HOLY CRAP!
YOU CAN SEE RIGHT THROUGH
   MY GHOST SUIT!
MARGE WAS RIGHT,
I SHOULDA WORN UNDERPANTS!

HALLOWEEN CAROLS

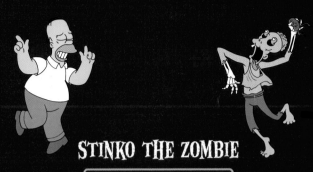

STINKO THE ZOMBIE

(SUNG TO THE TUNE OF
"FROSTY THE SNOWMAN")

STINKO THE ZOMBIE,
WAS A CORPSE WITHOUT A SOUL.
WITH A SINGLE TOOTH HANGING BY THE ROOT
AND TWO EYES MADE OUT OF TOES.

DOWN THROUGH THE VILLAGE,
WITH HIS KIDNEYS IN HIS HANDS,
CHILDREN SMELLED DECAY AS THEY LAUGHED
   AND PLAYED
A GAME OF DODGE BALL WITH HIS GLANDS.

THERE MUST HAVE BEEN SOME MAGIC
IN A CORPSE THAT SKIPS AND JOGS.
BUT THE KIDS KNEW THEY'D MADE A MISTAKE
WHEN THEY FED HIM TO THE DOGS.

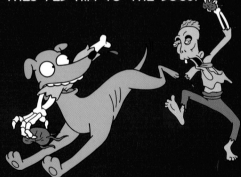

STINKO THE ZOMBIE,
WAS NOW A WORTHLESS PILE OF FLESH,
BUT HE SAID GOODBYE, AND FOR A FUN
   DEAD GUY,
YOU WILL ALWAYS HAVE JOHN TESH.*

SLOPPITY SLOP SLOP,
PLOPPITY PLOP PLOP,
LOOK AT STINKO GO!

CHUNKITY CHUNK CHUNK
CLUNKITY CLUNK
LEAVING PINK STAINS IN THE SNOW!

*THAT'S RIGHT, I MADE FUN OF JOHN TESH! WHAT'S *HE*
GONNA DO ABOUT IT? SEND OUT HIS *GOON PATROL* LIKE
LAST TIME? THEY DON'T SCARE ME. I'VE BEEN BEATEN BY
MUCH BETTER COMPOSERS' GOON PATROLS THAN *HIS*! MARVIN
HAMLISCH'S BOYS PUT A HOLE IN MY THROAT THAT STILL
BUBBLES WHEN I TALK! SO *BRING IT ON*, TESHY!

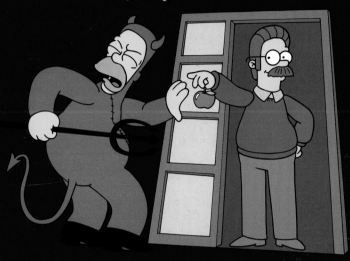

THE TWELFTH DAY OF SPOOK NIGHT

(SUNG TO THE TUNE OF
"TWELVE DAYS OF CHRISTMAS")

ON THE TWELFTH DAY OF SPOOK NIGHT
MY FLANDERS GAVE TO ME...

TWELVE STUPID APPLES
ELEVEN BIBLE VERSES
TEN STINKIN' HEALTH BARS
WHERE THE HELL'S THE CANDY?!
I'LL GET MY OWN DAMN CANDY!
DON'T TELL ME YOU DON'T EAT CANDY!
GUESS I'LL SETTLE FOR THIS BLENDER
AND I COULD USE THESE SPEAKERS
I'LL TAKE THESE FIVE GOLDEN THINGS!
FOUR CALLING CARDS
THREE FRENCH PENS
TWO CD PLAYERS
AND A PARTRIDGE IN A PEAR TREE!

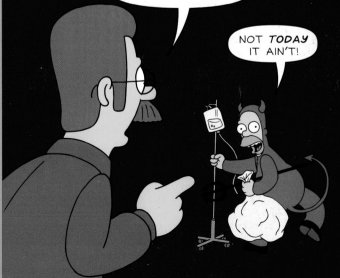

BUT THAT'S NOT
A PARTRIDGE IN A PEAR
TREE! THAT'S GRANNY'S
I.V. STAND!

NOT *TODAY*
IT AIN'T!

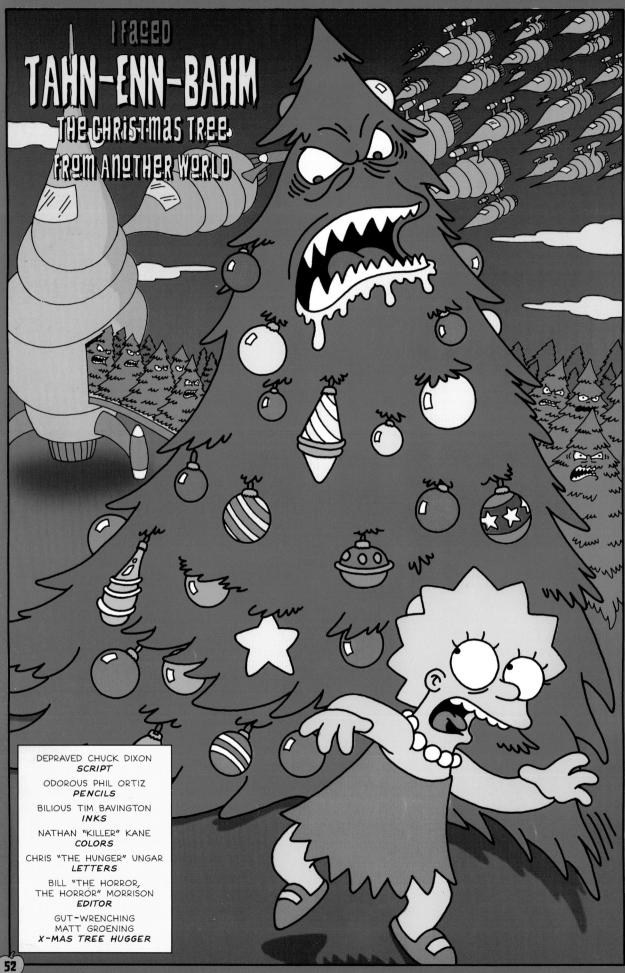

I FACED

TAHN-ENN-BAHM
THE CHRISTMAS TREE FROM ANOTHER WORLD

DEPRAVED CHUCK DIXON
SCRIPT

ODOROUS PHIL ORTIZ
PENCILS

BILIOUS TIM BAVINGTON
INKS

NATHAN "KILLER" KANE
COLORS

CHRIS "THE HUNGER" UNGAR
LETTERS

BILL "THE HORROR,
THE HORROR" MORRISON
EDITOR

GUT-WRENCHING
MATT GROENING
X-MAS TREE HUGGER

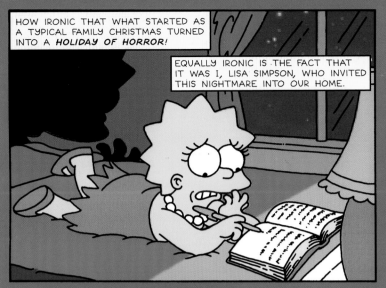

HOW IRONIC THAT WHAT STARTED AS A TYPICAL FAMILY CHRISTMAS TURNED INTO A *HOLIDAY OF HORROR!*

EQUALLY IRONIC IS THE FACT THAT IT WAS I, LISA SIMPSON, WHO INVITED THIS NIGHTMARE INTO OUR HOME.

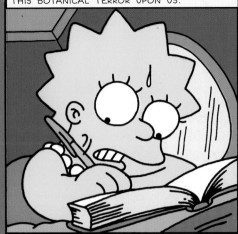

AND WITH IRONY SO DEEP IT REACHES THE SECOND FLOOR WINDOWS, IT WAS *MY* ENVIRONMENTAL AWARENESS THAT BROUGHT THIS BOTANICAL TERROR UPON US.

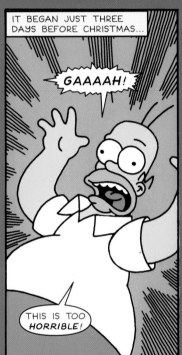

IT BEGAN JUST THREE DAYS BEFORE CHRISTMAS...

GAAAAH!

THIS IS TOO *HORRIBLE!*

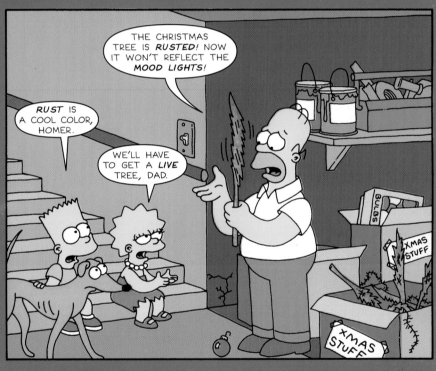

THE CHRISTMAS TREE IS *RUSTED!* NOW IT WON'T REFLECT THE *MOOD LIGHTS!*

RUST IS A COOL COLOR, HOMER.

WE'LL HAVE TO GET A *LIVE* TREE, DAD.

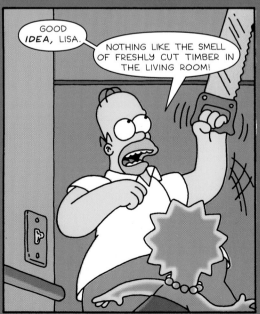

GOOD *IDEA*, LISA.

NOTHING LIKE THE SMELL OF FRESHLY CUT TIMBER IN THE LIVING ROOM!

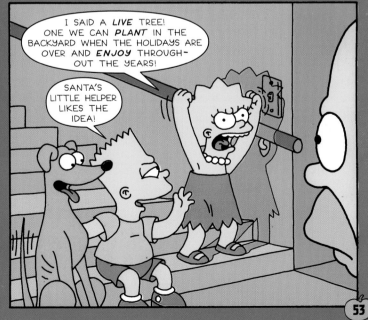

I SAID A *LIVE* TREE! ONE WE CAN *PLANT* IN THE BACKYARD WHEN THE HOLIDAYS ARE OVER AND *ENJOY* THROUGH- OUT THE YEARS!

SANTA'S LITTLE HELPER LIKES THE IDEA!

KRUSTY'S KRISTMAS KUT-O-RAMA!
KUT YOUR OWN TREE AND SAVE A BUNDLE!
A DIVISION OF KRUSTCO STRIP MINING ENTERPRISES.
LOUSY, NO GOOD...
WE COULD BE GOING TO KRUSTY'S.
AW, HOMEY, IT'LL BE AN ADVENTURE. LIKE AN OLD FASHIONED CHRISTMAS.
OLD FASHIONED CHRISTMAS, MY BUTT!
NEXT YOU'LL BE WANTING US TO SPEND ALL STUPID CHRISTMAS MORNING IN STUPID CHURCH.
AND WHAT WOULD BE WRONG WITH THAT?
JUST FORTY-FIVE MINUTES WE'LL NEVER SEE AGAIN!
WAY TO RUIN CHRISTMAS, MOM!
SHUT UP, BOY!
WHAT'D I DO?
IT'S NOT YOUR MOTHER WHO'S RUINING CHRISTMAS--
LIVE AND LET LIVE CHRISTMAS TREE FARM
--IT'S LISA.
HOMER!
WELL, IT IS!

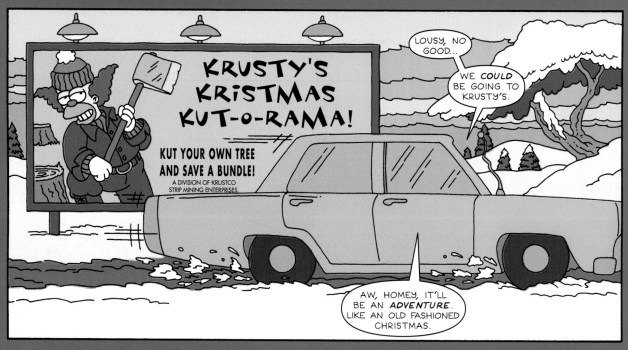

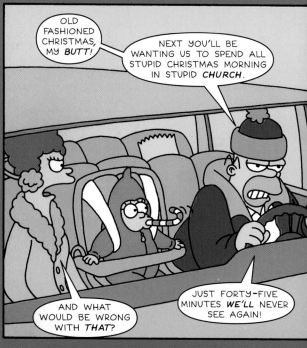

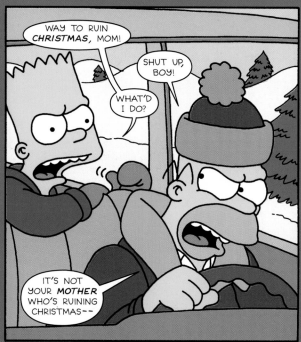

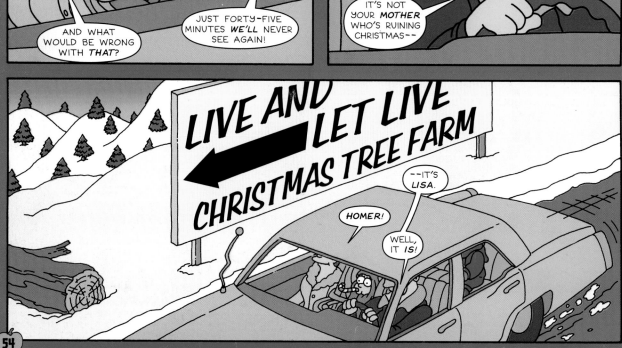

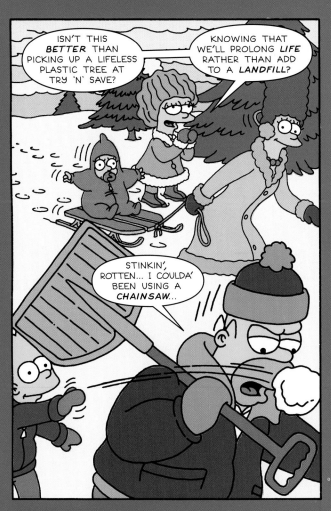

ISN'T THIS *BETTER* THAN PICKING UP A LIFELESS PLASTIC TREE AT TRY 'N' SAVE?

KNOWING THAT WE'LL PROLONG *LIFE* RATHER THAN ADD TO A *LANDFILL*?

STINKIN', ROTTEN... I COULDA' BEEN USING A *CHAINSAW*...

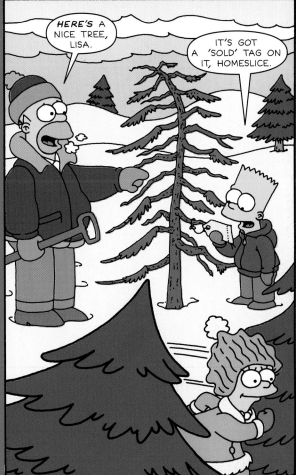

HERE'S A NICE TREE, LISA.

IT'S GOT A 'SOLD' TAG ON IT, HOMESLICE.

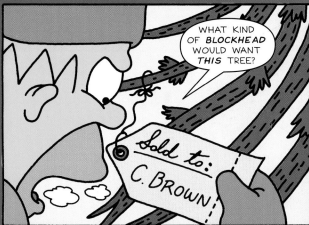

WHAT KIND OF *BLOCKHEAD* WOULD WANT *THIS* TREE?

Sold to: C. BROWN!

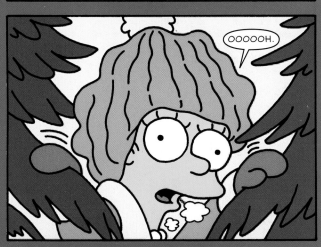

OOOOOH.

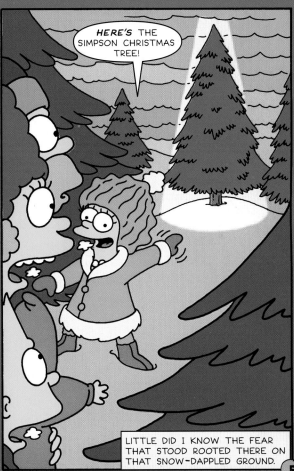

HERE'S THE SIMPSON CHRISTMAS TREE!

LITTLE DID I KNOW THE FEAR THAT STOOD ROOTED THERE ON THAT SNOW-DAPPLED GROUND.

THERE'S NO PRICE ON THIS TREE, SIR.
I NEVER SAW THAT ONE--
UM, I MEAN I DIDN'T GET AROUND TO TAGGING IT, MAN.
HMMMM.
A HUNDRED BUCKS.
Love
OW!
OW!
OW!
BART!
STOP SAYING OW!
IT WASN'T ME!
OH, THANK YOU, DAD!
SOME DAY WE'LL STAND IN THE SHADE OF THIS BEAUTIFUL--
WHAT KIND OF TREE IS THIS?
YOU'RE
:GASP!:
WELL
:GASP!:
COME!
WHO CARES AS LONG AS THERE'S PRESENTS UNDER IT!
DON'T FORGET TO WATER THE TREE, HOMEY!
UHHHHHHH...

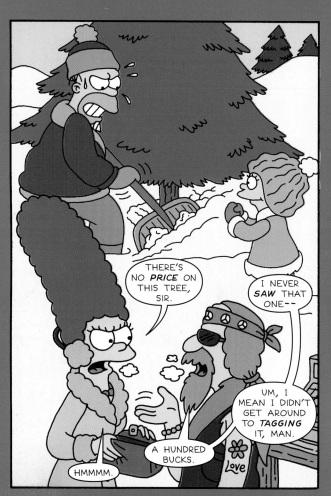

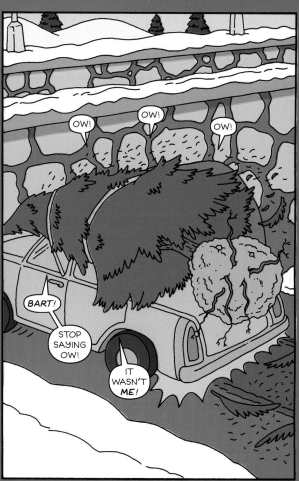

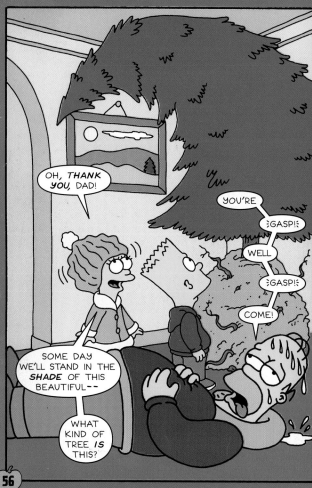

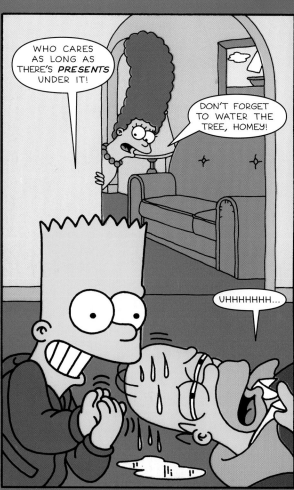

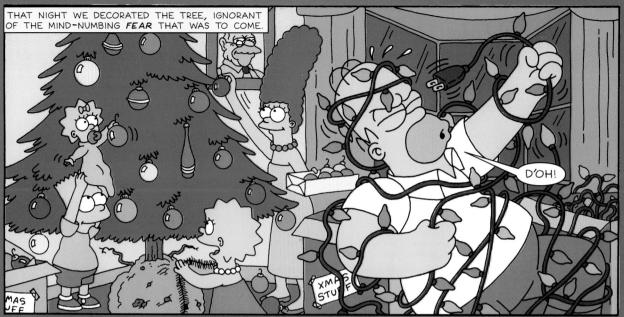

THAT NIGHT WE DECORATED THE TREE, IGNORANT OF THE MIND-NUMBING *FEAR* THAT WAS TO COME.

D'OH!

BUT STILL THE GENUS OF OUR FAMILY TREE PUZZLED ME.

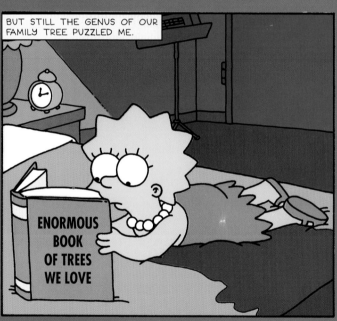

ENORMOUS BOOK OF TREES WE LOVE

I COULDN'T FIND ITS SPECIES IN ANY OF MY BOOKS.

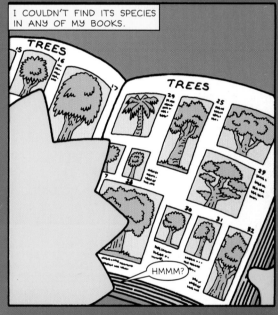

TREES

TREES

HMMM?

WHILE MY PARENTS AND SIBLINGS SLEPT, I WENT TO THE LIVING ROOM TO EXAMINE THE TREE.

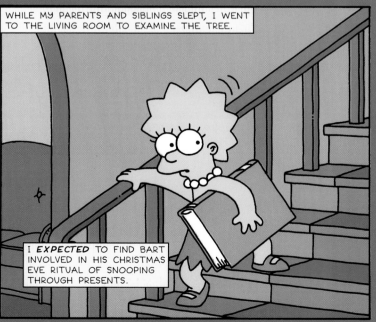

I *EXPECTED* TO FIND BART INVOLVED IN HIS CHRISTMAS EVE RITUAL OF SNOOPING THROUGH PRESENTS.

INSTEAD, I MADE THE MOST FRIGHTENING DISCOVERY OF MY YOUNG LIFE.

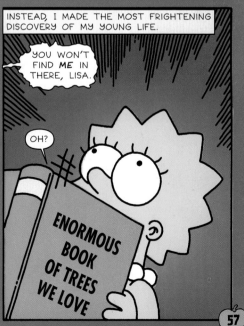

YOU WON'T FIND *ME* IN THERE, LISA.

OH?

ENORMOUS BOOK OF TREES WE LOVE

GAAAAAAAAAAH!
YES... YES... DON'T HOLD YOUR TERROR BACK.
I *TOLD* THE OTHERS YOURS WOULD BE A SIMPLE RACE TO CONQUER.
UH--UH-- *OTHERS*?
I AM BUT A *VANGUARD* FOR AN ALIEN INVASION FROM A FAR-OFF STAR SYSTEM.
MY NAME IS TAHN-ENN-BAHM. AND I AM BUT ONE OF *BILLIONS*. EVEN *NOW* AN ARMADA WAITS IN ORBIT FOR *MY* SIGNAL.
I COME FROM A WORLD WHOSE NAME YOUR KIND CANNOT EVEN *PRONOUNCE*.
BECAUSE IF YOU ACCENT THE THIRTIETH SYLLABLE WRONG IT MEANS 'BIG BUTT.'
I *TOLD* YOU WE SHOULD HAVE COME SOONER. NOW WE'LL *NEVER* GET A SPACE!
D'OH!

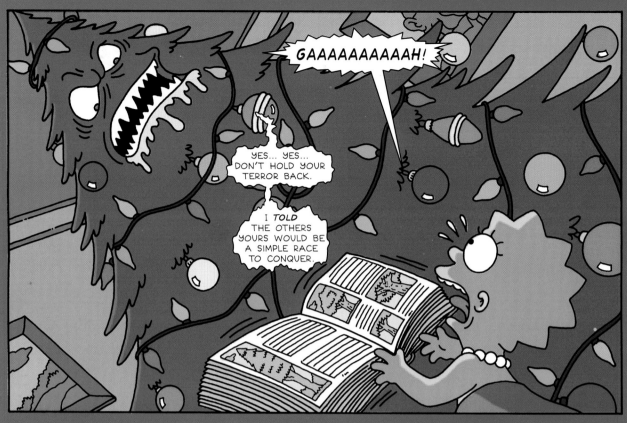

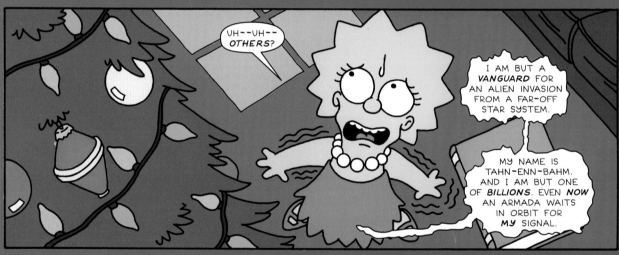

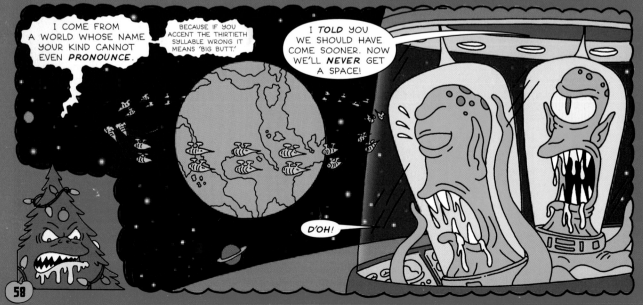

WHEN I TELL THEM OF YOUR WEAKNESS, MY BROTHERS WILL LAND IN FORCE IN ALL OF YOUR WORLD'S CAPITALS.
HEY! HOW MUCH DID THOSE TREES CONTRIBUTE?
YOUR ENTIRE POPULATION WILL BE THROWN INTO A PANIC!
OH, GREAT! JUST AS WE FIND A CURE FOR MALE IMPOTENCE OUR RACE IS DOOMED!
I MUST DEVELOP A MANURE-FLAVORED SQUISHEE!
ER, UH--I GUESS THERE GOES ANY HOPE OF RE-ELECTION.
ARE THEY TOBACCO TREES?
WELL, ARE THEY?
AND WHEN WE HAVE CRUSHED ALL RESISTANCE, WE WILL RULE SUPREME!
YOU WILL SPEND YOUR DAYS TENDING TO OUR EVERY NEED. WORSHIPING US EVERY DAY!
AND FOR THOSE WHO RESIST, THERE IS A SPECIAL FATE...
QUICKEE GRO IS PEOPLE!
QUICKEE GRO IS PEOPLE!
QUICKEE GRO

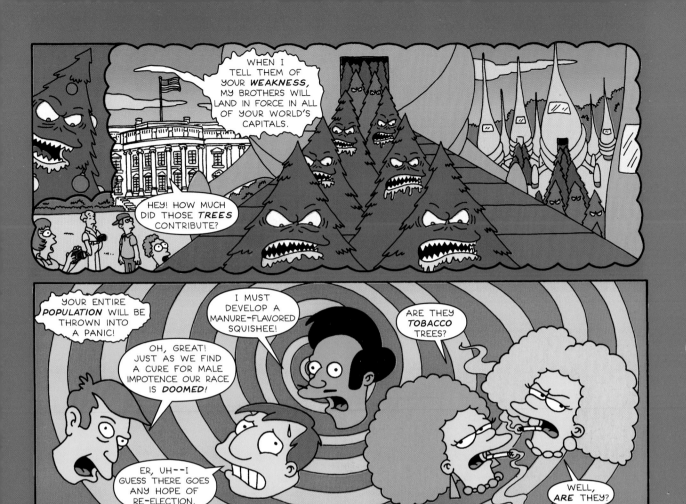

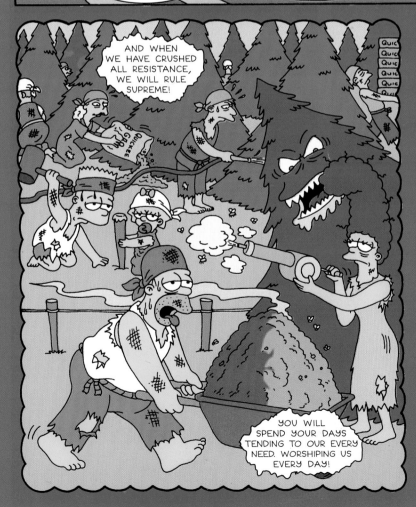

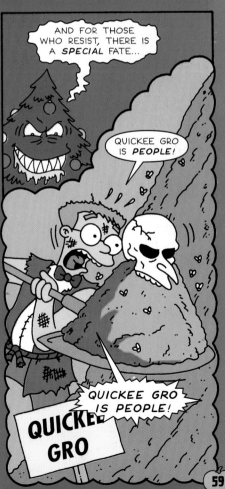

YES! RUN IN TERROR, EARTHLING!
SOON THERE WILL BE NOWHERE TO RUN!
SOON YOUR ENTIRE SPECIES WILL SEE THE FOREST FOR THE TREES!
HA HA HA HA HA HA!
WHA--?
WHAT ARE YOU DOING?
I THINK YOU NEED A LITTLE TRIM, ALIEN INTRUDER.
CAN YOU REALLY DO THAT, LISA?
I'VE HEARD YOUR WORSHIPFUL TONE WHEN SPEAKING OF PLANT LIFE.
CAN YOU CHOP DOWN A TREE?
EVEN A PLANET-PLUNDERING PINE LIKE MYSELF?
I...I...

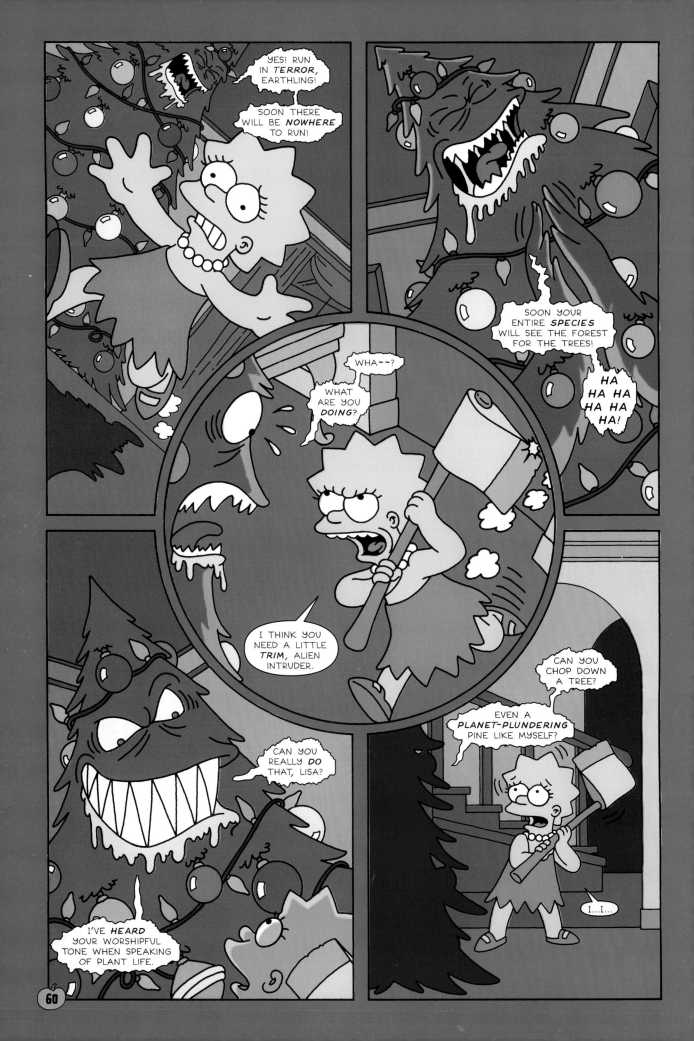

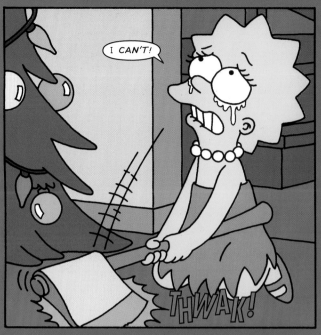

I CAN'T!

THWAK!

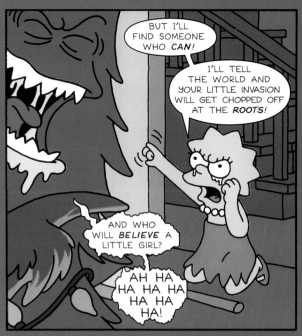

BUT I'LL FIND SOMEONE WHO *CAN*!

I'LL TELL THE WORLD AND YOUR LITTLE INVASION WILL GET CHOPPED OFF AT THE *ROOTS*!

AND WHO WILL *BELIEVE* A LITTLE GIRL?

AH HA HA HA HA HA HA!

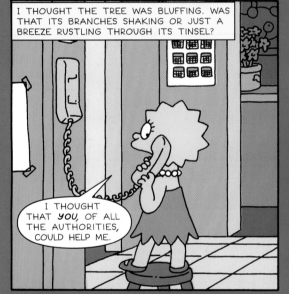

I THOUGHT THE TREE WAS BLUFFING. WAS THAT ITS BRANCHES SHAKING OR JUST A BREEZE RUSTLING THROUGH ITS TINSEL?

I THOUGHT THAT *YOU*, OF ALL THE AUTHORITIES, COULD HELP ME.

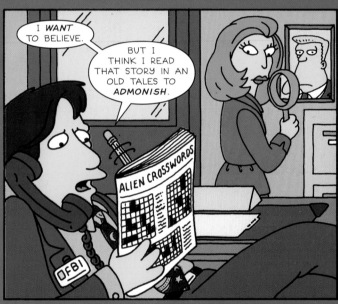

I *WANT* TO BELIEVE.

BUT I THINK I READ THAT STORY IN AN OLD TALES TO *ADMONISH*.

ALIEN CROSSWORDS

FBI

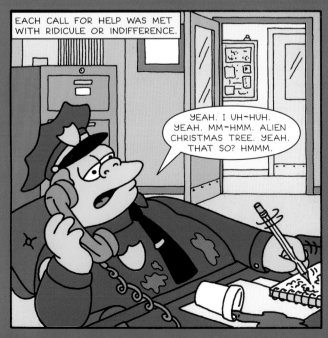

EACH CALL FOR HELP WAS MET WITH RIDICULE OR INDIFFERENCE.

YEAH. I UH-HUH. YEAH. MM-HMM. ALIEN CHRISTMAS TREE. YEAH. THAT SO? HMMM.

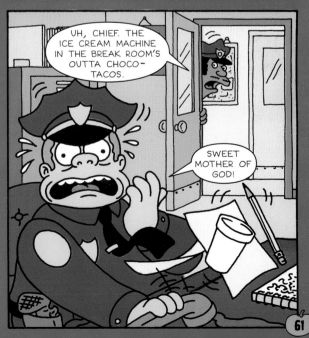

UH, CHIEF. THE ICE CREAM MACHINE IN THE BREAK ROOM'S OUTTA CHOCO-TACOS.

SWEET MOTHER OF GOD!

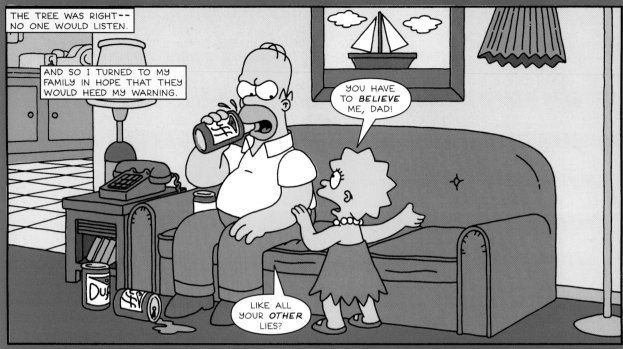

THE TREE WAS RIGHT-- NO ONE WOULD LISTEN.

AND SO I TURNED TO MY FAMILY IN HOPE THAT THEY WOULD HEED MY WARNING.

YOU HAVE TO *BELIEVE* ME, DAD!

LIKE ALL YOUR *OTHER* LIES?

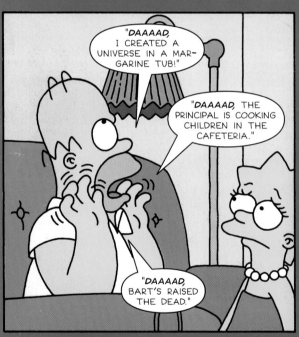

"*DAAAAD*, I CREATED A UNIVERSE IN A MARGARINE TUB!"

"*DAAAAD*, THE PRINCIPAL IS COOKING CHILDREN IN THE CAFETERIA."

"*DAAAAD*, BART'S RAISED THE DEAD."

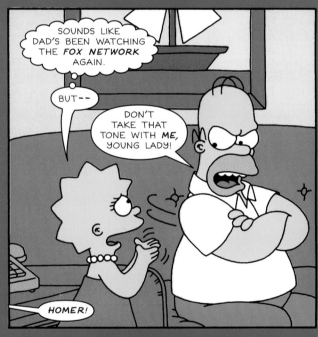

SOUNDS LIKE DAD'S BEEN WATCHING THE *FOX NETWORK* AGAIN.

BUT--

DON'T TAKE THAT TONE WITH *ME*, YOUNG LADY!

HOMER!

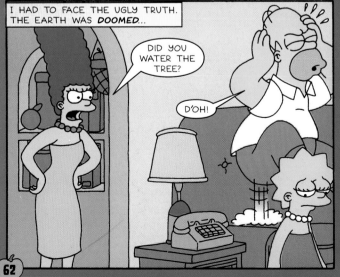

I HAD TO FACE THE UGLY TRUTH. THE EARTH WAS *DOOMED*...

DID YOU WATER THE TREE?

D'OH!

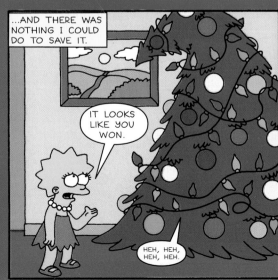

...AND THERE WAS NOTHING I COULD DO TO SAVE IT.

IT LOOKS LIKE YOU WON.

HEH, HEH, HEH, HEH.

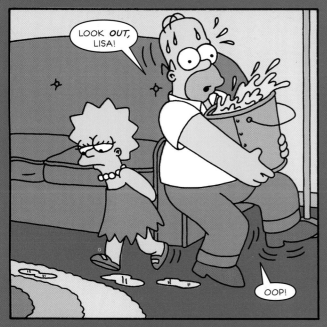

LOOK *OUT*, LISA!

OOP!

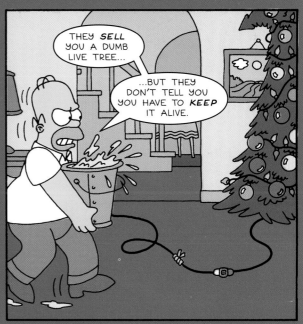

THEY *SELL* YOU A DUMB LIVE TREE...

...BUT THEY DON'T TELL YOU YOU HAVE TO *KEEP* IT ALIVE.

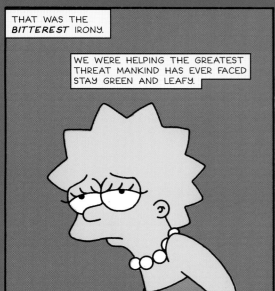

THAT WAS THE *BITTEREST* IRONY.

WE WERE HELPING THE GREATEST THREAT MANKIND HAS EVER FACED STAY GREEN AND LEAFY.

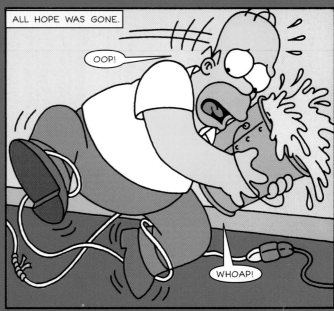

ALL HOPE WAS GONE.

OOP!

WHOAP!

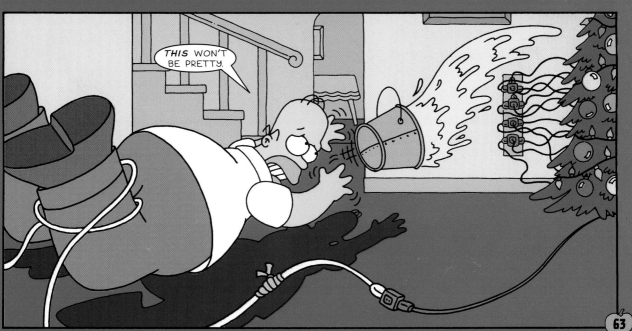

THIS WON'T BE PRETTY.

EEEEEYAAAAAAAAAAA!
STUPID SMOKE DETECTOR!
THAT'S NOT THE SMOKE DETECTOR. THAT'S AN ALIEN DEATH SCREAM.
STUPID ALIEN DEATH-SCREAM!
TAHN-ENN-BAHM IS DEAD!
THE EARTH-LINGS ARE TOO POWERFUL!
FLEE!
AND SO THE THREAT WAS ENDED. NOT BY WAR OR SCIENCE.
MARGE?
THE TREE'S WATERED.
AT LEAST NOW EVERYONE CAN FORGET THE TIME I BURNED UP THE TREE.
BUT BY A BUCKET OF WATER AND TWO LEFT FEET, EARTH WAS SAVED.
THAT'S WHAT SHE THINKS.
HA HA HA HA HA HA HA HA HA HA HA HA HA HA HA HA HA HA HA HA HA HA HA
THE END???????????????

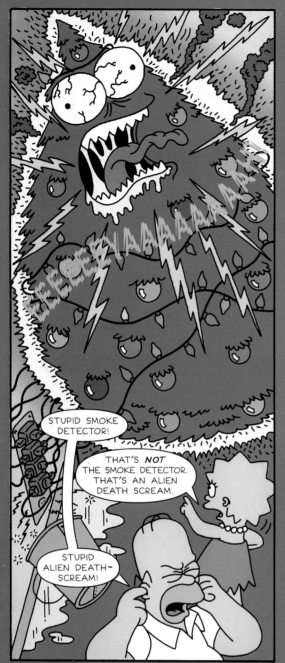

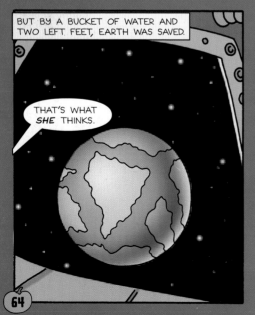

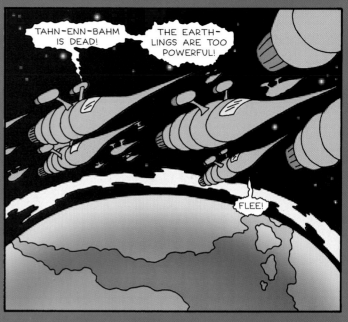

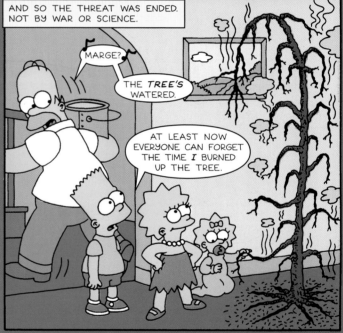

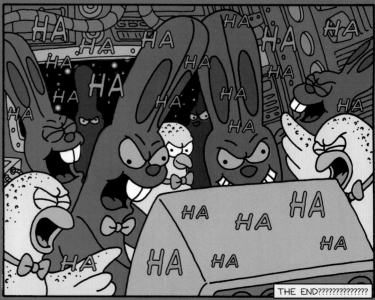

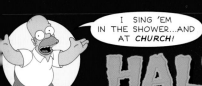

I SING 'EM IN THE SHOWER...AND AT *CHURCH!*

MORE OF HOMER'S HALLOWEEN CAROLS

IT CAME UPON A MIDNIGHT BEER

(SUNG TO THE TUNE OF "IT CAME UPON A MIDNIGHT CLEAR")

IT CAME UPON A MIDNIGHT BEER, SURROUNDED BY BOTTLES AND LIDS, OF HOW AT THE END OF THIS HALLOWEEN NIGHT...

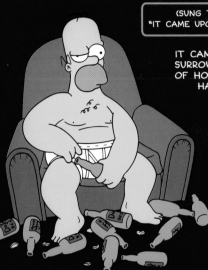

...I FORGOT TO PICK UP THE KIDS!

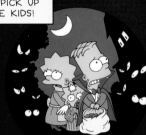

PUMPKIN FIGHT

(SUNG TO THE TUNE OF "SILENT NIGHT")

SILENT NIGHT, QUIET NIGHT, AFTER OUR PUMPKIN FIGHT. CHUNKS OF PULP FLYING THROUGH THE AIR, A STEM IS STUCK IN MY UNDERWEAR.

WE'VE RUINED MILHOUSE'S HOOOME... THANK GOD, IT'S MILHOUSE'S HOME.

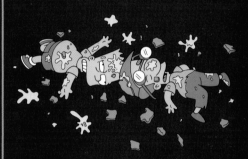

WE THREE KINGS
(AS ELVIS STAND)

(SUNG TO THE TUNE OF "WE THREE KINGS")

WE THREE KINGS AS ELVIS STAND. OUR COSTUMES SHOW THE LIFE OF THE MAN:

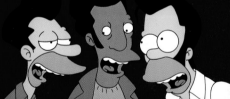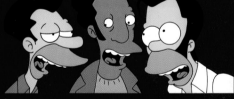

OLD AND WISER...

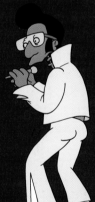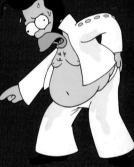

HOT, YOUNG GEYSER...

AND THE ONE WHO DIED *ON THE CAN!*

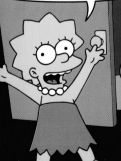

♪ THE BOAR'S HEAD IN HAND BEAR I BEDECKED WITH BAYS AND ROSEMAR-Y! AND I PRAY YOU MY MASTERS BE MERR-Y, QUOT ESTES IN CONVIVIO! ♪

WHAT THE HELL WAS *THAT?!*

A CHRISTMAS CAROL FROM SEVENTEENTH-CENTURY ENGLAND.

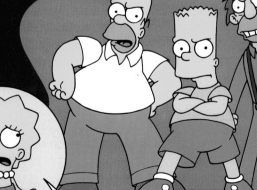

I JUST THOUGHT, YOU KNOW, MAYBE...

UMM...

PUMPKIN FIGHT?

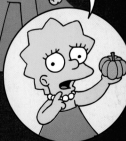

ELBARTO WAS HERE
I AM THE *PUMPKIN KING*!!!!
AH!!! WE'VE BEEN ATTACKED FROM THE REAR!
PUMPKIN FIGHHHHHT!!
YES, BUT YOU ARE SLAIN BY *GOURD GIRL* IN ISSUE #213.
I SITTED IN A PUMPKIN AND IT FEELS LIKE *POTTY*!
YOU'RE ONE *FRIENDLY* PUMPKIN!
ER, AH, TWO OF MY BROTHERS *DIED* THIS WAY.

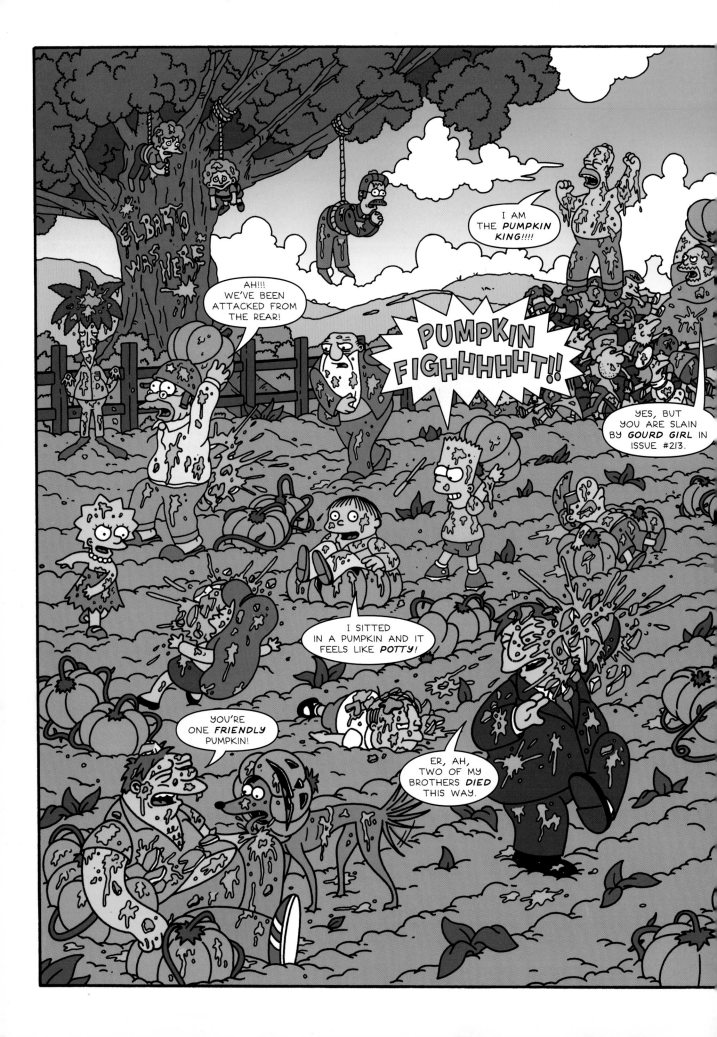

WOULD SOMEONE PLEASE THINK OF **THE CHILDREN**?!
AIM FOR THE FACE, MAGGIE! AIM FOR THE **FACE**!
BUR-HEY!
YOU WANTED THANKSGIVIN' DINNER? WELL, START LICKIN'!
GET OOT A ME PUMPKIN PATCH! **GET OOOOOOOOT**!
I'VE HAD **BETTER-SMELLING** HOLIDAYS.

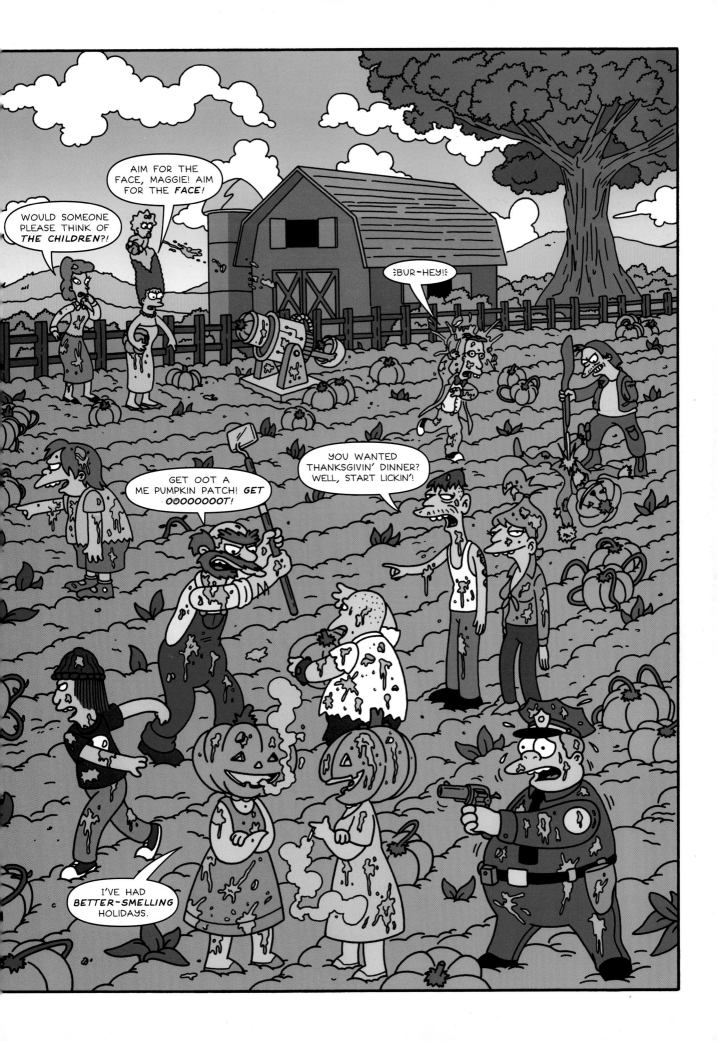

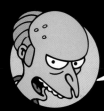

IT HAS BEEN BROUGHT TO MY ATTENTION THAT A TALE IN THIS "COMIC BOOK" MADE MENTION OF YOURS TRULY IN A LESS THAN *PERFECT LIGHT*. APPARENTLY, I WAS PORTRAYED BY MR. ABE SIMPSON AS A *BACKSTABBING OPPORTUNIST* AS WELL AS A GENTLEMAN OF *CHINESE EXTRACTION*.

OF COURSE, I BEAR NO *ILL WILL* TOWARD MY ORIENTAL BRETHREN. WHY, WITHOUT THEM I COULDN'T BUILD MY RAILROAD TO THE MOON. BUT A BACKSTABBER?! *NEVER!* AND AN OPPORTUNIST?! I'D SOONER BOIL MY OWN MOTHER!**

NEEDLESS TO SAY I COULD SHUT THIS BOOK DOWN IN AN *INSTANT*. BUT I PREFER TO FIGHT SLANDER WITH *STYLE*, WORDS WITH *WIT*. SO WITHOUT FURTHER ADO, I GIVE YOU MY OWN *DANSE MACABRE*, A TALE I LIKE TO CALL...

*SEE "BURNS V. JOHANSEN: 1953"
**SEE "BURNS V. MRS. BURNS: 1948"

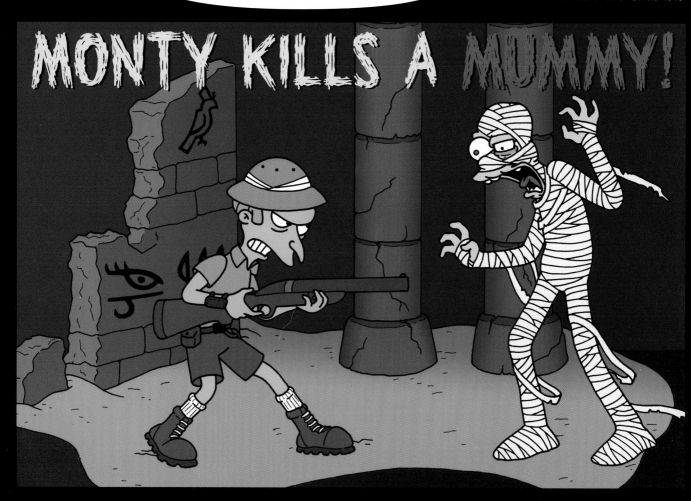

MONTY KILLS A MUMMY!

THE YEAR WAS 1936. THE PLACE, THE ETERNALLY SHIFTING SANDS OF LOWER AEGYPT. PROFESSOR SMITHERS AND I HAD BEEN CONTRACTED TO TRAVEL TO THE ANCIENT RUINS BY AN EMPLOYER OBSESSED WITH OBTAINING RELIGIOUS ARTIFACTS. NICE GERMAN FELLOW WHOSE NAME ELUDES ME. ANYHOO...
SMITHERS AND I HAD JUST SPENT TWENTY GRUELING DAYS TRAVELING UP THE NILE WITH ONE GOAL IN MIND, THE GOLDEN DEATH MASK OF KING ANKHENATEN! IT WAS SAID THAT HE WHO WORE THE DEATH MASK COULD LOOK DIRECTLY INTO THE VERY SOUL OF HIS FELLOW MAN. I PLANNED TO USE IT TO FIND OUT WHY SMITHERS INSISTED I WEAR TIGHT SLACKS. WITH TWO HUNDRED AEGYPTIAN PORTERS, WE SET OFF FROM THE BANKS OF THE RIVER ON A JOURNEY THAT PROVED QUITE UNEVENTFUL FOR US (THOUGH SOMEWHAT EVENTFUL FOR A HUNDRED AEGYPTIAN PORTERS AND A LARGE CROCODILE.) EVENTUALLY WE REACHED OUR DESTINATION, THE PYRAMID OF THE GREAT PHARAOH HIMSELF! WE IMMEDIATELY SET TO DIGGING IN HOPES OF UNEARTHING THE TREASURES WITHIN. OF COURSE, I DIDN'T SEE OUR EFFORTS AS GRAVE ROBBING, BUT RATHER AS "POST CORPOREAL ASSET REALLOCATION," OR "GRAVE ROBBING." EITHER WAY, SOME OF THE MORE SUPERSTITIOUS NATIVES INSISTED ON WARNING ME THAT OPENING THE TOMB WOULD RESULT IN THE "PHARAOH'S CURSE." IN FACT, ONE

AEGYPTIAN SIMPLY WOULD NOT SHUT UP ABOUT THE CURSE, BLATHERING ON AND ON IN THE MOST COWARDLY WAY, EVEN HIDING BEHIND THE MULES SO HE WOULD NOT BE CHOSEN FOR WORK DETAIL. OH, THE MISTS OF TIME HAVE CAST A SHROUD ON MY MEMORY FOR NAMES, EVEN ON THE NAME OF THAT CRINGING JACKAMOUNT. NO, WAIT, IT'S COMING...I'M STARTING TO REMEMBER...WHY, I BELIEVE IT WAS SOME FOOL NAMED ABE SIMPSON! YES, ABRAHAM SIMPSON, THE MOST COWERING, QUAILING, PLUCKLESS, ONE-LEGGED AEGYPTIAN DAY-LABORER THE WORLD HAS EVER KNOWN! BUT I DIGRESS. FOR ON THAT NIGHT WE DISCOVERED WHAT HAD BEEN HIDDEN FOR THOUSANDS OF YEARS...A SECRET PASSAGE INTO THE HEART OF THE VERY TOMB ITSELF! ARMED WITH ONLY AN ELEPHANT GUN AND THE TWELVE PORTERS WHO CARRIED IT, I CREPT CAUTIOUSLY INTO THE GAPING MAW OF THE PASSAGEWAY. WAS THAT THE LOW MOAN OF A CENTURIES-DEAD EMPEROR, OR JUST THE DUSTY CAVERN WIND? I TOOK TWO, MAYBE THREE STEPS INSIDE WHEN SUDDENLY THE DOOR SLAMMED SHUT! THERE I WAS, FACE TO FACE WITH THE MOST HIDEOUS MUMMY CREATURE I HAD EVER SEEN! GRABBING THE ELEPHANT GUN, I LEVELED IT AT THE ATTACKING ZOMBIE AND SQUEEZED THE TRIGGER...BUT HEARD ONLY A CLICK! SOMEONE HAD FORGOTTEN TO LOAD THE ELEPHANT GUN! UPON INQUIRY I DISCOVERED THAT WAS ABE SIMPSON'S JOB. NO SURPRISE THERE, FOR AS WE ALL KNEW, ABE SIMPSON WAS NOT ONLY A COWARD, BUT A COMPLETELY INEPT DUNDERHEAD! WHO POURED MOTOR OIL IN THE CANTEENS? ABE SIMPSON! WHO CLEANED THE SURVEY EQUIPMENT WITH COUGH SYRUP? ABE SIMPSON! WHO TRIED TO DELOUSE THE--

CONSARN IT, BURNS! THAT'S ENOUGH!

CAN'T STAND THE HEAT, EH, SIMPSON? EVERYTHING YOU SAY ABOUT ME IS A DADBURN LIE! LOOKS LIKE SOMEONE DOESN'T LIKE BEING CALLED AEGYPTIAN. WHA-JE-PHA-- ARE YOU KIDDING? I LOVE EGYPTIANS! I ONCE SPENT CHRISTMAS IN AN EGYPTIAN CAT HOUSE! BUT I AIN'T NO COWARD! AND I AIN'T NO DUNDERHEAD! YOU SHOULD HAVE THOUGHT OF THAT BEFORE CALLING ME A BACKSTABBING OPPORTUNIST! YOU MESS WITH THE BURNS, YOU GET THE HORNS! AND I HAVEN'T EVEN GOTTEN TO THE PART WHERE ABE ACCIDENTALLY SMEARS HIMSELF IN BUTTER AND GETS EATEN BY THE MUMMY! OH YEAH?! I MEANT TO DO THAT, SO I COULD BURST OUT OF THE MUMMY'S STOMACH AND SAVE THE DAY! THINK YOU CAN USURP MY STORY, EH? WELL, THE PARTS OF THE MUMMY TURNED INTO LITTLE MUMMIES AND BEGAN EATING SIMPSON'S HEAD! THEY DID NOT! THEY MOST CERTAINLY DID!

OH, MY CRAP! WOULD YOU GEEZERS JUST SHUT UP?! IT'S LIKE SOMEONE PUT A PILE OF PRUNES ON THE RECORD PLAYER!

WHO THE DEVIL ARE YOU?! I'M HOMER SIMPSON, AND I'VE GOT MY OWN GHOST STORY TO TELL. IT'S CALLED...

THE MYSTERY OF WHY OLD PEOPLE WON'T SHUT UP!

ONCE UPON A TIME THERE WAS THIS CRAZY OLD GUY AND HE WAS...HE COULD...HE

APU ON RIGEL 7
Gee, Mr. Burns, what quasi-legal means did you employ to get the Russians to part with their top-secret teleport?
Well, Smithers, when I was just a lad I won a bet with Catherine the Great!
Freshly Doug TenNapel Writer/Artist
Crawling Chris Ungar Letters
Nathan "Nosferatu" Kane Colors
Bill Morbidson Editor
Monstrous Matt Groening BEM (Bug-Eyed Master)
Lucky you. She'd have won if the rope didn't break.
I didn't collect my winnings, allowing the interest to compound over the years. It's a little trick I learned from the I.R.S.
So last week, when the Russian economy was at its weakest in years, I demanded the full payment of my debt. It was worth 8 billion, million rubles—enough to bankrupt Russia!
Sir, you are quite the financial genius!

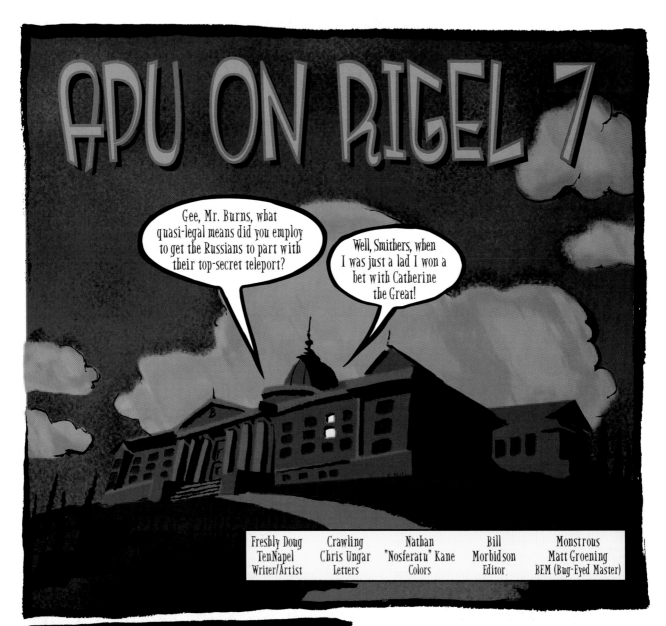

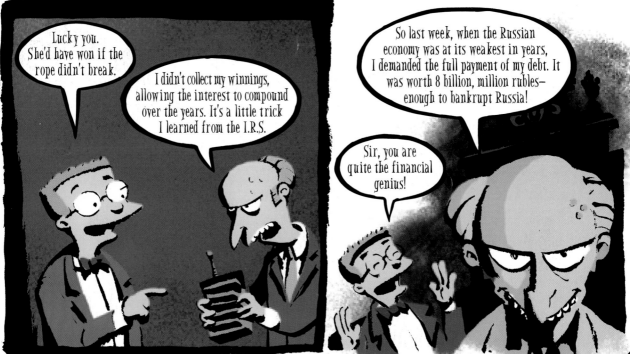

And now, Smithers, let us behold my long-awaited teleport! Bow down to it, Smithers! Bow down!
Mr. Burns, I don't mean to question your omniscience, but the teleport looks more like a Kwik-E-Mart hot dog warmer.
Confound those pesky Russkies!
Look at the bright side, sir, we can warm our weenies on it!
KWIK E MART
If this is a hot dog warmer, where is my particle teleport?!
Uh, Mr. Burns, may I get up now?

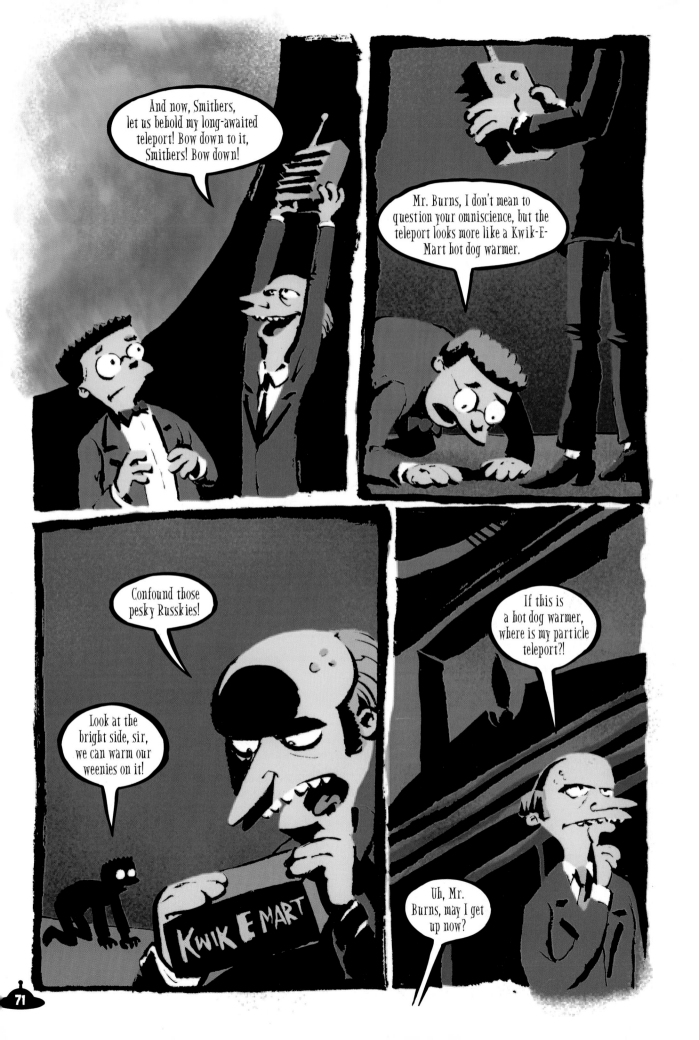

At last! My Kwik-E-Mart brand hot dog warmer has arrived. Without it, I cannot free my choice edibles from their clammy, gelatinous casing.
SQUI
Mmm...claaaaammy, gelatinous casing.
Mr. Homer! You should not eat raw pork. You will get worms!
Nonsense! I've eaten raw hot dogs my whole life, and I've never had a problem with worms!
PLOP!
SCOOT! SCOOT!
SCOOT SCOOT!
SCOOT SCOOT!

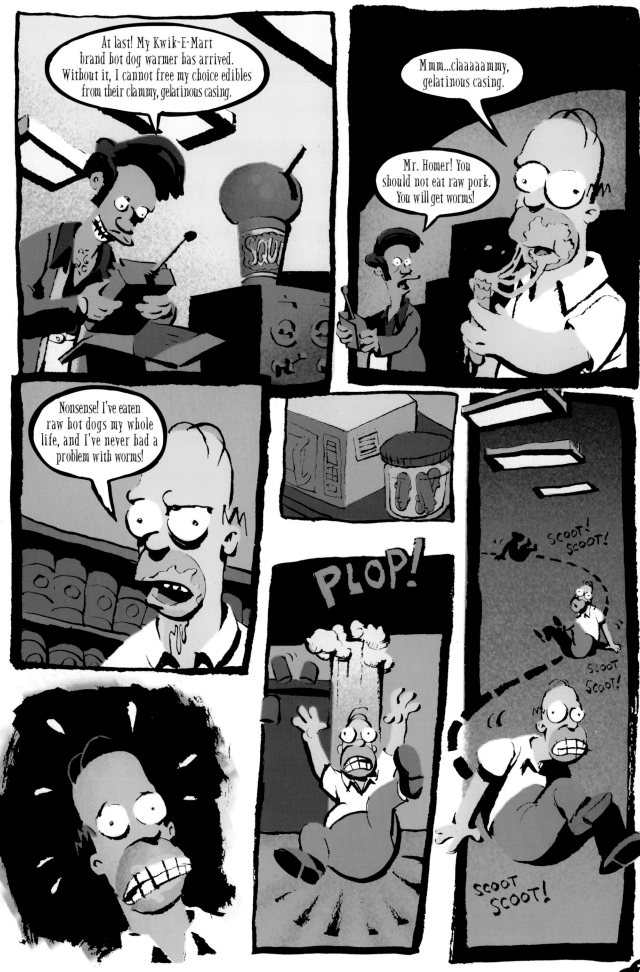

I wonder where the customary Kwik-E-Mart logo is? It is a seal of virtual quality on all Kwik-E-Mart products, from re-heating devices to security cameras.
Uh, shouldn't we warm a few hot dogs on it to make sure it works?!
Hey, there seems to be Chinese writing all over it!
That is not Chinese. It is Russian! Luckily all children in India must learn at least 7 languages to properly compete in the international business world!
Hey! I'll bet C3PO was from India! He knows over 71,000 languages!
Do not be a moron. C3PO was not from India! He was from England!
Woops!
By the six arms of Shiva! You dropped my Kwik-E-Mart brand hot dog warmer!
CLUNK!
ZAP!
CLICK!

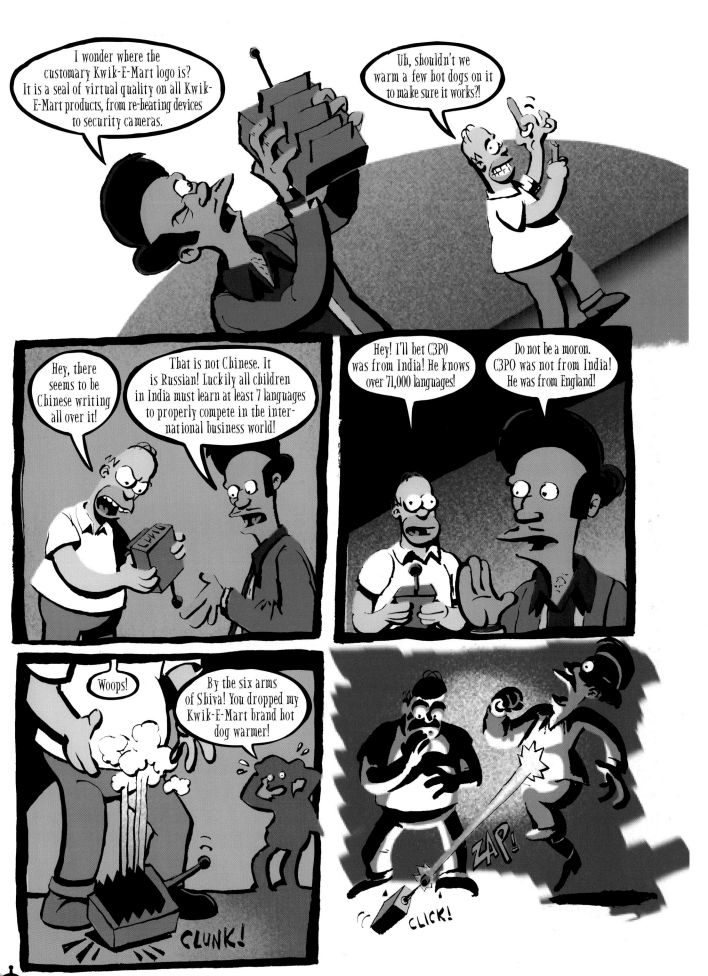

Where did this windstorm come from? I hope Mr. Homer did not consume all of the nacho chili while my back was turned.
Where am I?!
I haven't felt this strange since I sat too close to my grand-father's hookah.
I am uncontrollably falling toward that planet! I pray to Vishnu that I land on something soft!

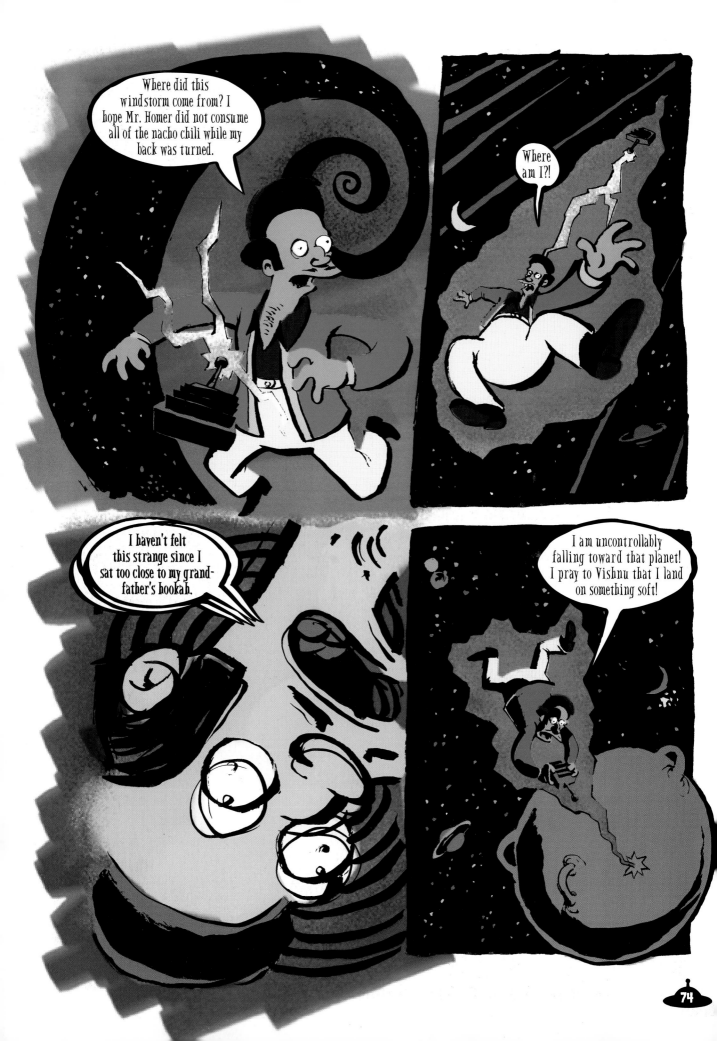

KODOS, MY FELLOW CONSPIRATOR! MY LOYAL SISTER! OUR TIME HAS COME!
WE MUST OVERTHROW THE EVIL DICTATOR AND FREE OUR COMRADES!
I dare not answer or he will see that I have murdered his beloved sister who has no doubt reincarnated into a higher life form–like a sea monkey.
KODOS?
I accidentally killed your sister, Kodos, when I materialized on top of her.

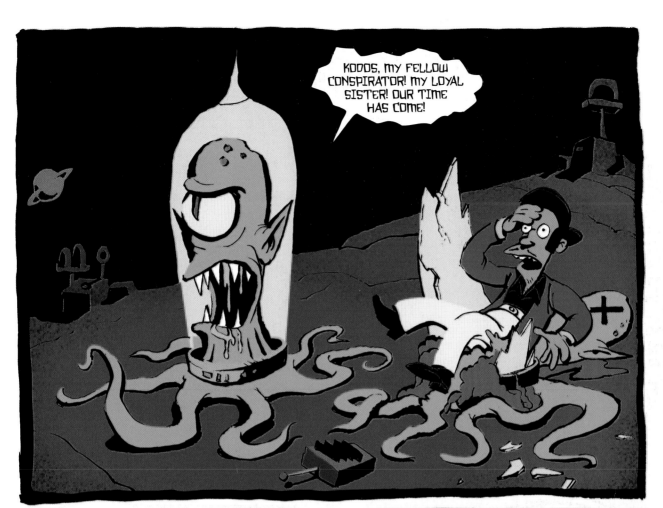

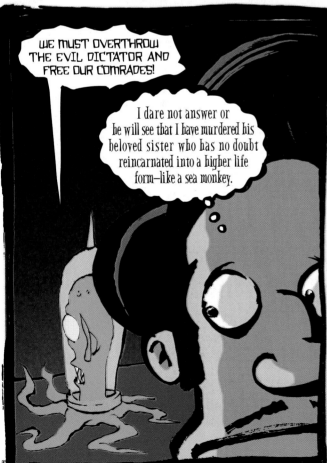

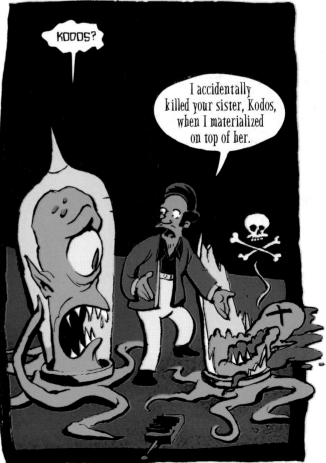

FOOLISH EARTH MAN! DO YOU KNOW HOW MANY TIMES I'VE HEARD THE EXCUSE, "I JUST MATERIALIZED ON TOP OF HER"?! KODOS WAS THE ONLY RIGELIAN WITH THE FIGHTING ABILITY TO OVERTHROW THE DICTATOR WHO HAS DOOMED MY PEOPLE TO SLAVERY!
I am sorry about the hardship to your alien race, but I must go now!
My teleportation apparatus appears to be defunct. The warranty must have just expired.
HA HA, FOOLISH EARTH MAN! YOUR TELEPORTATION DEVICE IS BROKEN! AND ONLY I HAVE THE KNOWLEDGE TO FIX IT!
It is customary in my religion to help those who destroy your siblings.
REALLY?
Well, no, but it would be nice if you helped me.
I KNOW! WE CAN HELP EACH OTHER!
What kind of ridiculous religion is that?!
I WILL FIX YOUR TELEPORTER IF YOU HELP ME DESTROY THE EVIL RIGELIAN DICTATOR!
To destroy a corrupt dictator of another civilization is completely offensive to my religion, but okay.

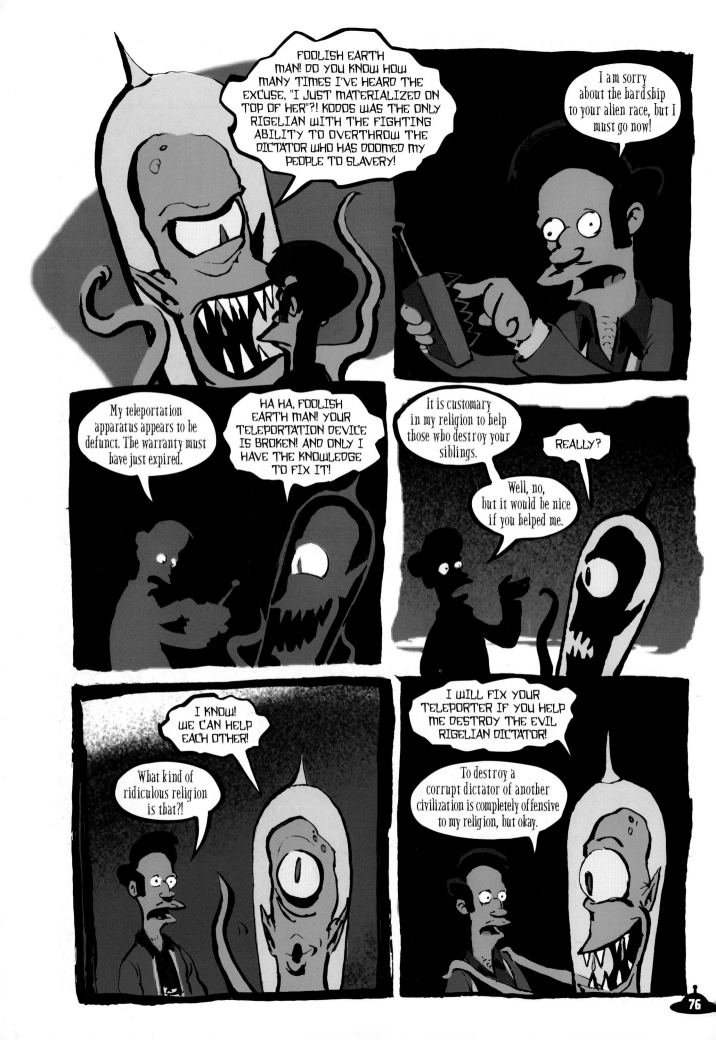

How did this dictator take over your world?
HE HAD SUPERIOR FIGHTING SKILLS WITH HIS "BOARD AND NAIL" TECHNIQUE. HE OVERTHREW OUR PREVIOUS PRESIDENT WHOM WE PUT INTO POWER WITH A DEMOCRATIC ELECTION.
You have democratic elections?
WELL, IT ISN'T EXACTLY DEMOCRATIC. OURS IS NOT A LEGITIMATE DEMOCRACY LIKE YOUR UNITED STATES. OUR ELECTIONS ARE BOUGHT BY SPECIAL INTEREST GROUPS WHO FLOOD THE MEDIA WITH INFLAMMATORY AND EXAGGERATED ADVERTISING TO INFLUENCE A POORLY INFORMED PUBLIC.
Why do we climb this mountain? Could we not just sneak in through the back door?
THE DICTATOR WANTED KODOS AND I KILLED. YOU CAN'T IMAGINE WHAT IT'S LIKE TO BE AN ILLEGAL ALIEN IN YOUR OWN HOME LAND!
WE MADE IT! I SHOULD CALL YOU APU THE CLIMBER!
Thank you, my Rigelian brother.

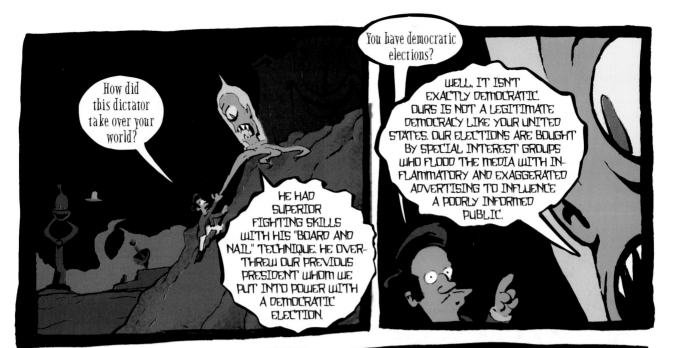

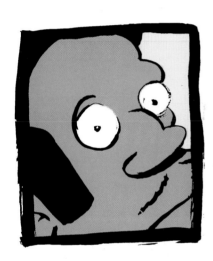

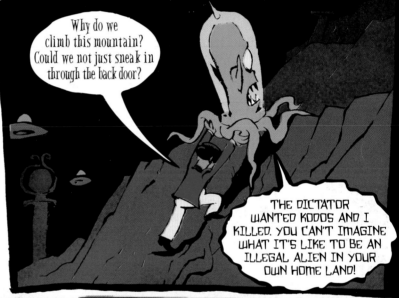

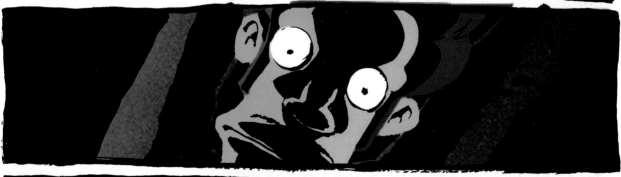

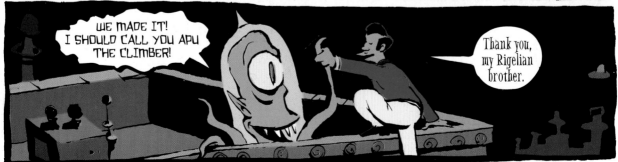

I DON'T GET IT, THE WHOLE TOWN IS EMPTY!
Perhaps there is a sports event being broadcast on television.
IMPOSSIBLE. WE STOPPED WATCHING TELEVISED SPORTS EVENTS AFTER WE EVOLVED BEYOND THE IQ OF A PARAKEET.
AND NOW MY RIGELIAN SLAVES, WE MUST BUILD A BRIDGE TO THE FUTURE! A MILLION POINTS OF LIGHT! WE MUST RACIALLY CLEANSE THE UNIVERSE OF...
ALAS! A CROWD GATHERS IN THE TOWN COURTYARD! THE DICTATOR IS FEEDING MY PEOPLE MORE PROPAGANDA! HE MUST BE STOPPED!
Yes, my oppressed brother!

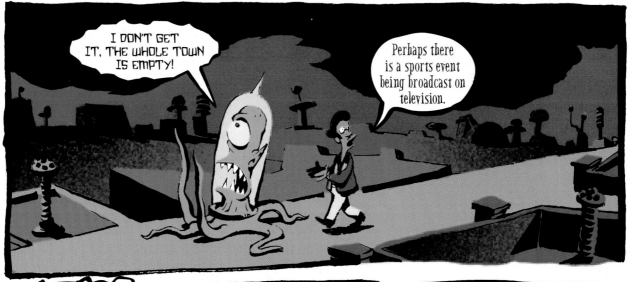

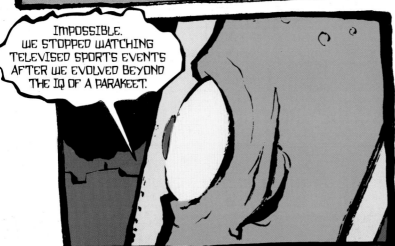

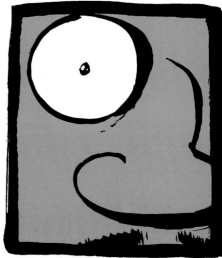

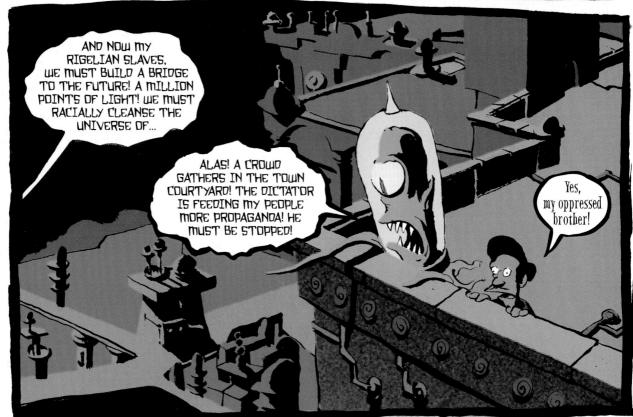

I PROMISE A COMPLIMENTARY COW AND PROBE FOR EVERY ALIEN! ALL YOU HAVE TO DO IS WORSHIP ME!
HOORAY! WE WORSHIP YOU!
SIR, YOU MAKE A GREAT DICTATOR!
DON'T INTERRUPT ME SMITHOS THE BROWN! AND DON'T CALL ME TATOR!
BURNZAK! YOU HAVE OPPRESSED MY PEOPLE ENOUGH!
My people must be avenged!
ZZZZZZ
Your brain weapons will not sway us!
POOF!

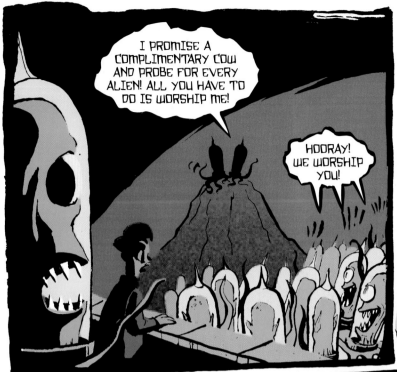

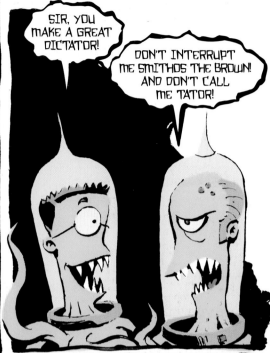

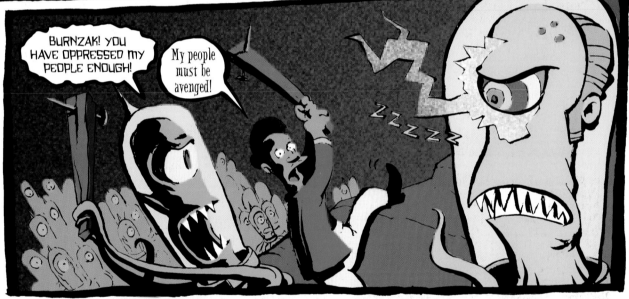

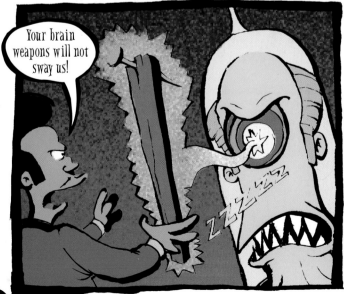

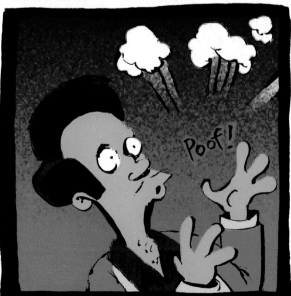

Run as fast as you can.
GET ON THE SHUTTLE!
JUMP ON MY BACK MR. BURNS—I MEAN, BURNZAK!
SIR, IT IS A PRIVILEGE AND AN HONOR TO BE GROUND TO HAMBURGER WHILE YOU CLIMB TO SAFETY.

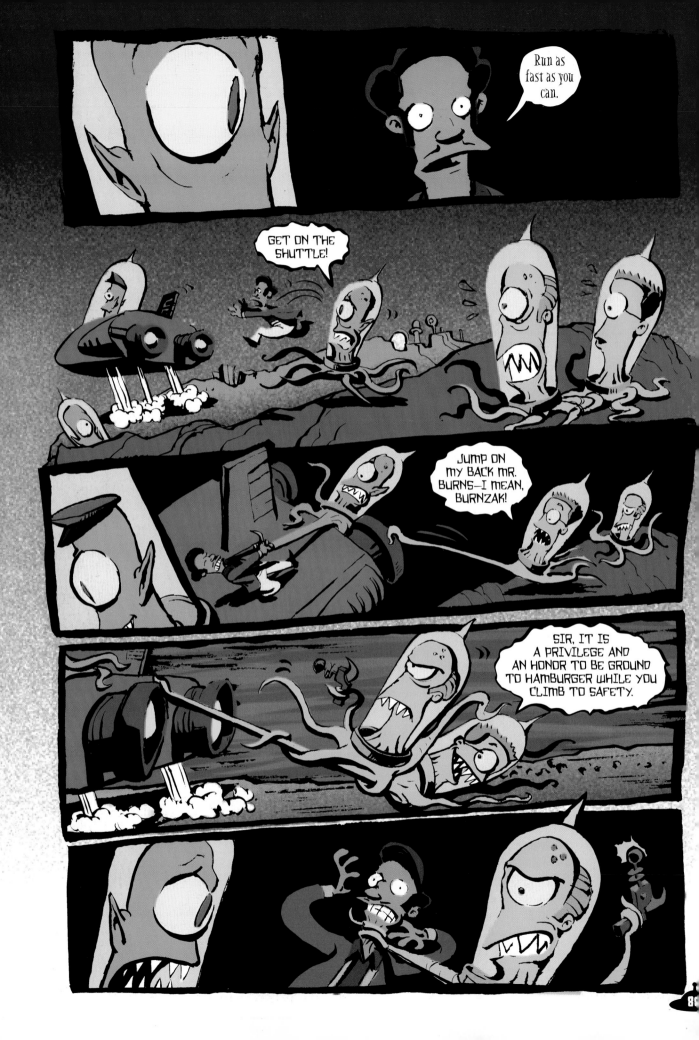

NOOOOOOO!
The only substance hard enough to penetrate Burnzak's head is...
ZAP
...a Kwik-E-Mart donut!
Once again, Kwik-E-Mart food is so much more than edible!

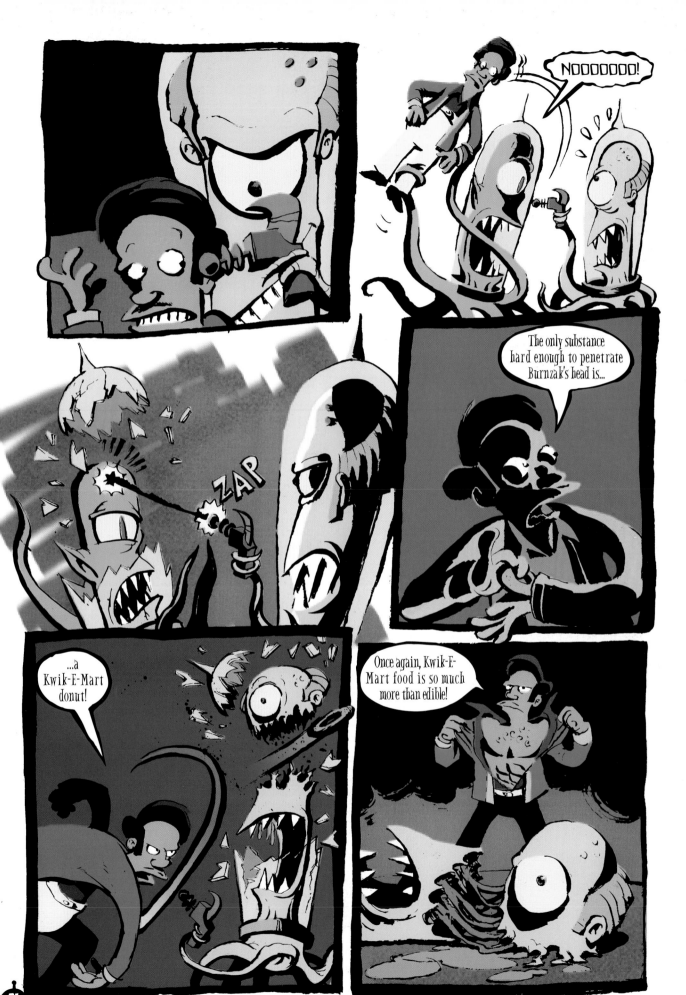

Kang, wake up! This is not a time for blissful slumber.
By the six arms of Ganesha, the 7-headed serpent of the apocalypse and the Monkey Prince, open your eye, Kang!
Open your eye!
Oh, gross, I touched his EYE!

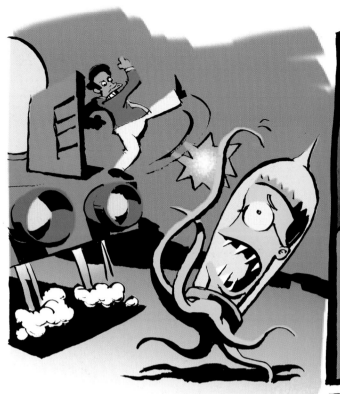

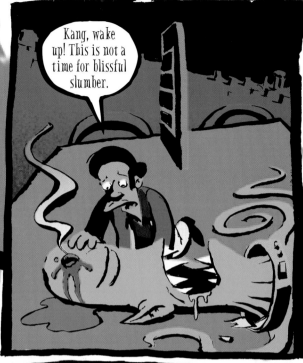

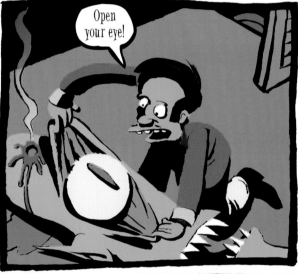

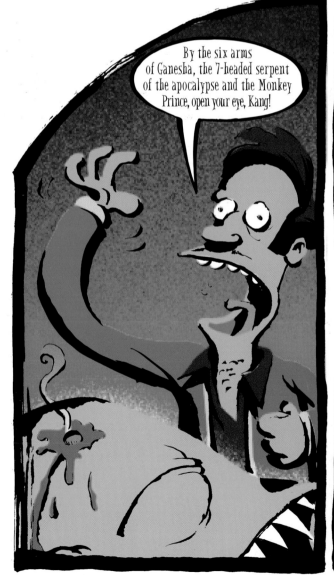

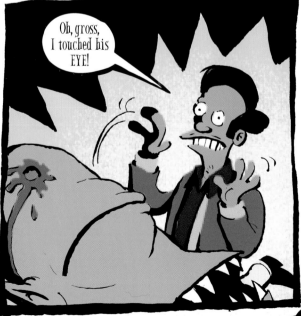

APU THE CLIMBER!
Kang! My companion! You are alive!
OF COURSE I'M ALIVE. I JUST HAD TO TAKE A QUICK NAP AFTER DESTROYING BURNZAK.
Does this mean that you will fix my teleport machine?
I'LL FIX IT AND SHOW YOU HOW I GOT MY NAME AT THE SAME TIME!
WOOSH!
KANG!
ZAP!

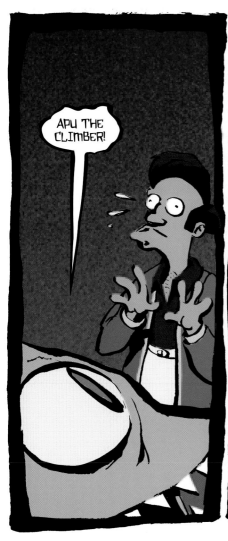

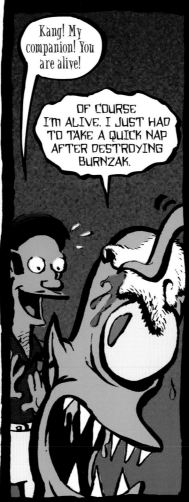

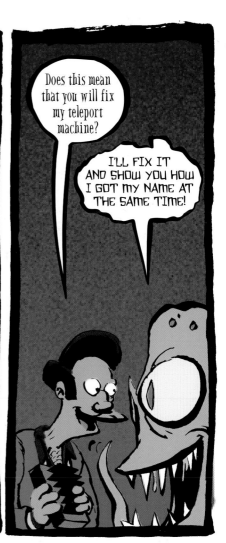

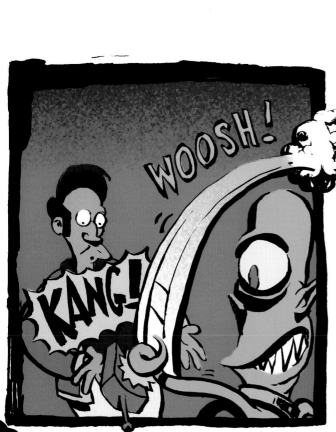

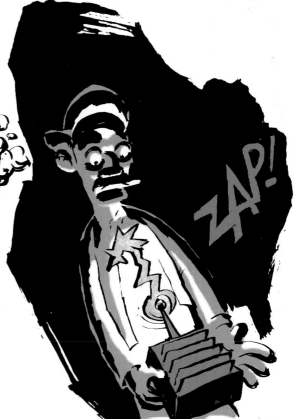

I'LL BE RIGHT HERE.
ZZZ
Mmmm... Wiiiild Cherry.
SQUISH
Home at last! I am so happy to be on a planet of higher life forms!
Brain freeze! Brain Freeze!

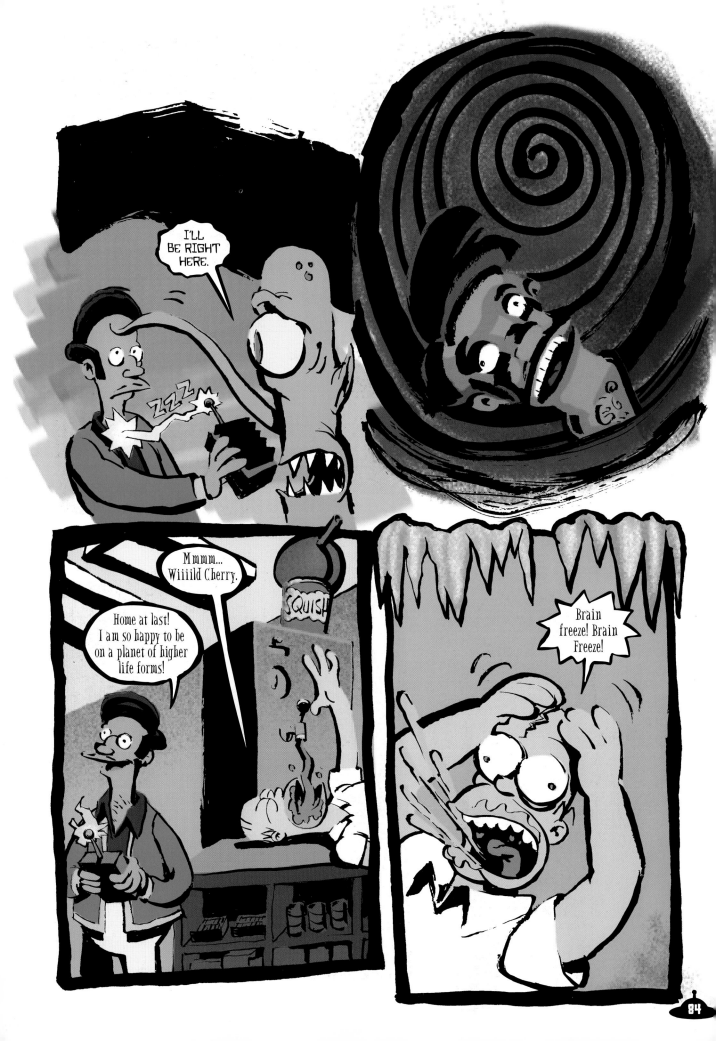

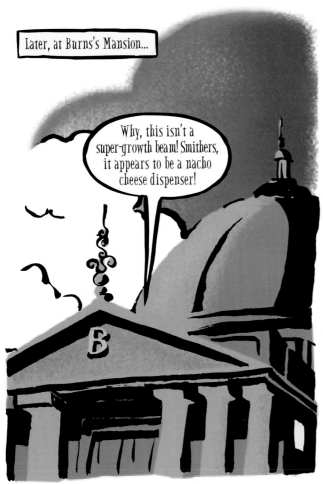

Later, at Burns's Mansion...

Why, this isn't a super-growth beam! Smithers, it appears to be a nacho cheese dispenser!

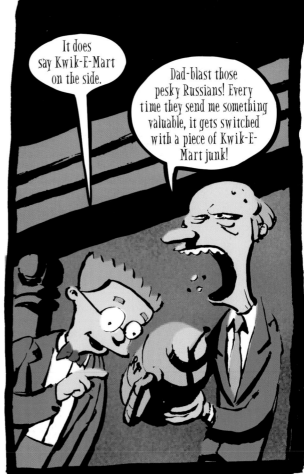

It does say Kwik-E-Mart on the side.

Dad-blast those pesky Russians! Every time they send me something valuable, it gets switched with a piece of Kwik-E-Mart junk!

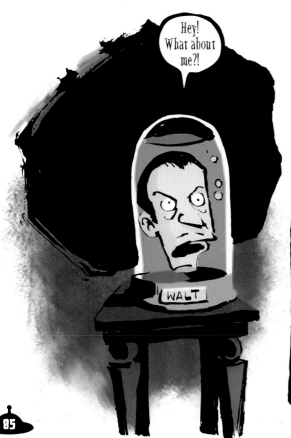

Hey! What about me?!

WALT

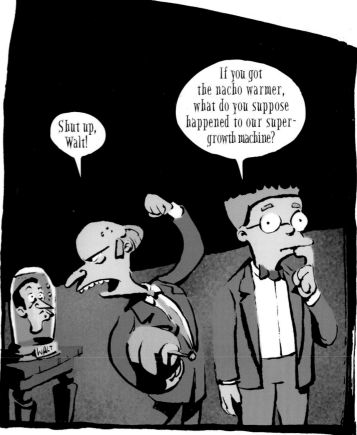

Shut up, Walt!

If you got the nacho warmer, what do you suppose happened to our super-growth machine?

WALT

KWIK E MART
KWIK E MART
JACK POT $
DUFF RIP OFF
Ha-ha!

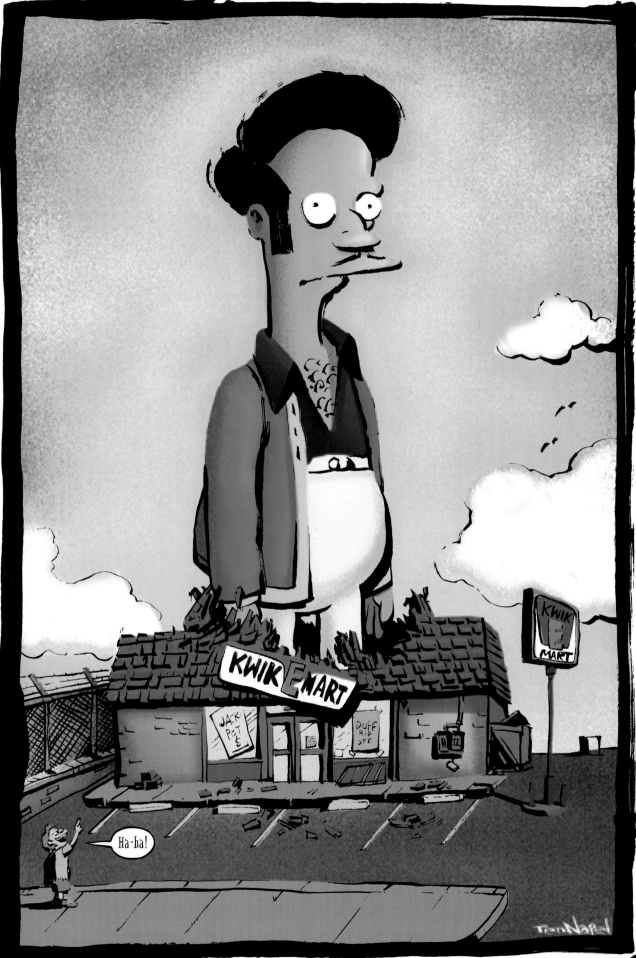

What do you get when you pay six comic actors what you should have spent on an X4000 Anti-Rigellian Missile Shield?...**HILARITY!**

GROVEL AT THE FEET OF THE ALMIGHTY CRITICS:

"Hooray! I suffered only mild intestinal discomfort!"

—*TV Guide*

"I laughed when I heard they were supposed to be humans."

—*Sacramento Bee*

"Kodchel's hair was sexually attractive and generally louse-free!"

—*Star Tribune*

"Sometimes they remind me of MY friends and why I chose to eat them."

—Matt Roush, *USA Today*

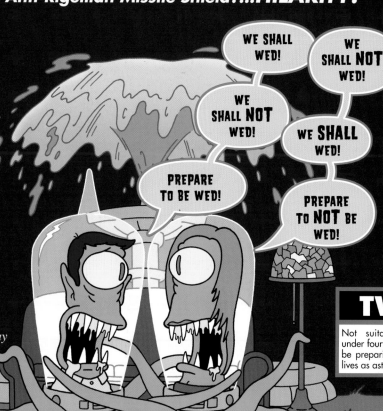

TV-14

Not suitable for humans under fourteen as they should be preparing for their future lives as astro-slaves.

Our actresses are starved in cages, keeping them kindling thin, the way you like them!

Kangoss and Kodchel star in

FRIENDLY FRIENDLY FRIENDS

They are just like your real friends, only they never will be!

YOU WILL PIERCE YOUR SIDES WITH THE COLORFUL ANTICS OF...

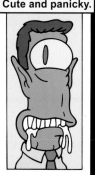

Kangdler:
Cute and panicky.

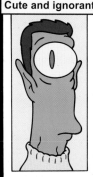

Kangoey:
Cute and ignorant.

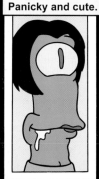

Kodica:
Panicky and cute.

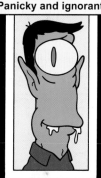

Kangoss:
Panicky and ignorant.

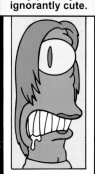

Kodchel:
Cutely panicky and ignorantly cute.

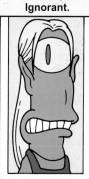

Khoedbe:
Ignorant.

YOU WILL LAUGH SO HARD YOU WILL FORGET YOU ARE BEING MINCED!

Watch *Friendly Friendly Friends* on Thursdays!

Placed between a program you cannot remember and another you would choose to forget.

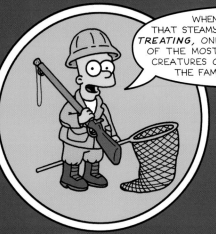

WHEN BUSHWACKING THROUGH THAT STEAMY JUNGLE KNOWN AS *TRICK-OR-TREATING*, ONE MUST BE *PREPARED* FOR SOME OF THE MOST *VICIOUS* AND *UNPREDICTABLE* CREATURES ON THE PLANET. CREATURES OF THE FAMILY "CANDIUS GIVEUS OUTUS."

UNDERSTANDING THEIR *HABITS* CAN MEAN THE DIFFERENCE BETWEEN A *SACK FULL OF CANDY* AND A *SACKFUL OF SQUAT*. SO HOLD ON TO YOUR PUMPKINS AS I TAKE YOU ON...

BART'S TRICK-OR-TREATING SAFARI

The Fruit Bat

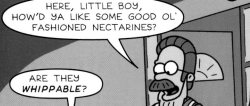

HERE, LITTLE BOY, HOW'D YA LIKE SOME GOOD OL' FASHIONED NECTARINES?

ARE THEY *WHIPPABLE*?

Unprepare-o:
The Man of a Thousand Surprises

OF COURSE I KNEW IT WAS HALLOWEEN! NOW LET'S SEE... GARAGE REMOTE, ASTHMA INHALER...WHO WANTS A FLIP-FLOP?

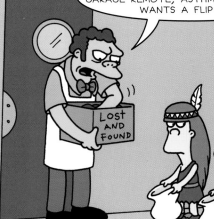

LOST AND FOUND

The Interrogator

AND WHAT ARE *YOU* SUPPOSED TO BE?!

A GHOST.

WHAT KIND OF GHOST?

UMM... PIRATE?

WHAT KIND OF PIRATE?

DUTCH?

WHAT KIND OF DUTCH?

LOWLAND?

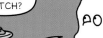

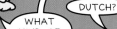
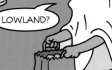

The Hiders

LOOKS LIKE WE GOT A COUPLE A HIDERS.

THANK GOD WE DIDN'T WHIP *ALL* THE NECTARINES AT FLANDERS' HOUSE!

SEYMOUR! I TOLD YOU TO BUY SOME CANDY!

BUT, MOTHER. I WAS SURE THE CHILDREN WOULD STILL BE DOING THEIR *HOMEWORK*!

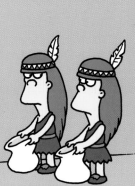
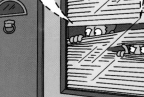
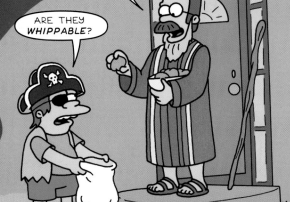

Trick-or-Trailer Park
PLEASE TELL ME THOSE ARE "GUMMY" WORMS...
DEPENDS HOW LONG YA COOK 'EM.
Dan Blather
COWBOY, EH? IN MY DAY THEY DIDN'T HAVE COWBOYS, SEEING AS THERE WARN'T NO SUCH THING AS COWS...ONLY PIGS. EVERY FRIDAY, AFTER THE ROUNDUP THEY'D RIDE INTO TOWN. "HERE COME THE PIG BOYS!" YOU'D YELL. THEN YOU'D PUT ON YOUR FINEST LACE STOCKINGS AND...
STOP!! FOR THE LOVE OF GOD! NO MORE!!!
Captain Creepy
COME CLOSER, CHILDREN! I HAVE A TASTY ASSORTMENT OF LINDY POPS, SWEETMEATS, AND "GRAHAMED" CRACKERS FOR THE URCHIN WHO BEST FITS THE SHACKLES.
The Jackpot
OH, YEAH?! WELL, HERE'S A KING-SIZE JUMBO MUSKETEERS BAR!
JUMBO?! AFTER TWELVE YEARS OF MARRIAGE I KNOW ALL TOO WELL WHAT YOU CALL "JUMBO!"
HARPY!
GUTLESS!
LET'S MOVE ON TO THE TEN POUNDS OF REESE'S PIECES YOU MENTIONED...
AND FINALLY, THE MOST DREADED BEAST OF THEM ALL...
The Homer
NO CANDY. GO HOME.

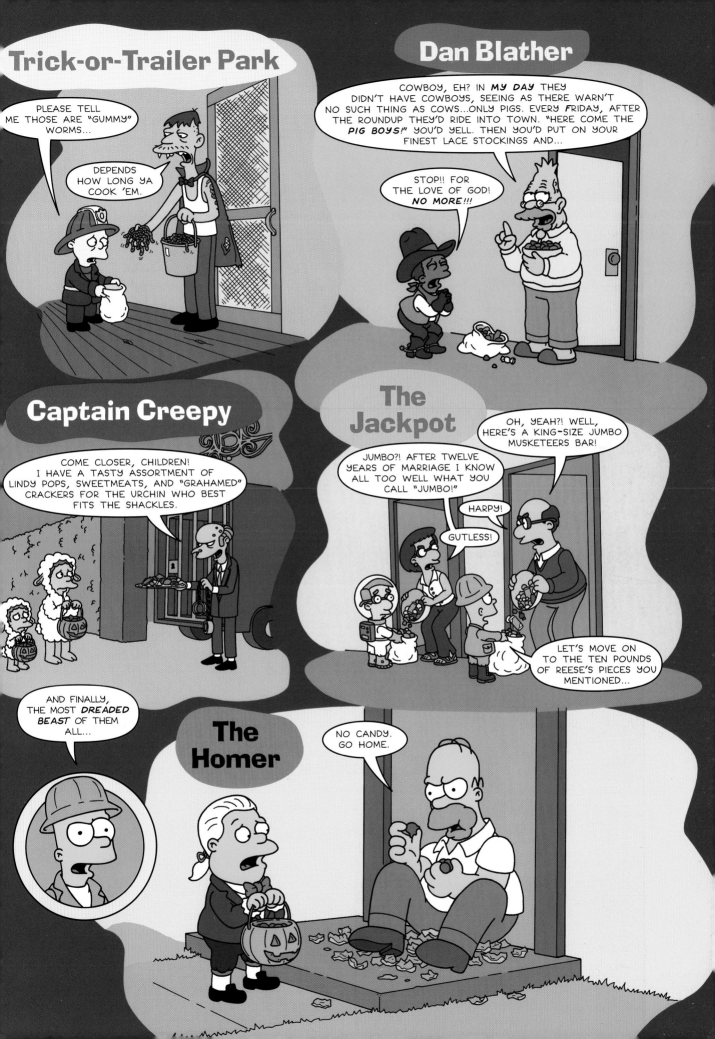

SOMETIMES I'M A BOY, BUT TONIGHT, I'M A *LADYBUG!*
RALPH WIGGUM'S
Trail of Treats!
7:14–MEETING OF THE MINDS.
AHHH! THE OLD MAN HAS A SCARY FACE!!!
SPRINGFIELD RETIREMENT CASTLE
AHHH! THE MOON MAN WANTS TO EAT MY *BRAIN!!*
7:58–DOES A GOOD DEED.
HEY, MISTER! A BOY AND A GIRL ARE ALL ALONE, AND THEY GOT THEIR LIPS *STUCK TOGETHER!* YOU BETTER GO *HELP* THEM!
YES...HELP THEM...
LOVER'S LANE
8:10–ACCIDENTALLY PURCHASED BY DRUNKEN MAN.
I'LL TAKE THE BEER...AND THE LADYBUG.
DUFF BEER
AN EXCELLENT CHOICE.
JERKY SALE
8:14–GOES HOME TO BED.
8:24–REALIZES IT'S NOT HIS HOME.
8:33–AT LAST, TRICK-OR-TREAT VICTORY.
HOORAY! I GOT AN *ONION!*
8:42–A NIGHT WELL SPENT.
AND THEN OUR BRACES GOT STUCK, AND WE WOULD HAVE DIED IF THE LITTLE BOY HADN'T SENT THIS *NICE MAN* TO HELP.
THAT'S ONE *SMART* LITTLE BOY!
HE SURE IS!

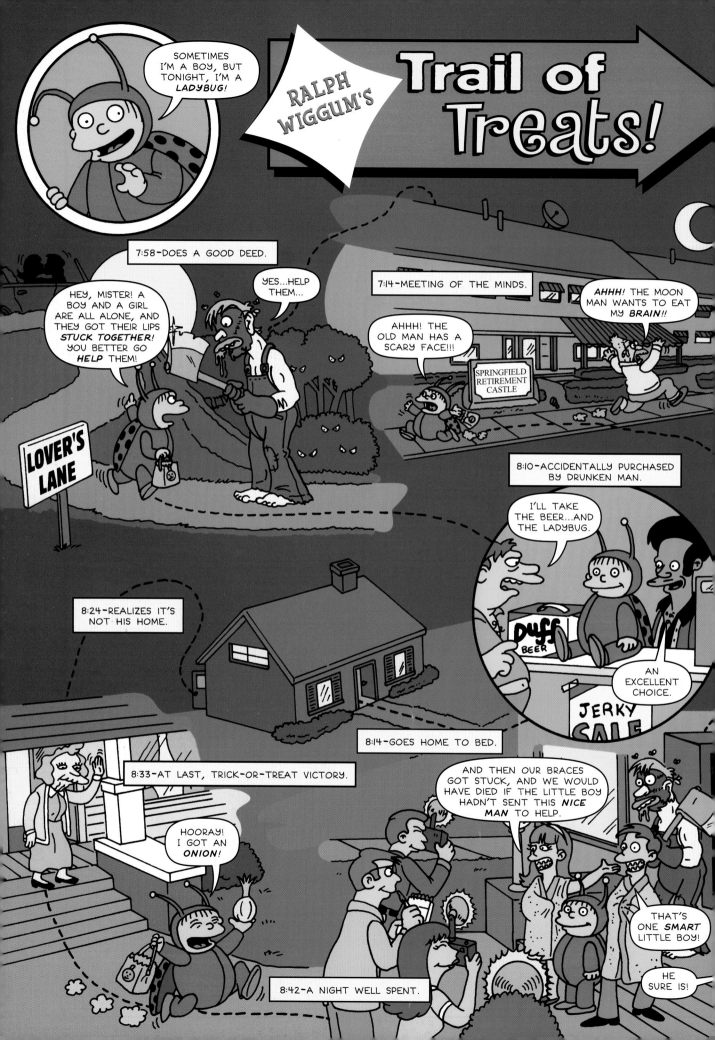

:15–THE NIGHT BEGINS...
I'M A LADYBUG, AND I'M GOING TO GET SOME CANDY!
YOU SURE ARE, RALPHIE! AND AS SOON AS I CHECK OUT THE NOISE IN THE ALLEY,
I'M GONNA BE WITH YOU THE WHOLE TIME!
WHUMP!!
THANKS FOR THE COSTUME! I'M GOING AS A PIGGY!
OINK, OINK MEOW!
YOUR BAG'S KIND OF EMPTY, RALPH. HERE, HAVE A LOLLIPOP.
6:21–MEETS FELLOW TRICK-OR-TREATER.
NO THANKS, LISA. I'M ONLY SUPPOSED TO TAKE CANDY FROM STRANGERS.
7:03–PRETENDS HE'S A DUCK.
QUACK, QUACK, MEOW!
6:52–MEETS NEW FRIENDS.
DANGER!
TOXIC WASTE
I'M A LADYBUG!
AIN'T THAT CUTE!?
ALMOST MAKES YA FORGET YOU'RE ABOUT TO GET A KNIFE IN THE EYE!
LEGITIMATE BUSINESSMAN'S CLUB
AHH! MUMMY!
NO... DADDY!
HA HA HA HA HA HA
PLEASE KILL THE MUMMY.

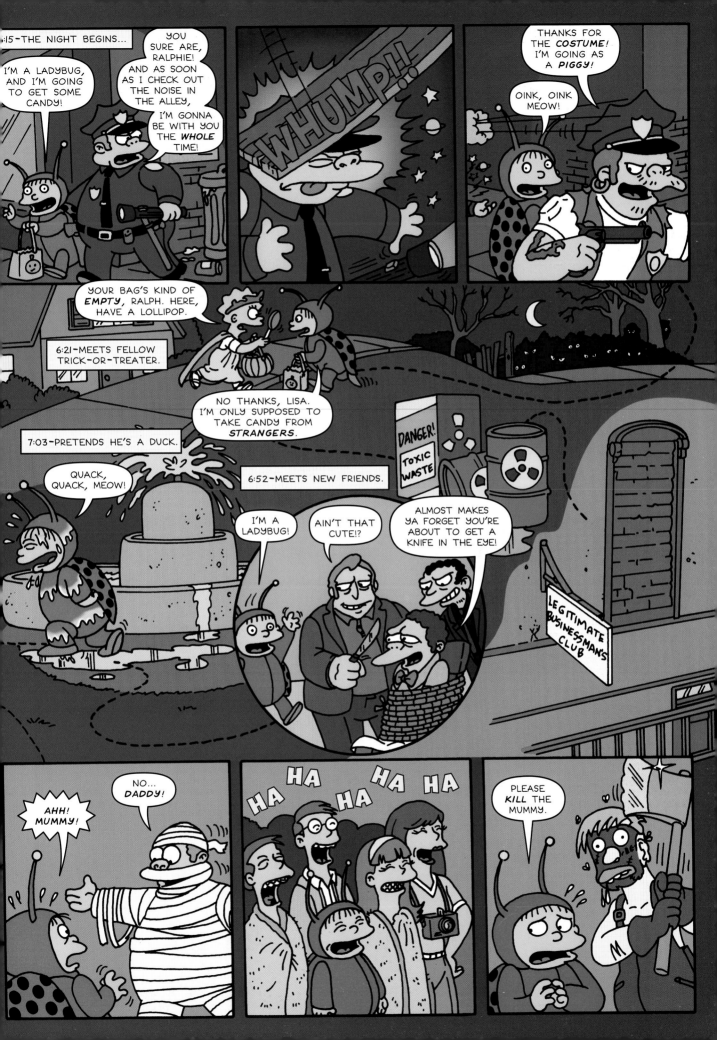

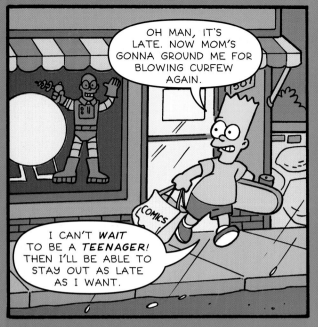

OH MAN, IT'S LATE. NOW MOM'S GONNA GROUND ME FOR BLOWING CURFEW AGAIN.

I CAN'T *WAIT* TO BE A *TEENAGER!* THEN I'LL BE ABLE TO STAY OUT AS LATE AS I WANT.

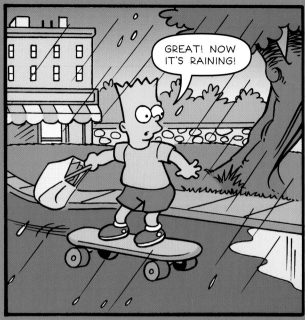

GREAT! NOW IT'S RAINING!

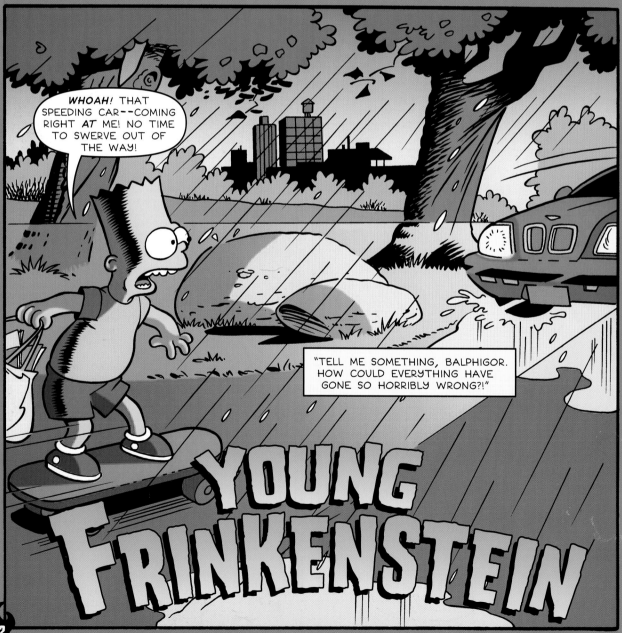

WHOAH! THAT SPEEDING CAR--COMING RIGHT *AT* ME! NO TIME TO SWERVE OUT OF THE WAY!

"TELL ME SOMETHING, BALPHIGOR. HOW COULD EVERYTHING HAVE GONE SO HORRIBLY WRONG?!"

YOUNG FRINKENSTEIN

SCRIPT
SHRILL BILL
MORRISON

PENCILS
DANGEROUS
DAN DECARLO

INKS
ALLEN "GRAVE"
ROBERTS

COLORS
ART "OF DARKNESS"
VILLANUEVA

LETTERING
CREEPY-CRAWLIN'
KAREN BATES

ANGRY VILLAGER #1
MALIGNANT
MATT GROENING

"I NEVER ACTUALLY MEANT FOR THINGS TO TURN OUT LIKE THIS. I ONLY WANTED TO CREATE LIFE ꞓBUR-HEYꞓ-- TO *ANIMATE* THAT WHICH WAS ꞓWOO-HOYꞓ PREVIOUSLY *DEAD!* I REMEMBER THE FEELING OF RAUCOUS JUBILATION ON THAT FATEFUL NIGHT WHEN ALL MY MONTHS OF THEORETICAL HYPOTHENIZATION AND EXPERIMENTAL JERKING AROUND FINALLY PAID OFF!"

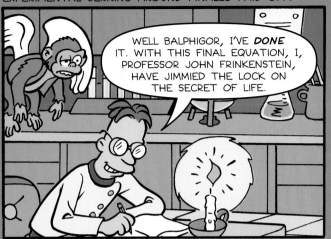

WELL BALPHIGOR, I'VE **DONE** IT. WITH THIS FINAL EQUATION, I, PROFESSOR JOHN FRINKENSTEIN, HAVE JIMMIED THE LOCK ON THE SECRET OF LIFE.

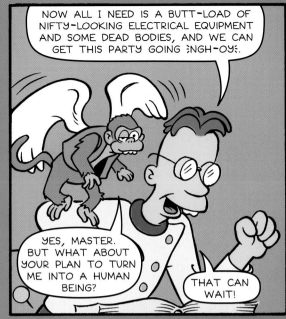

NOW ALL I NEED IS A BUTT-LOAD OF NIFTY-LOOKING ELECTRICAL EQUIPMENT AND SOME DEAD BODIES, AND WE CAN GET THIS PARTY GOING ꞓNGH-OYꞓ.

YES, MASTER. BUT WHAT ABOUT YOUR PLAN TO TURN ME INTO A HUMAN BEING?

THAT CAN WAIT!

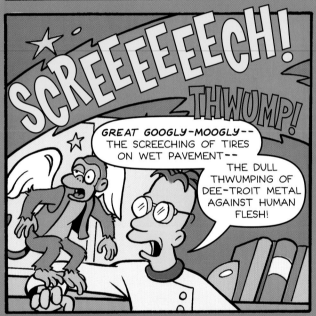

SCREEEEEECH!

THWUMP!

GREAT GOOGLY-MOOGLY-- THE SCREECHING OF TIRES ON WET PAVEMENT--

THE DULL THWUMPING OF DEE-TROIT METAL AGAINST HUMAN FLESH!

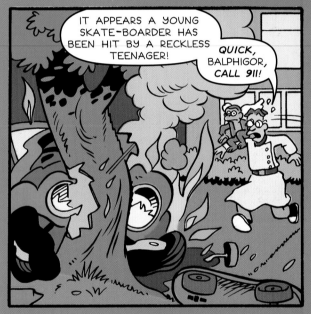

IT APPEARS A YOUNG SKATE-BOARDER HAS BEEN HIT BY A RECKLESS TEENAGER!

QUICK, BALPHIGOR, *CALL 911!*

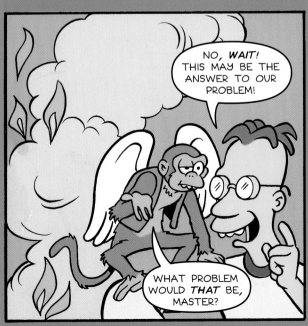

NO, *WAIT!* THIS MAY BE THE ANSWER TO OUR PROBLEM!

WHAT PROBLEM WOULD *THAT* BE, MASTER?

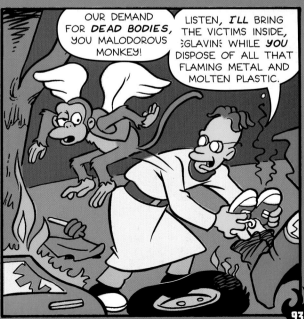

OUR DEMAND FOR *DEAD BODIES*, YOU MALODOROUS MONKEY!

LISTEN, *I'LL* BRING THE VICTIMS INSIDE, ꞓGLAVINꞓ WHILE *YOU* DISPOSE OF ALL THAT FLAMING METAL AND MOLTEN PLASTIC.

SOON...
I'M IN LUCK! BOTH VICTIMS APPEAR TO BE QUITE DEAD :FLA-HAVEN:. NOW LET'S SEE WHAT WE HAVE TO WORK WITH.
HMMM...WELL, THIS SPIKY-HAIRED YOUNGSTER'S BODY WAS BADLY MANGLED, BUT I BELIEVE I CAN STILL USE THE HEAD.
IT'S A LITTLE SCARRED, AND THERE IS SOME MINOR **BRAIN LEAKAGE**, BUT NOTHING A GOOD METAL PLATE CAN'T FIX.
BLECH! THIS TEENAGER'S **BODY** IS INTACT, BUT HIS **FACE** WAS **HORRIBLY DISFIGURED**!
I BELIEVE THAT'S JUST **ACNE**, MASTER.
YEE-GADS! WELL, NO CREATURE OF **MINE** IS GOING TO WALK AROUND LOOKING LIKE **THAT**! WE'LL TAKE THE HEAD OF THE BOY AND TRANSPLANT IT ONTO THE TEENAGER'S BODY.
WE'LL NEED TO PURCHASE SOME ELABORATE ELECTRICAL DOO-WHACKIES! THANK GOODNESS FOR ALL THE **MILLIONS** I'VE MADE FROM PATENTING AND SELLING MY LATEST INVENTION, CHEWABLE STEROIDS!

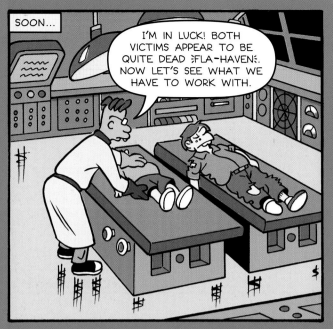

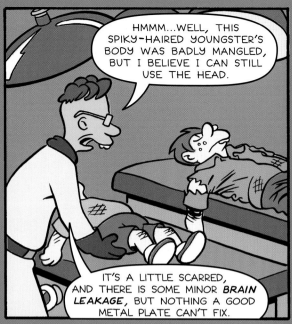

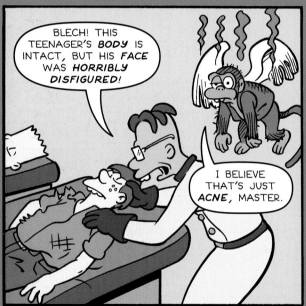

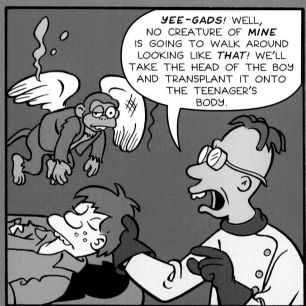

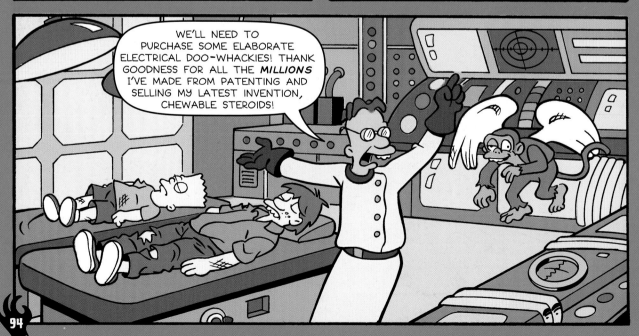

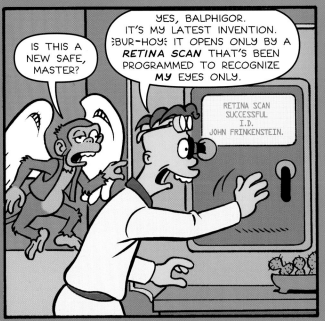

IS THIS A NEW SAFE, MASTER?

YES, BALPHIGOR. IT'S MY LATEST INVENTION. {BUR-HOY} IT OPENS ONLY BY A *RETINA SCAN* THAT'S BEEN PROGRAMMED TO RECOGNIZE *MY* EYES ONLY.

RETINA SCAN SUCCESSFUL I.D. JOHN FRINKENSTEIN.

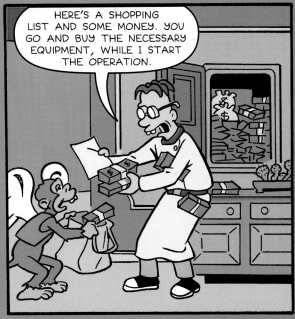

HERE'S A SHOPPING LIST AND SOME MONEY. YOU GO AND BUY THE NECESSARY EQUIPMENT, WHILE I START THE OPERATION.

"SOON, EVERYTHING WAS READY--THE CREATURE, THE LABORATORY, AND OF COURSE, THE TRADITIONAL PRE-EXPERIMENT LUCKY PLATE OF MINI-BURGERS {NA-WOYGLE}!"

"THE MOMENT OF TRUTH WAS *UPON* US!"

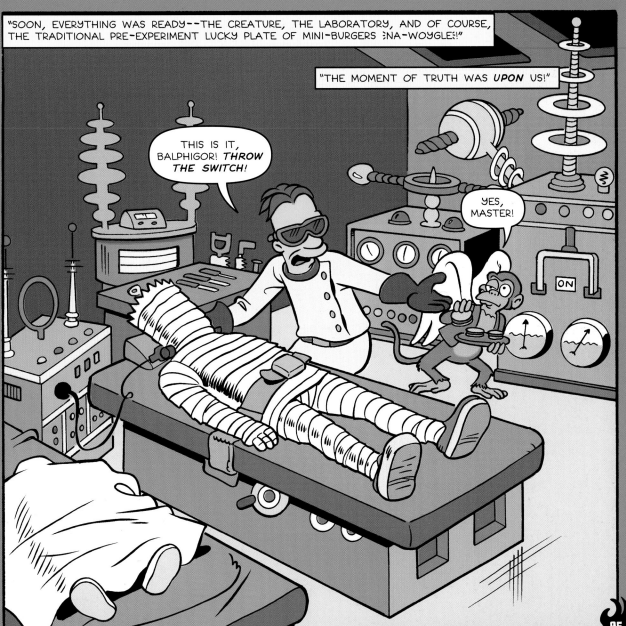

THIS IS IT, BALPHIGOR! *THROW THE SWITCH!*

YES, MASTER!

ON

SHWUK!
BZZZAAAAK!
THIS IS INCREDIBLE!
QUICK, BALPHIGOR! ⸗GULK⸗ GET ME A REFRESHING BEVERAGE TO WASH THIS SLIDER DOWN WITH!
KA-ZZZAP!
ALLRIGHTY THEN, THAT SHOULD DO IT! ⸗WOO-HOY⸗ KILL THE POWER!

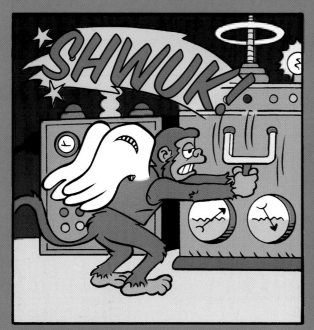

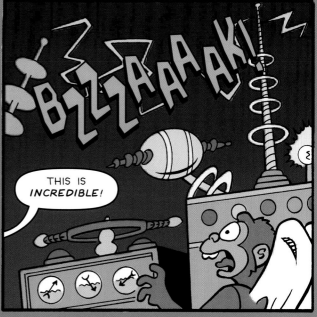

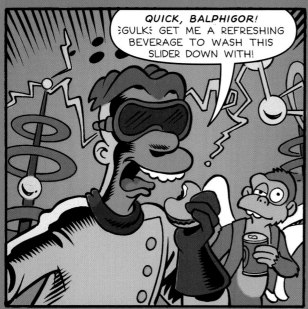

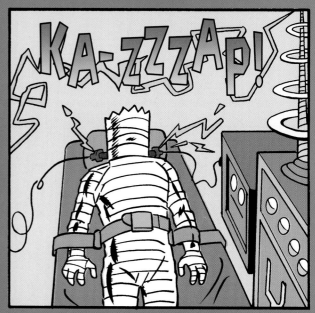

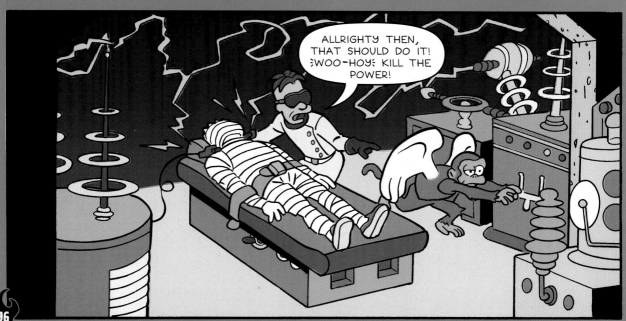

LOOK, BALPHIGOR! IT'S ALIVE! ALIVE! WITH THE WALKING AND THE SNARLING AND VILLAGERS FLEEING IN TERROR FROM DEATH ON TWO LEGS, FLINGING SMALL CHILDREN INTO A LAKE AND...
GOOD LORD, WHAT HAVE I DONE?!

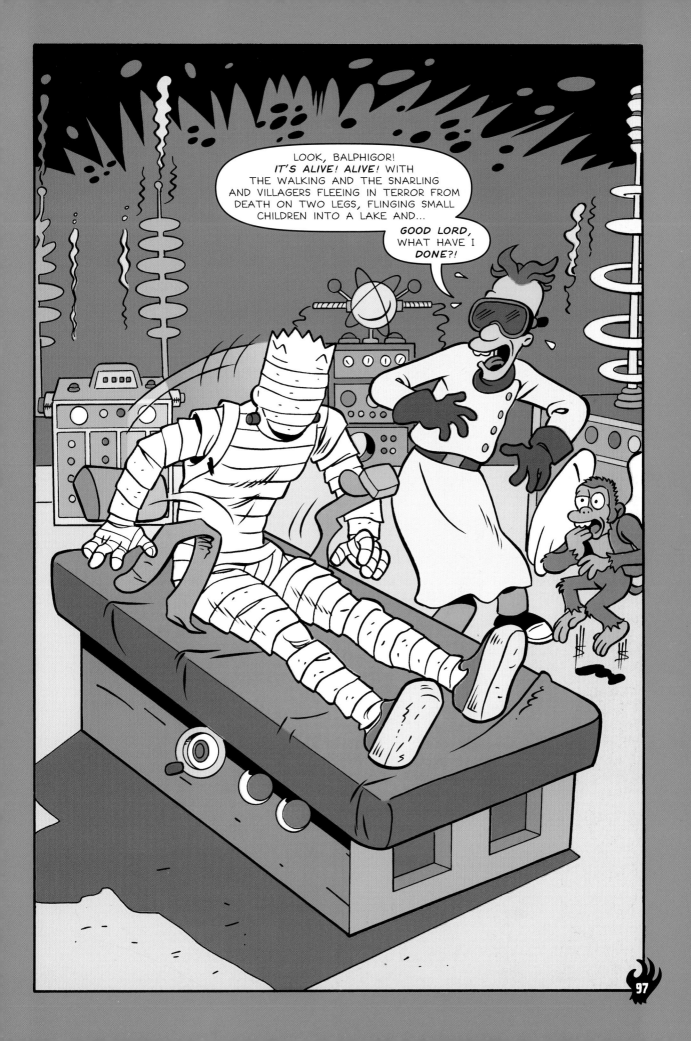

HEY, WHAT'S GOING ON HERE, MAN? WHO TURNED OUT THE LIGHTS?
IT **SPEAKS!** MAYBE IT'S NOT A MONSTER AFTER ALL.
HERE, LET'S GET IT OUT OF THOSE BANDAGES!
I'M **BART SIMPSON**. WHO THE HELL ARE **YOU**?
ACTUALLY, I'M YOUR CREATOR, PROFESSOR JOHN FRINKENSTEIN.
SORRY DOC, BUT **MY** CREATORS WERE HOMER AND MARGE SIMPSON, AND FROM WHAT I'M TOLD, GOD.
ER, YES, BUT--
NOW IF YOU DON'T MIND, I GOTTA GET HOME BEFORE I'M GROUNDED FOR LIFE.
WHAT THE-- **HEY!** THIS ISN'T **MY** BODY!
THAT'S WHAT I WAS TRYING TO EXPLAIN!
YOU WERE KILLED IN A TERRIBLE ACCIDENT. I PUT **YOUR** HEAD ON A **TEENAGER'S** BODY AND BROUGHT YOU BACK TO LIFE.
NO WAY! YOU MEAN I'M A **TEEN-AGER?!**
WOO-HOO! I'M A TEENAGER!

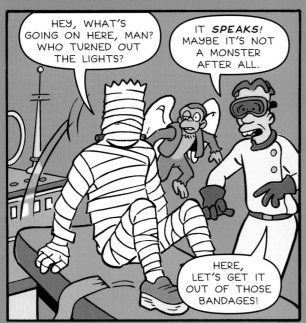

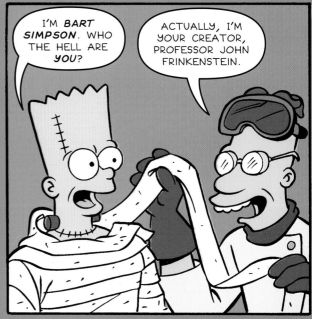

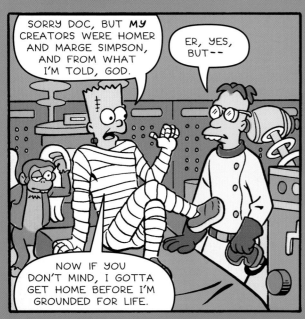

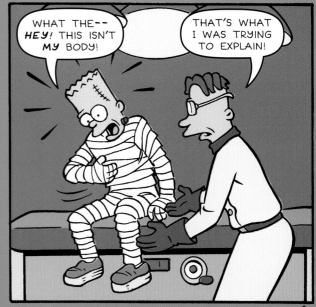

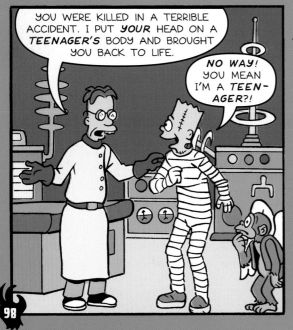

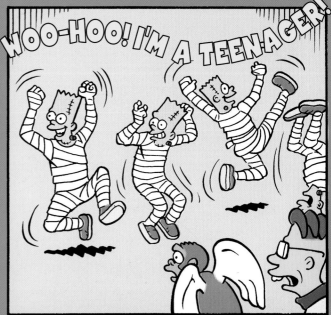

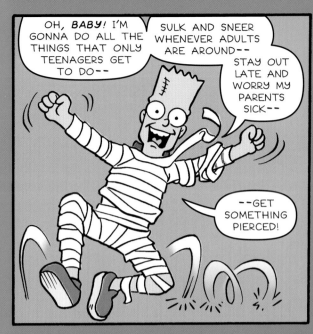
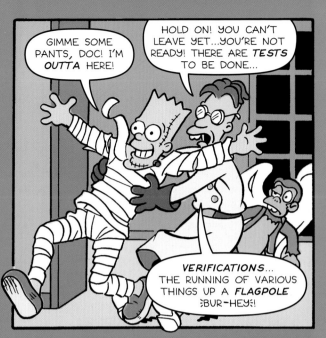

OH, *BABY!* I'M GONNA DO ALL THE THINGS THAT ONLY TEENAGERS GET TO DO--

SULK AND SNEER WHENEVER ADULTS ARE AROUND-- STAY OUT LATE AND WORRY MY PARENTS SICK--

--GET SOMETHING PIERCED!

GIMME SOME PANTS, DOC! I'M *OUTTA* HERE!

HOLD ON! YOU CAN'T LEAVE YET...YOU'RE NOT READY! THERE ARE *TESTS* TO BE DONE...

VERIFICATIONS... THE RUNNING OF VARIOUS THINGS UP A *FLAGPOLE* ɛBUR-HEYɛ!

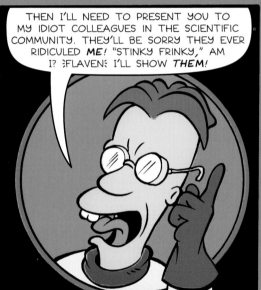

THEN I'LL NEED TO PRESENT YOU TO MY IDIOT COLLEAGUES IN THE SCIENTIFIC COMMUNITY. THEY'LL BE SORRY THEY EVER RIDICULED *ME*! "STINKY FRINKY," AM I? ɛFLAVENɛ I'LL SHOW *THEM*!

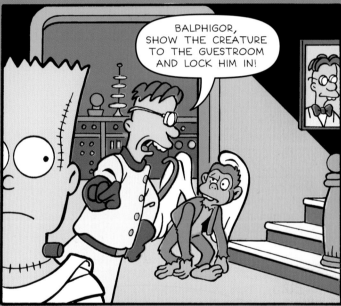

BALPHIGOR, SHOW THE CREATURE TO THE GUESTROOM AND LOCK HIM IN!

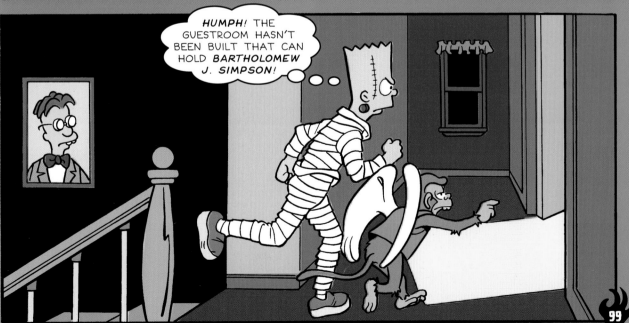

HUMPH! THE GUESTROOM HASN'T BEEN BUILT THAT CAN HOLD *BARTHOLOMEW J. SIMPSON!*

SOON...

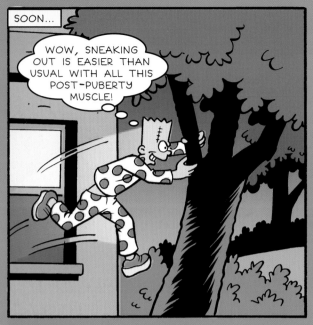

WOW, SNEAKING OUT IS EASIER THAN USUAL WITH ALL THIS POST-PUBERTY MUSCLE!

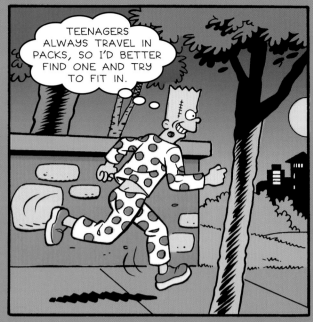

TEENAGERS ALWAYS TRAVEL IN PACKS, SO I'D BETTER FIND ONE AND TRY TO FIT IN.

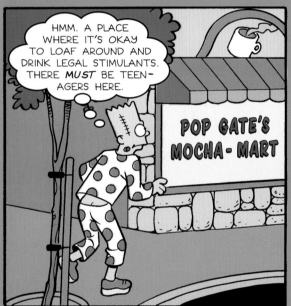

HMM. A PLACE WHERE IT'S OKAY TO LOAF AROUND AND DRINK LEGAL STIMULANTS. THERE *MUST* BE TEEN-AGERS HERE.

POP GATE'S MOCHA-MART

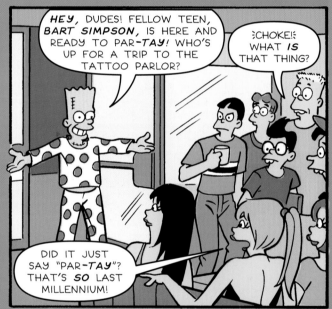

HEY, DUDES! FELLOW TEEN, *BART SIMPSON,* IS HERE AND READY TO PAR-*TAY*! WHO'S UP FOR A TRIP TO THE TATTOO PARLOR?

:CHOKE!: WHAT *IS* THAT THING?

DID IT JUST SAY "PAR-*TAY*"? THAT'S *SO* LAST MILLENNIUM!

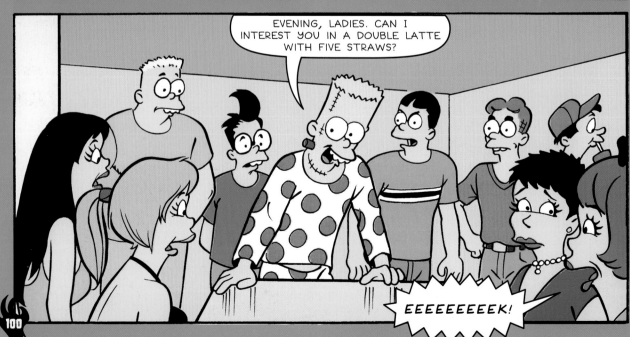

EVENING, LADIES. CAN I INTEREST YOU IN A DOUBLE LATTE WITH FIVE STRAWS?

EEEEEEEEEEK!

GULP MAYBE WEARING PAJAMAS OUT IN PUBLIC WASN'T SUCH A GOOD IDEA.
C'MON, MEN! WE'VE GOT TO PROTECT OUR WOMEN FROM THIS MONSTER! **GET IT!**
HEY GUYS, I'M NOT AN *IT!* I'M A ***HIM!*** C'MON, BACK OFF!
STAY AWAY— ***OOPS!***
UNGH!
WHACK!
OH MY GOSH! IT SMACKED DOWN **WARTHOG** LIKE HE WAS A **POTBELLY PIG!**
YIKES! I GUESS I DON'T KNOW MY OWN STRENGTH.
HEY, ***COOL!*** I ALWAYS WANTED TO SAY THAT!
I THINK THE MONSTER KILLED HIM!
WEEEEEEOOOOOO!
UH, OH! SOMEBODY MUST HAVE CALLED THE COPS! I'D BETTER VAMOOSE!

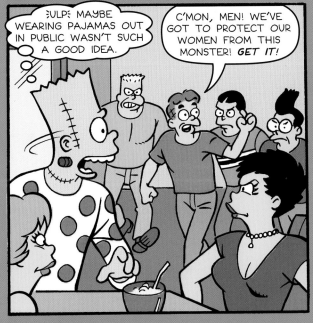

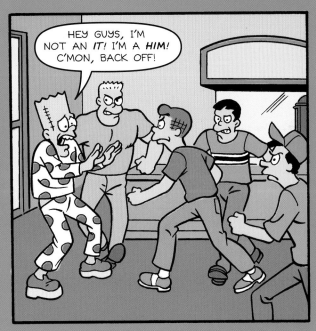

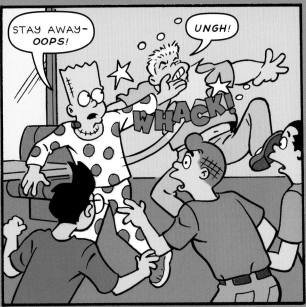

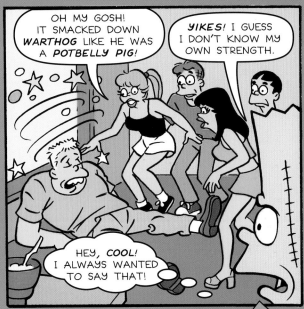

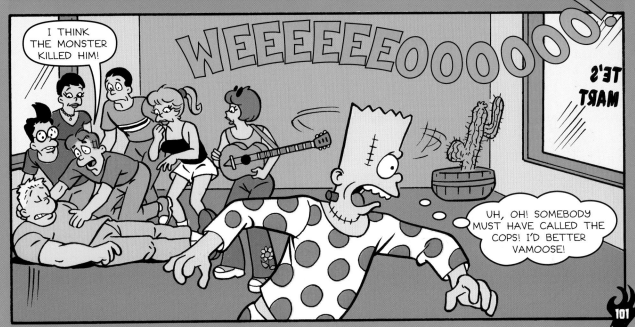

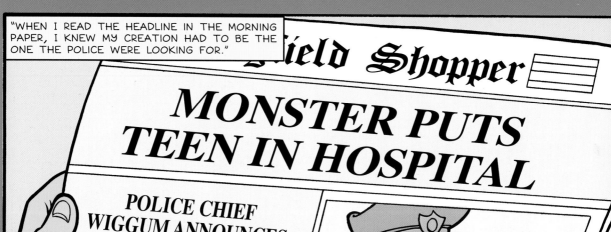

"WHEN I READ THE HEADLINE IN THE MORNING PAPER, I KNEW MY CREATION HAD TO BE THE ONE THE POLICE WERE LOOKING FOR."

field Shopper

MONSTER PUTS TEEN IN HOSPITAL

POLICE CHIEF WIGGUM ANNOUNCES MANHUNT, VACATION

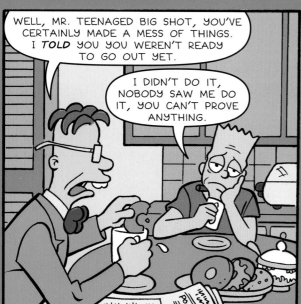

WELL, MR. TEENAGED BIG SHOT, YOU'VE CERTAINLY MADE A MESS OF THINGS. I *TOLD* YOU YOU WEREN'T READY TO GO OUT YET.

I DIDN'T DO IT, NOBODY SAW ME DO IT, YOU CAN'T PROVE ANYTHING.

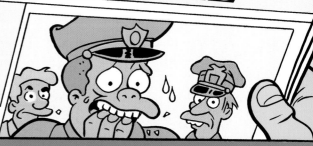

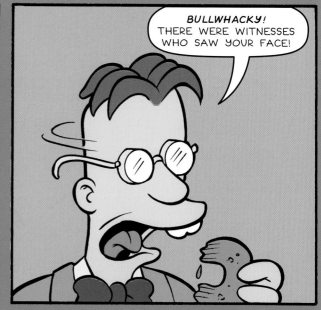

BULLWHACKY! THERE WERE WITNESSES WHO SAW YOUR FACE!

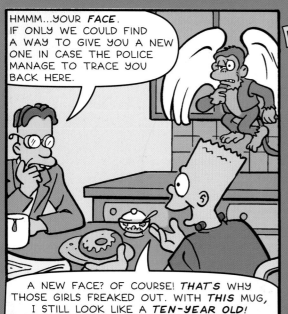

HMMM...YOUR *FACE*. IF ONLY WE COULD FIND A WAY TO GIVE YOU A NEW ONE IN CASE THE POLICE MANAGE TO TRACE YOU BACK HERE.

A NEW FACE? OF COURSE! *THAT'S* WHY THOSE GIRLS FREAKED OUT. WITH *THIS* MUG, I STILL LOOK LIKE A *TEN-YEAR OLD*!

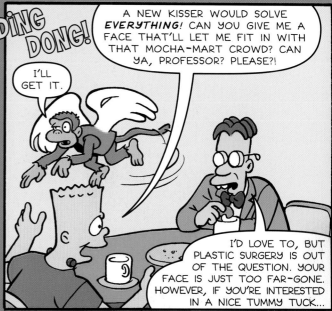

DING DONG!

I'LL GET IT.

A NEW KISSER WOULD SOLVE *EVERYTHING!* CAN YOU GIVE ME A FACE THAT'LL LET ME FIT IN WITH THAT MOCHA-MART CROWD? CAN YA, PROFESSOR? PLEASE?!

I'D LOVE TO, BUT PLASTIC SURGERY IS OUT OF THE QUESTION. YOUR FACE IS JUST TOO FAR-GONE. HOWEVER, IF YOU'RE INTERESTED IN A NICE TUMMY TUCK...

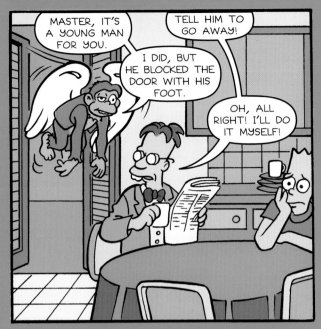

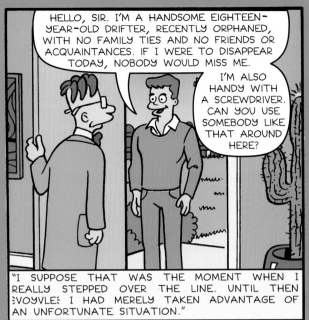

"I SUPPOSE THAT WAS THE MOMENT WHEN I REALLY STEPPED OVER THE LINE. UNTIL THEN ÷VOYLE÷ I HAD MERELY TAKEN ADVANTAGE OF AN UNFORTUNATE SITUATION."

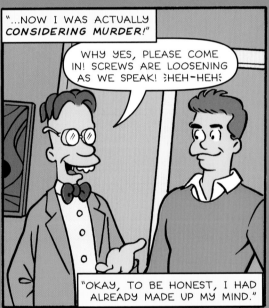

"...NOW I WAS ACTUALLY **CONSIDERING MURDER!**"

"OKAY, TO BE HONEST, I HAD ALREADY MADE UP MY MIND."

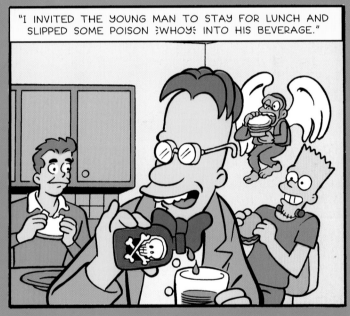

"I INVITED THE YOUNG MAN TO STAY FOR LUNCH AND SLIPPED SOME POISON ÷WHOY÷ INTO HIS BEVERAGE."

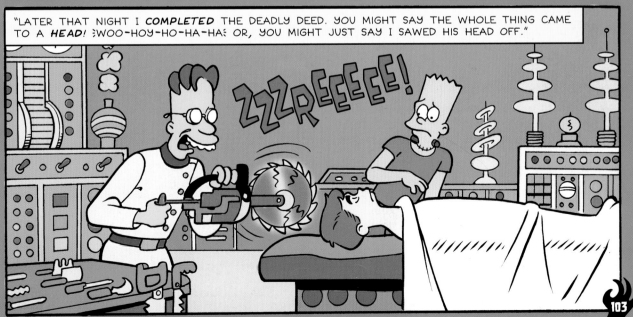

"LATER THAT NIGHT I **COMPLETED** THE DEADLY DEED. YOU MIGHT SAY THE WHOLE THING CAME TO A **HEAD!** ÷WOO-HOY-HO-HA-HA÷ OR, YOU MIGHT JUST SAY I SAWED HIS HEAD OFF."

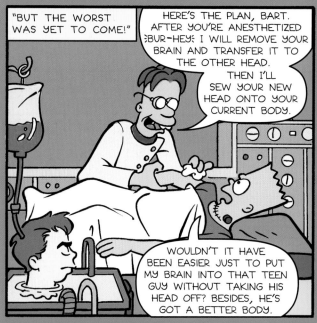

"BUT THE WORST WAS YET TO COME!"

HERE'S THE PLAN, BART. AFTER YOU'RE ANESTHETIZED ≈BUR-HEY≈ I WILL REMOVE YOUR BRAIN AND TRANSFER IT TO THE OTHER HEAD.
THEN I'LL SEW YOUR NEW HEAD ONTO YOUR CURRENT BODY.

WOULDN'T IT HAVE BEEN EASIER JUST TO PUT MY BRAIN INTO THAT TEEN GUY WITHOUT TAKING HIS HEAD OFF? BESIDES, HE'S GOT A BETTER BODY.

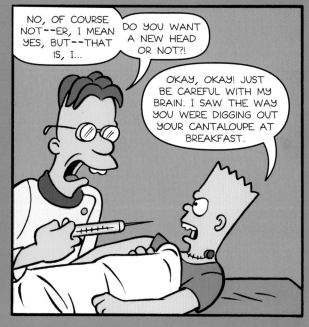

NO, OF COURSE NOT--ER, I MEAN YES, BUT--THAT IS, I...

DO YOU WANT A NEW HEAD OR NOT?!

OKAY, OKAY! JUST BE CAREFUL WITH MY BRAIN. I SAW THE WAY YOU WERE DIGGING OUT YOUR CANTALOUPE AT BREAKFAST.

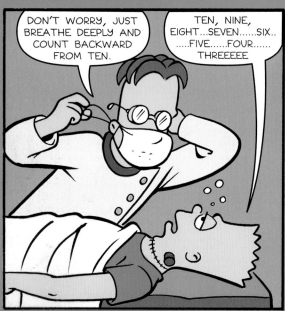

DON'T WORRY, JUST BREATHE DEEPLY AND COUNT BACKWARD FROM TEN.

TEN, NINE, EIGHT...SEVEN......SIX.. .....FIVE......FOUR...... THREEEEE

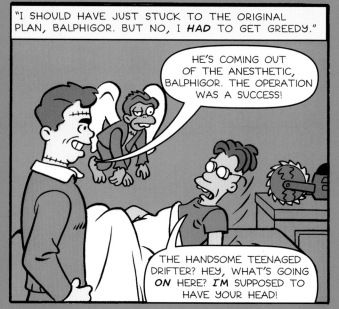

"I SHOULD HAVE JUST STUCK TO THE ORIGINAL PLAN, BALPHIGOR. BUT NO, I *HAD* TO GET GREEDY."

HE'S COMING OUT OF THE ANESTHETIC, BALPHIGOR. THE OPERATION WAS A SUCCESS!

THE HANDSOME TEENAGED DRIFTER? HEY, WHAT'S GOING *ON* HERE? *I'M* SUPPOSED TO HAVE YOUR HEAD!

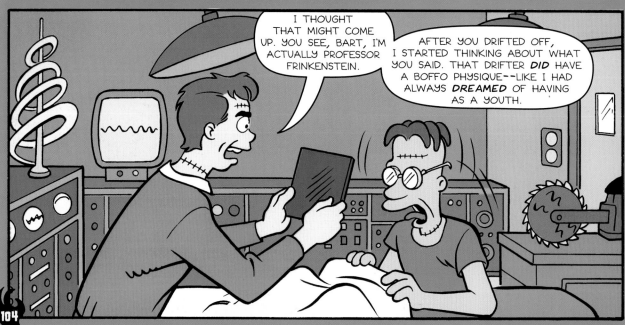

I THOUGHT THAT MIGHT COME UP. YOU SEE, BART, I'M ACTUALLY PROFESSOR FRINKENSTEIN.

AFTER YOU DRIFTED OFF, I STARTED THINKING ABOUT WHAT YOU SAID. THAT DRIFTER *DID* HAVE A BOFFO PHYSIQUE--LIKE I HAD ALWAYS *DREAMED* OF HAVING AS A YOUTH.

SO I DECIDED TO TRANSFER MY BRAIN TO HIS HEAD AND REATTACHED IT TO HIS BODY. THEN I PUT YOUR BRAIN INTO MY OLD GOOFY HEAD AND STITCHED IT ONTO YOUR BODY.
AY CARUMBA! I DON'T KNOW WHAT'S MORE DISTURBING--HAVING YOUR HEAD OR WONDERING HOW YOU MANAGED TO TRANSPLANT YOUR OWN BRAIN!
NOW, WITH MY INTELLIGENCE, MONEY, AND GOOD LOOKS, I CAN RULE THE WORLD!
FIRST I'LL NEED A FEW HUNDRED THOUSAND DOLLARS FOR SOME SPIFFY THREADS AND A NEW ROLLS ROYCE--SAY, WHY WON'T THIS SAFE OPEN?
ACCESS DENIED!
JULIUS H. KELP! THIS RETINA SCANNER WON'T RECOGNIZE MY NEW EYES! IT'S ONLY PROGRAMMED TO RECOGNIZE MY OLD ONES!
OH, REALLY? YOU MEAN THESE? WELL, WHO NEEDS TO BE A TEENAGER WHEN YOU CAN BE INCREDIBLY RICH?!
"HOW COULD EVERYTHING HAVE GONE SO HORRIBLY WRONG? WITHOUT A FORTUNE TO FUND MY EXPERIMENTS, I'M JUST YOUR AVERAGE GOOD-LOOKING TEENAGE HEARTTHROB."
IF IT'S ANY CONSOLATION, MASTER, I'M VERY HAPPY WITH MY NEW HUMAN HEAD!
I'VE GOT MONEY TO BURN! DOUBLE MOCHA LATTES FOR EVERYBODY!
OH, SHUT UP, YOU CACOPHONOUS CHIMP!
THE END

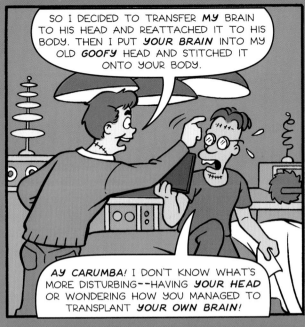

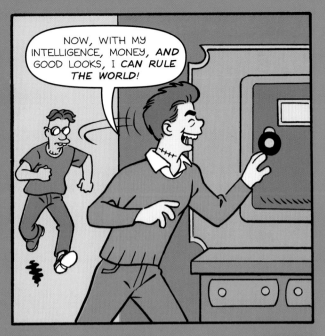

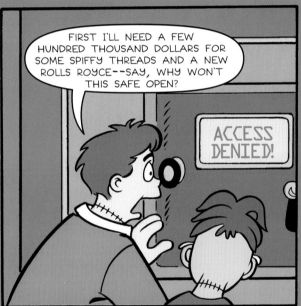

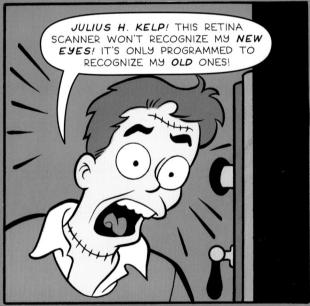

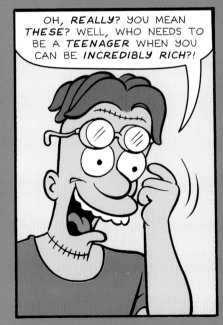

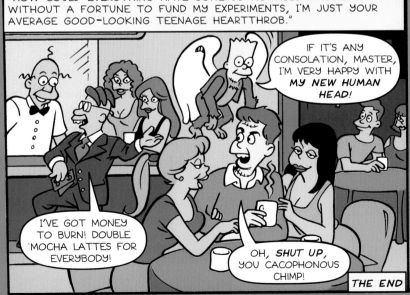

Why do you feel so warm and fuzzy? Is it a deadly fungal infection from the asteroid Gamulon? Perhaps. Or perhaps it is...

KOPRAH!

Koprah says: "You shall OBEY!"

YOU GO, KANGFRIEND!

I AM FORCED TO ENJOY YOU!

She will hug you till your ribs crack!

BY WATCHING, YOU WILL LEARN HOW TO...

- Hire a trainer to teach you how to eat.
- Hire a thought doctor to teach you how to feel.
- Hire a second thought doctor to teach you how to feel about eating the trainer and the thought doctor.

LEARN KOPRAH'S FAVORITE RECIPES!

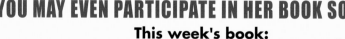

Add 2 cups of fat
Stir
Eat

CAN MALE HUMANS WATCH?

SURE!*

YOU MAY EVEN PARTICIPATE IN HER BOOK SOCIETY!

This week's book:
Something You Will Not Complete.

THE CRITICS CHEER:

"Koprah has been there. She knows the pain of sleeping on a giant stack of currency."
—*Newsday*

"Two! Four! Six! Eight! I cannot wait to ovulate!"
—*Foreign Affairs Quarterly*

*Males who watch will be shot.

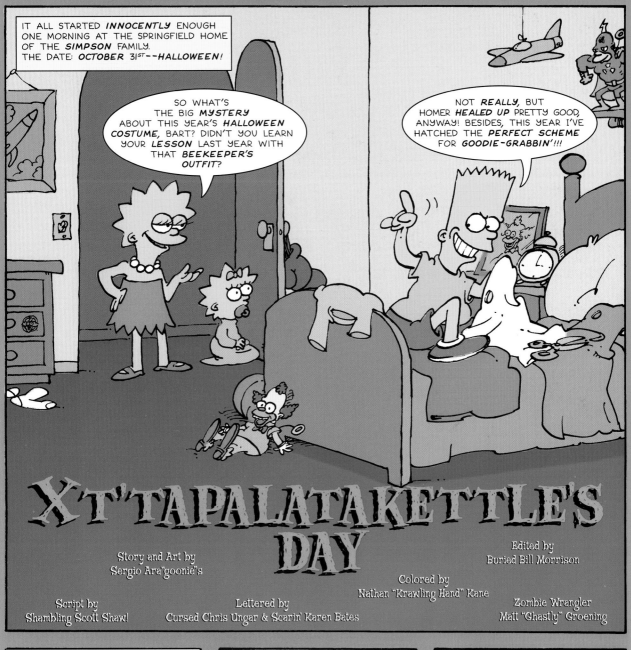

IT ALL STARTED *INNOCENTLY* ENOUGH ONE MORNING AT THE SPRINGFIELD HOME OF THE *SIMPSON* FAMILY. THE DATE: *OCTOBER 31ST--HALLOWEEN!*

SO WHAT'S THE BIG *MYSTERY* ABOUT THIS YEAR'S *HALLOWEEN COSTUME*, BART? DIDN'T YOU LEARN YOUR *LESSON* LAST YEAR WITH THAT *BEEKEEPER'S OUTFIT?*

NOT *REALLY*, BUT HOMER *HEALED UP* PRETTY GOOD, ANYWAY! BESIDES, THIS YEAR I'VE HATCHED THE *PERFECT SCHEME* FOR *GOODIE-GRABBIN'!!!*

Xt'Tapalatakettle's Day

Story and Art by
Sergio Ara'goonie's

Edited by
Buried Bill Morrison

Colored by
Nathan "Krawling Hand" Kane

Script by
Shambling Scott Shaw!

Lettered by
Cursed Chris Ungar & Scarin' Karen Bates

Zombie Wrangler
Matt "Ghastly" Groening

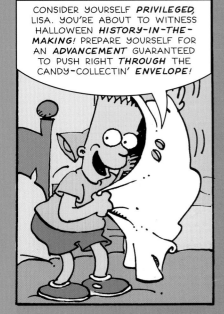

CONSIDER YOURSELF *PRIVILEGED*, LISA. YOU'RE ABOUT TO WITNESS HALLOWEEN *HISTORY-IN-THE-MAKING!* PREPARE YOURSELF FOR AN *ADVANCEMENT* GUARANTEED TO PUSH RIGHT *THROUGH* THE CANDY-COLLECTIN' *ENVELOPE!*

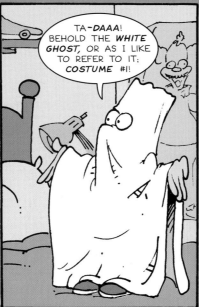

TA-DAAA! BEHOLD THE *WHITE GHOST*, OR AS I LIKE TO REFER TO IT; *COSTUME #1!*

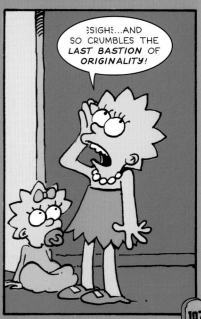

⊰SIGH⊱...AND SO CRUMBLES THE *LAST BASTION* OF *ORIGINALITY!*

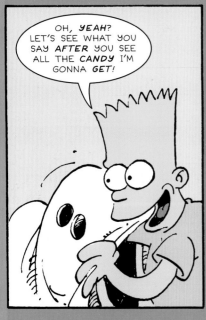

OH, *YEAH?* LET'S SEE WHAT YOU SAY *AFTER* YOU SEE ALL THE *CANDY* I'M GONNA *GET!*

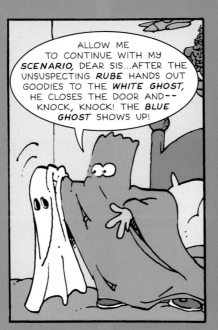

ALLOW ME TO CONTINUE WITH MY *SCENARIO,* DEAR SIS...AFTER THE UNSUSPECTING *RUBE* HANDS OUT GOODIES TO THE *WHITE GHOST,* HE CLOSES THE DOOR AND-- KNOCK, KNOCK! THE *BLUE GHOST* SHOWS UP!

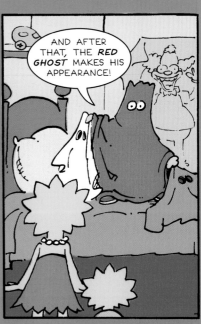

AND AFTER THAT, THE *RED GHOST* MAKES HIS APPEARANCE!

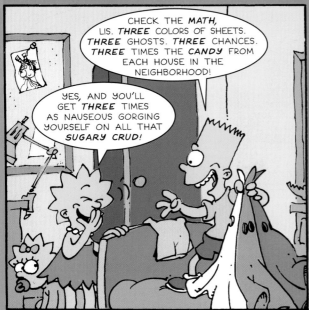

CHECK THE *MATH,* LIS. *THREE* COLORS OF SHEETS. *THREE* GHOSTS. *THREE* CHANCES. *THREE* TIMES THE *CANDY* FROM EACH HOUSE IN THE NEIGHBORHOOD!

YES, AND YOU'LL GET *THREE* TIMES AS NAUSEOUS GORGING YOURSELF ON ALL THAT *SUGARY CRUD!*

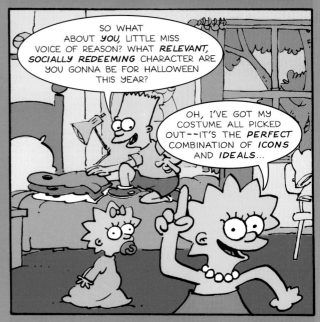

SO WHAT ABOUT *YOU,* LITTLE MISS VOICE OF REASON? WHAT *RELEVANT, SOCIALLY REDEEMING* CHARACTER ARE YOU GONNA BE FOR HALLOWEEN THIS YEAR?

OH, I'VE GOT MY COSTUME ALL PICKED OUT--IT'S THE *PERFECT* COMBINATION OF *ICONS* AND *IDEALS...*

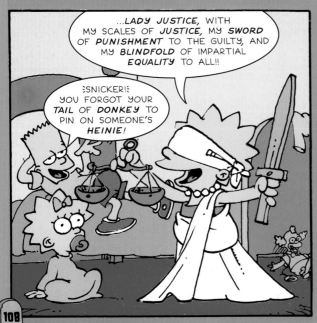

...*LADY JUSTICE,* WITH MY SCALES OF *JUSTICE,* MY *SWORD* OF *PUNISHMENT* TO THE GUILTY, AND MY *BLINDFOLD* OF IMPARTIAL *EQUALITY* TO ALL!!

⌐SNICKER!⌐ YOU FORGOT YOUR *TAIL* OF *DONKEY* TO PIN ON SOMEONE'S *HEINIE!*

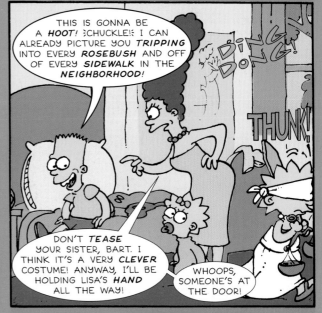

THIS IS GONNA BE A *HOOT!* ⌐CHUCKLE!⌐ I CAN ALREADY PICTURE YOU *TRIPPING* INTO EVERY *ROSEBUSH* AND OFF OF EVERY *SIDEWALK* IN THE *NEIGHBORHOOD!*

DON'T *TEASE* YOUR SISTER, BART. I THINK IT'S A VERY *CLEVER* COSTUME! ANYWAY, I'LL BE HOLDING LISA'S *HAND* ALL THE WAY!

WHOOPS, SOMEONE'S AT THE DOOR!

DING DONG!

THUNK!

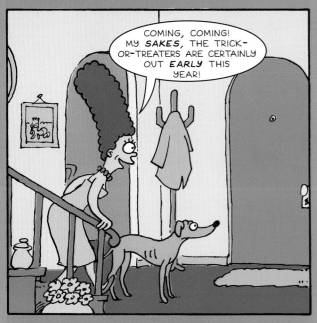

COMING, COMING! MY *SAKES*, THE TRICK-OR-TREATERS ARE CERTAINLY OUT *EARLY* THIS YEAR!

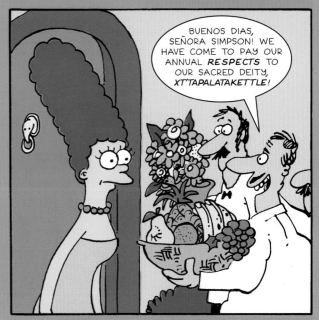

BUENOS DIAS, SEÑORA SIMPSON! WE HAVE COME TO PAY OUR ANNUAL *RESPECTS* TO OUR SACRED DEITY, *XT'TAPALATAKETTLE!*

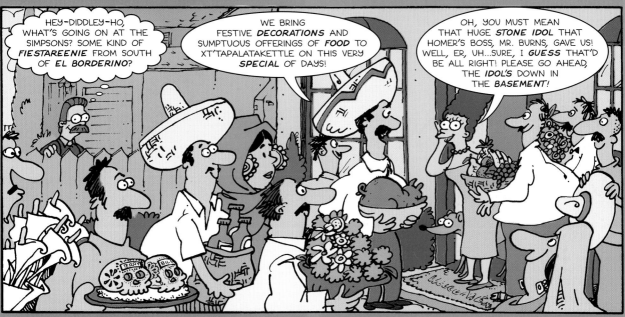

HEY-DIDDLEY-HO, WHAT'S GOING ON AT THE SIMPSONS? SOME KIND OF *FIESTAREENIE* FROM SOUTH OF *EL BORDERINO?*

WE BRING FESTIVE *DECORATIONS* AND SUMPTUOUS OFFERINGS OF *FOOD* TO XT'TAPALATAKETTLE ON THIS VERY *SPECIAL* OF DAYS!

OH, YOU MUST MEAN THAT HUGE *STONE IDOL* THAT HOMER'S BOSS, MR. BURNS, GAVE US! WELL, ER, UH...SURE, I *GUESS* THAT'D BE ALL RIGHT! PLEASE GO AHEAD, THE *IDOL'S* DOWN IN THE *BASEMENT!*

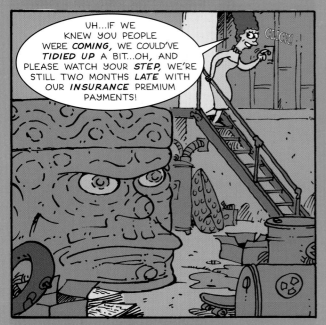

UH...IF WE KNEW YOU PEOPLE WERE *COMING*, WE COULD'VE *TIDIED UP* A BIT...OH, AND PLEASE WATCH YOUR *STEP*, WE'RE STILL TWO MONTHS *LATE* WITH OUR *INSURANCE* PREMIUM PAYMENTS!

CLICK!

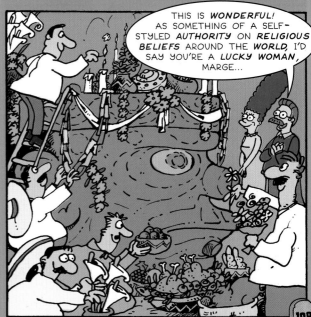

THIS IS *WONDERFUL!* AS SOMETHING OF A SELF-STYLED *AUTHORITY* ON *RELIGIOUS BELIEFS* AROUND THE *WORLD*, I'D SAY YOU'RE A *LUCKY WOMAN*, MARGE...

109

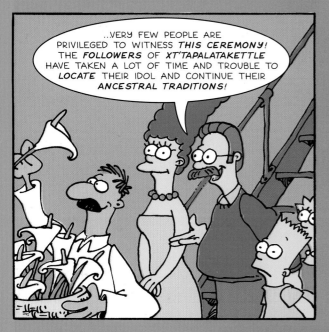

...VERY FEW PEOPLE ARE PRIVILEGED TO WITNESS *THIS CEREMONY!* THE *FOLLOWERS* OF *XT'TAPALATAKETTLE* HAVE TAKEN A LOT OF TIME AND TROUBLE TO *LOCATE* THEIR IDOL AND CONTINUE THEIR *ANCESTRAL TRADITIONS!*

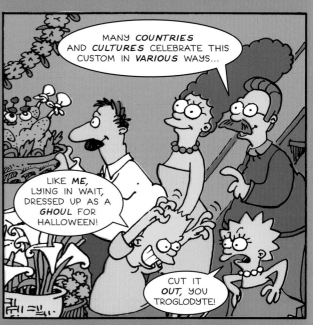

MANY *COUNTRIES* AND *CULTURES* CELEBRATE THIS CUSTOM IN *VARIOUS* WAYS...

LIKE *ME*, LYING IN WAIT, DRESSED UP AS A *GHOUL* FOR HALLOWEEN!

CUT IT *OUT*, YOU TROGLODYTE!

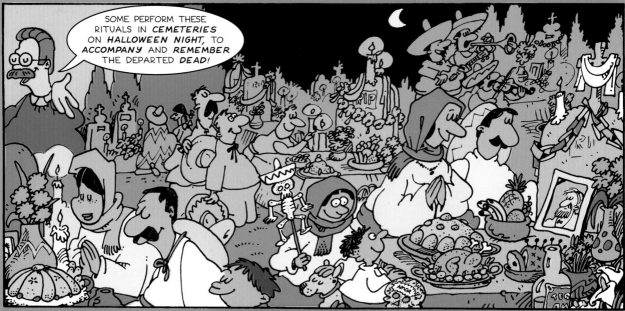

SOME PERFORM THESE RITUALS IN *CEMETERIES* ON *HALLOWEEN NIGHT*, TO *ACCOMPANY* AND *REMEMBER* THE DEPARTED *DEAD!*

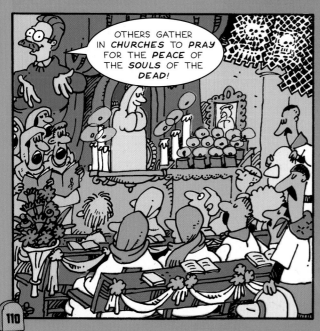

OTHERS GATHER IN *CHURCHES* TO *PRAY* FOR THE *PEACE* OF THE *SOULS* OF THE *DEAD!*

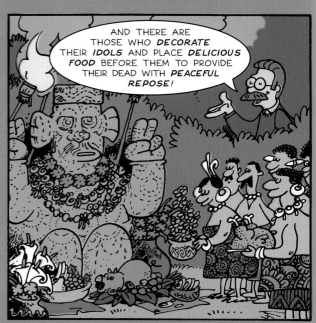

AND THERE ARE THOSE WHO *DECORATE* THEIR *IDOLS* AND PLACE *DELICIOUS FOOD* BEFORE THEM TO PROVIDE THEIR DEAD WITH *PEACEFUL REPOSE!*

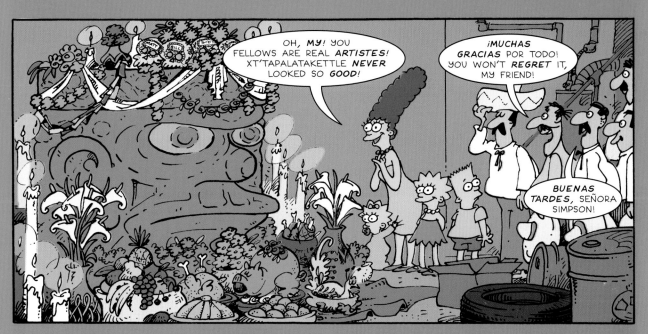

OH, *MY!* YOU FELLOWS ARE REAL *ARTISTES!* XT'TAPALATAKETTLE *NEVER* LOOKED SO *GOOD!*

¡MUCHAS *GRACIAS* POR TODO! YOU WON'T *REGRET* IT, MY FRIEND!

BUENAS TARDES, SEÑORA SIMPSON!

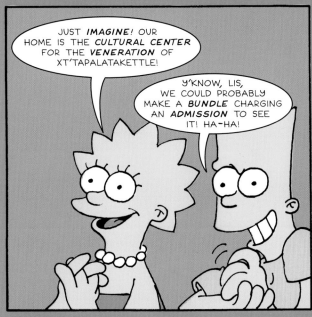

JUST *IMAGINE!* OUR HOME IS THE *CULTURAL CENTER* FOR THE *VENERATION* OF XT'TAPALATAKETTLE!

Y'KNOW, LIS, WE COULD PROBABLY MAKE A *BUNDLE* CHARGING AN *ADMISSION* TO SEE IT! HA-HA!

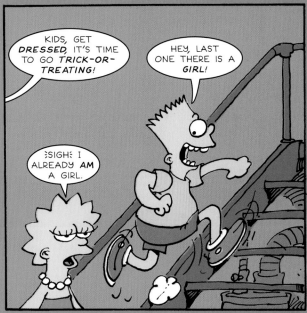

KIDS, GET *DRESSED,* IT'S TIME TO GO *TRICK-OR-TREATING!*

HEY, LAST ONE THERE IS A *GIRL!*

∷SIGH∷ I ALREADY *AM* A GIRL.

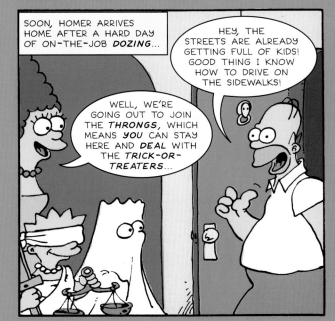

SOON, HOMER ARRIVES HOME AFTER A HARD DAY OF ON-THE-JOB *DOZING...*

HEY, THE STREETS ARE ALREADY GETTING FULL OF KIDS! GOOD THING I KNOW HOW TO DRIVE ON THE SIDEWALKS!

WELL, WE'RE GOING OUT TO JOIN THE *THRONGS,* WHICH MEANS *YOU* CAN STAY HERE AND *DEAL* WITH THE *TRICK-OR-TREATERS...*

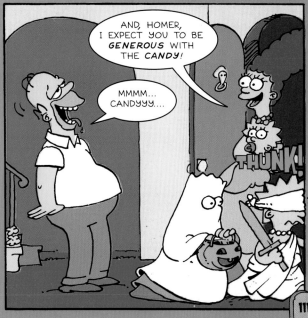

AND, HOMER, I EXPECT YOU TO BE *GENEROUS* WITH THE *CANDY!*

MMMM... CANDYYY....

THUNK!

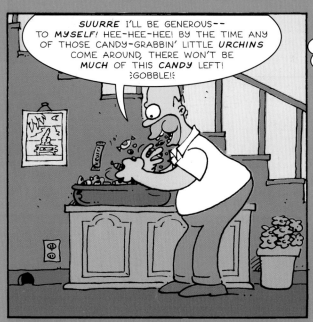

SUURRE I'LL BE GENEROUS-- TO **MYSELF**! HEE-HEE-HEE! BY THE TIME ANY OF THOSE CANDY-GRABBIN' LITTLE **URCHINS** COME AROUND, THERE WON'T BE **MUCH** OF THIS **CANDY** LEFT! ⸘GOBBLE‽

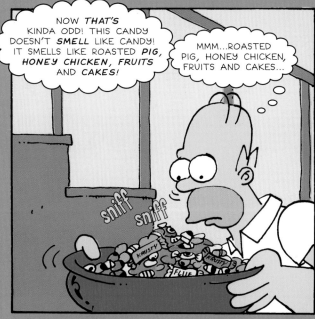

NOW **THAT'S** KINDA ODD! THIS CANDY DOESN'T **SMELL** LIKE CANDY! IT SMELLS LIKE ROASTED **PIG**, **HONEY CHICKEN, FRUITS** AND **CAKES**!

MMM...ROASTED PIG, HONEY CHICKEN, FRUITS AND CAKES...

sniff sniff

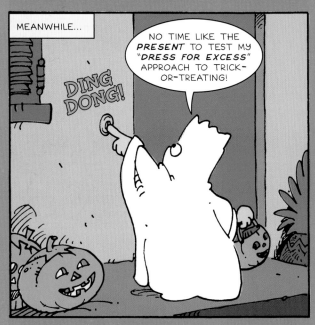

MEANWHILE...

NO TIME LIKE THE **PRESENT** TO TEST MY "**DRESS FOR EXCESS**" APPROACH TO TRICK-OR-TREATING!

DING DONG!

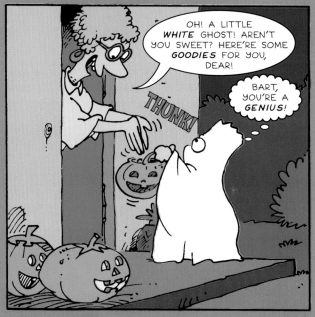

OH! A LITTLE **WHITE** GHOST! AREN'T YOU SWEET? HERE'RE SOME **GOODIES** FOR YOU, DEAR!

BART, YOU'RE A **GENIUS**!

THUNK!

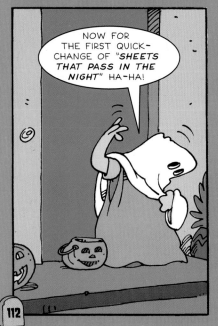

NOW FOR THE FIRST QUICK-CHANGE OF "**SHEETS THAT PASS IN THE NIGHT**" HA-HA!

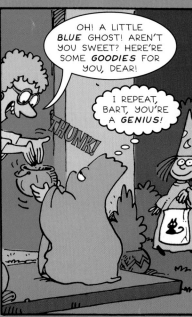

OH! A LITTLE **BLUE** GHOST! AREN'T YOU SWEET? HERE'RE SOME **GOODIES** FOR YOU, DEAR!

I REPEAT, BART, YOU'RE A **GENIUS**!

THUNK!

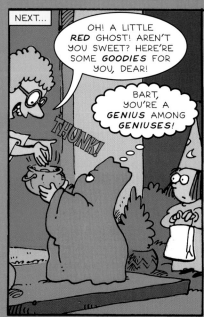

NEXT...

OH! A LITTLE **RED** GHOST! AREN'T YOU SWEET? HERE'RE SOME **GOODIES** FOR YOU, DEAR!

BART, YOU'RE A **GENIUS** AMONG **GENIUSES**!

THUNK!

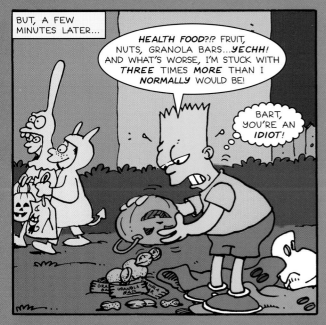

BUT, A FEW MINUTES LATER...

HEALTH FOOD?!? FRUIT, NUTS, GRANOLA BARS...*YECHH!* AND WHAT'S WORSE, I'M STUCK WITH *THREE* TIMES *MORE* THAN I *NORMALLY* WOULD BE!

BART, YOU'RE AN *IDIOT!*

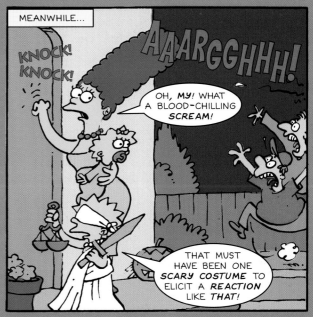

MEANWHILE...

KNOCK! KNOCK!

AAARGGHHH!

OH, *MY!* WHAT A BLOOD-CHILLING *SCREAM!*

THAT MUST HAVE BEEN ONE *SCARY COSTUME* TO ELICIT A *REACTION* LIKE *THAT!*

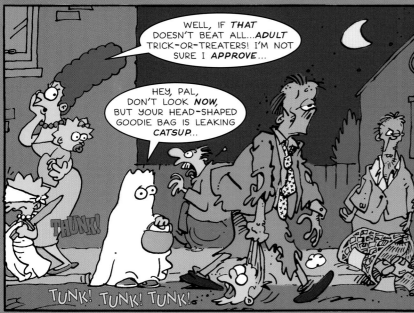

WELL, IF *THAT* DOESN'T BEAT ALL...*ADULT* TRICK-OR-TREATERS! I'M NOT SURE I *APPROVE...*

HEY, PAL, DON'T LOOK *NOW*, BUT YOUR HEAD-SHAPED GOODIE BAG IS LEAKING *CATSUP...*

THUNK!

TUNK! TUNK! TUNK!

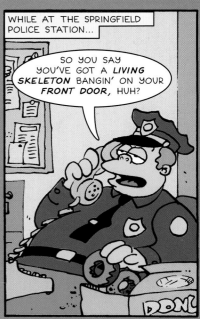

WHILE AT THE SPRINGFIELD POLICE STATION...

SO YOU SAY YOU'VE GOT A *LIVING SKELETON* BANGIN' ON YOUR *FRONT DOOR,* HUH?

DON

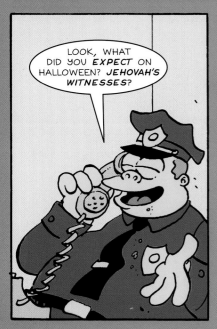

LOOK, WHAT DID YOU *EXPECT* ON HALLOWEEN? *JEHOVAH'S WITNESSES?*

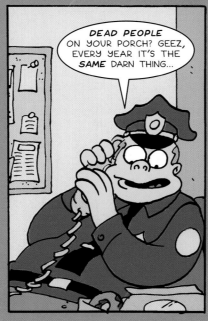

DEAD PEOPLE ON YOUR PORCH? GEEZ, EVERY YEAR IT'S THE *SAME* DARN THING...

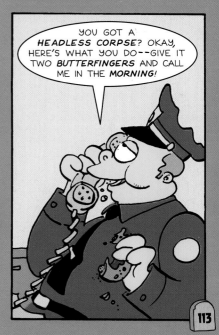

YOU GOT A *HEADLESS CORPSE?* OKAY, HERE'S WHAT YOU DO--GIVE IT TWO *BUTTERFINGERS* AND CALL ME IN THE *MORNING!*

MEANWHILE, ALL AROUND SPRINGFIELD...
WELL, SMITHERS, I WONDER WHAT THE POOR PEOPLE ARE DOING?
ERR...FROM THE LOOKS OF THINGS, THEY'RE NOT DOING SO WELL, MR. BURNS...
WELCOME TO SPRINGFIELD NUCLEAR POWER PLANT
KRUSTY BURGER
SNIFF! MY ENTIRE LIFE HAS BEEN BUT A PRELUDE TO THIS MAGIC MOMENT!
BUDDA BUDDA BUDDA POW!
BUT, KANG ACCORDING TO MY HISTORICAL RESEARCH, THIS DATE SHOULD BE IDEAL FOR THE INVASION OF EARTH.
PERHAPS ONE OF THESE FOOLISH EARTHLINGS CAN ELUCIDATE. NOW TELL ME, KODOS, WHICH ONE OF THEM IS ORSON WELLES?
WELCOME TO KRUSTYBURGER, MAY I TAKE YOUR--ARGHH!!!
MILITARY
MOE'S
AHEM... WORST WALKING DEAD MAKEUP EVER...
"TAKE ME TO YOUR COMIC BOOK & BASEBALL CAP"
GET OUT, BARNEY! MY NEW WALKING DEAD CLIENTELE KEEP COMPLAINING ABOUT YOUR OFFENSIVE BODY ODOR!!
AW, MOE, WHAT DO THEY KNOW? BELCHHH! THEY'RE DEAD! SOME OF THOSE GUYS DON'T EVEN HAVE NOSES ANY MORE!
...KENT BROCKMAN CONDUCTING ANOTHER OF MY ON-THE-STREET INTERVIEWS! I'M SPEAKING WITH BOTH LIVING AND DEAD LOCAL CITIZENS...
HELLO, EVERYBODY! FOR ONLY $49.95, I CAN GET YOU LOOKING LIKE NEW AGAIN!
HEY, GOOD LOOKIN', HOW ABOUT NIBBLING ON MY CLAVICLE!?!
C'MON, DUDE. GIMME BACK MY SKATEBOARD!
YOU HAVE THE RIGHT TO REMAIN SILENT: IF YOU CHOOSE TO GIVE UP THE RIGHT TO REMAIN SILENT, ANYTHING YOU SAY CAN AND WILL BE USED AGAINST...AW, GEE, FORGET IT!
I'M GONNA NEED A REPLACEMENT PATROL CAR DOWN HERE ASAP! YEAH, AND A FEW CANISTERS OF SOME OF THAT ANTI-WALKING-DEAD REPELLENT, TOO!
HUH? WHADDAYA MEAN, YOU "DON'T HAVE ANY ANTI-WALKING-DEAD REPELLENT?"

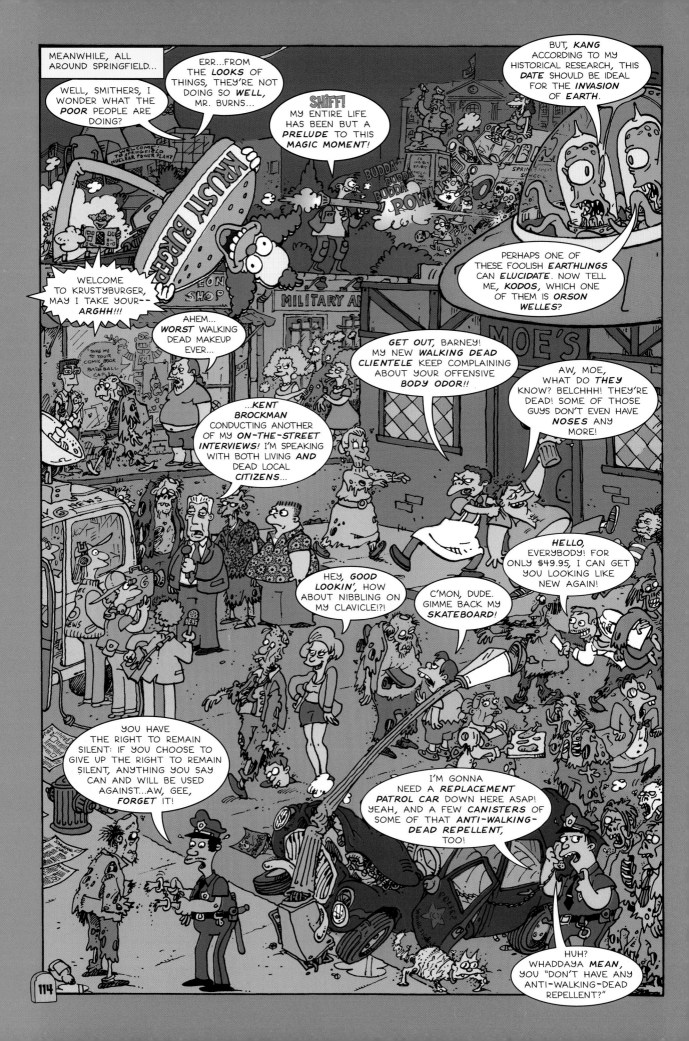

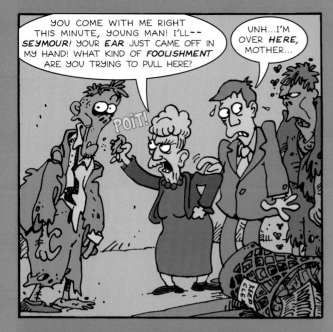

YOU COME WITH ME RIGHT THIS MINUTE, YOUNG MAN! I'LL-- *SEYMOUR!* YOUR *EAR* JUST CAME OFF IN MY HAND! WHAT KIND OF *FOOLISHMENT* ARE YOU TRYING TO PULL HERE?

UNH...I'M OVER *HERE*, MOTHER...

POIT!

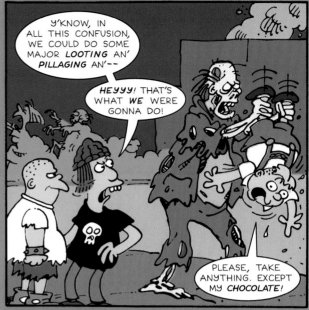

Y'KNOW, IN ALL THIS CONFUSION, WE COULD DO SOME MAJOR *LOOTING* AN' *PILLAGING* AN'--

HEYYY! THAT'S WHAT *WE* WERE GONNA DO!

PLEASE, TAKE ANYTHING. EXCEPT MY *CHOCOLATE!*

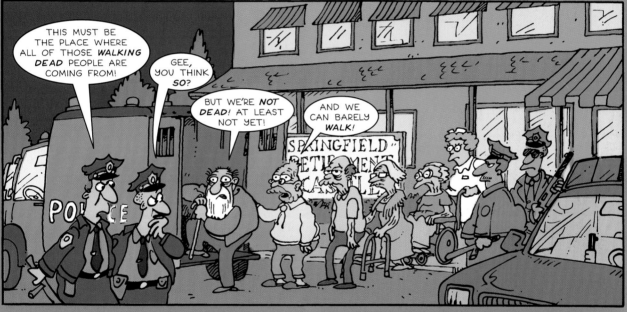

THIS MUST BE THE PLACE WHERE ALL OF THOSE *WALKING DEAD* PEOPLE ARE COMING FROM!

GEE, YOU THINK *SO?*

BUT WE'RE *NOT DEAD!* AT LEAST NOT YET!

AND WE CAN BARELY *WALK!*

SPRINGFIELD RETIREMENT CASTLE

POLICE

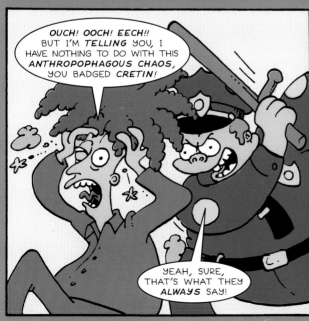

OUCH! OOCH! EECH!! BUT I'M *TELLING* YOU, I HAVE NOTHING TO DO WITH THIS *ANTHROPOPHAGOUS* CHAOS, YOU BADGED *CRETIN!*

YEAH, SURE, THAT'S WHAT THEY *ALWAYS* SAY!

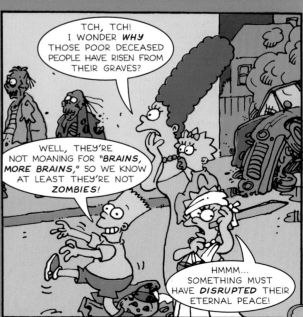

TCH, TCH! I WONDER *WHY* THOSE POOR DECEASED PEOPLE HAVE RISEN FROM THEIR GRAVES?

WELL, THEY'RE NOT MOANING FOR *"BRAINS, MORE BRAINS,"* SO WE KNOW AT LEAST THEY'RE NOT *ZOMBIES!*

HMMM... SOMETHING MUST HAVE *DISRUPTED* THEIR ETERNAL PEACE!

BURP!
THAT HORRIBLE SOUND CAME FROM OUR HOUSE! OH, I HOPE HOMIE'S ALL RIGHT!
NOW THAT'S SOMEONE WHO COULD USE MORE BRAINS!
OH, MY GOSH! WHAT IF HOMER--OH, HE COULDN'T HAVE! BUT WHAT IF HE DID--?
DID WHAT, MOM?
OH, NO, HOMER! YOU ATE ALL OF XT'TAPALATAKETTLE'S FOOD!
AND ALL OF THE DECORATIONS!
OOOHHH...
DAD! THAT STUFF WAS SUPPOSED TO KEEP THE DEAD IN A RESTFUL PEACE!
MATT
OH, HI, MARGE...GOT ANY AFTER-DINNER MINTS?
WELL, AT LEAST YOU'RE ALL RIGHT, I GUESS.
SO, LISA, WHAT DO YOU SUGGEST WE DO NOW?
I GUESS WE SHOULD RESTORE THE FOOD TO APPEASE THE DEAD!
"RESTORE THE FOOD?" HEY, I CAN DO THAT!
COME TO BED, HOMIE, YOU'VE ALREADY DONE MORE THAN ENOUGH DAMAGE FOR ONE DAY!
BUT HOW ARE WE GONNA DO THAT?
ALL THAT'S IN THE FRIDGE IS A HALF-FULL CAN OF DUFF, A ROTTING HEAD OF LETTUCE AND A BOX OF BAKING SODA!
APU!!!
SNAP!

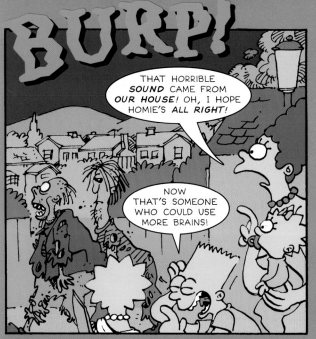

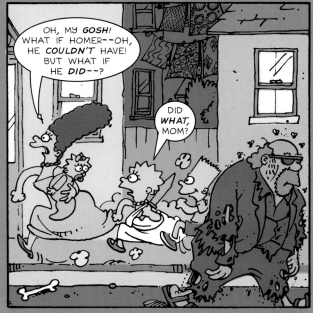

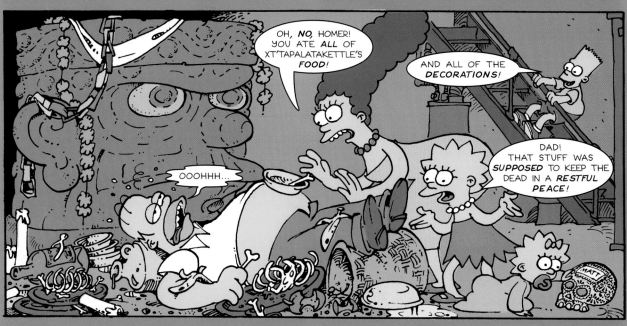

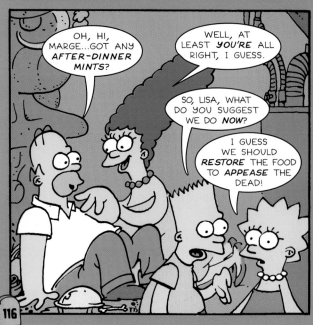

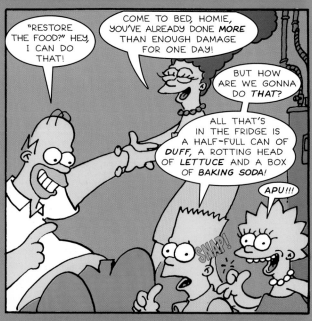

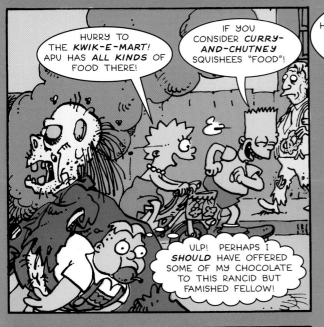

HURRY TO THE *KWIK-E-MART*! APU HAS *ALL KINDS* OF FOOD THERE!

IF YOU CONSIDER *CURRY-AND-CHUTNEY* SQUISHEES "FOOD"!

ULP! PERHAPS I *SHOULD* HAVE OFFERED SOME OF MY CHOCOLATE TO THIS RANCID BUT FAMISHED FELLOW!

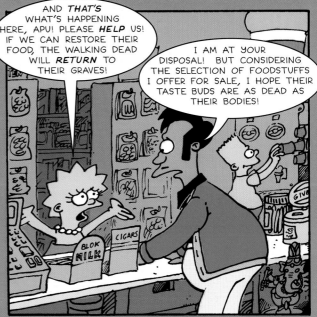

AND *THAT'S* WHAT'S HAPPENING HERE, APU! PLEASE *HELP* US! IF WE CAN RESTORE THEIR FOOD, THE WALKING DEAD WILL *RETURN* TO THEIR GRAVES!

I AM AT YOUR *DISPOSAL*! BUT CONSIDERING THE SELECTION OF FOODSTUFFS I OFFER FOR SALE, I HOPE THEIR TASTE BUDS ARE AS DEAD AS THEIR BODIES!

BLOK MILK

CIGARS

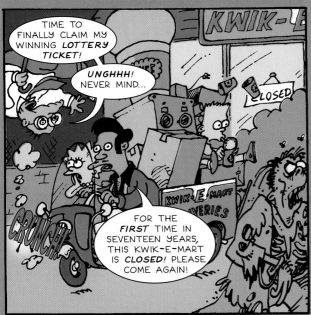

TIME TO FINALLY CLAIM MY WINNING *LOTTERY* TICKET!

UNGHHH! NEVER MIND...

CLOSED

FOR THE *FIRST* TIME IN SEVENTEEN YEARS, THIS KWIK-E-MART IS *CLOSED*! PLEASE COME AGAIN!

KWIK-E-MART GROCERIES

CRUNCH!

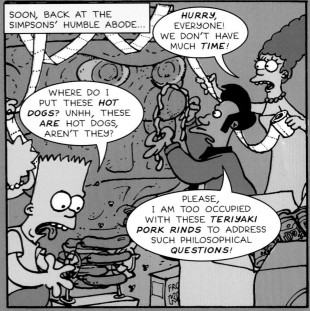

SOON, BACK AT THE SIMPSONS' HUMBLE ABODE...

HURRY, EVERYONE! WE DON'T HAVE MUCH *TIME*!

WHERE DO I PUT THESE *HOT DOGS*? UNHH, THESE *ARE* HOT DOGS, AREN'T THEY?

PLEASE, I AM TOO OCCUPIED WITH THESE *TERIYAKI PORK RINDS* TO ADDRESS SUCH PHILOSOPHICAL *QUESTIONS*!

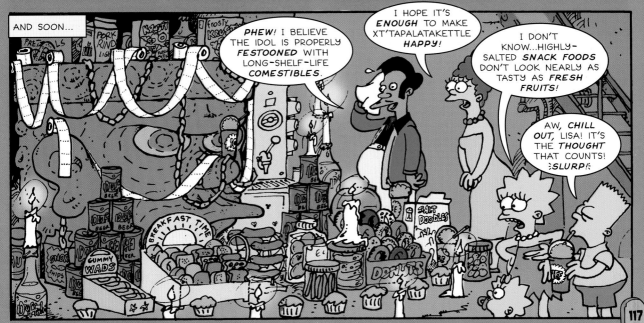

AND SOON...

PHEW! I BELIEVE THE IDOL IS PROPERLY *FESTOONED* WITH LONG-SHELF-LIFE *COMESTIBLES*.

I HOPE IT'S *ENOUGH* TO MAKE XT'TAPALATAKETTLE *HAPPY!*

I DON'T KNOW...HIGHLY-SALTED *SNACK FOODS* DON'T LOOK NEARLY AS TASTY AS *FRESH FRUITS!*

AW, *CHILL OUT*, LISA! IT'S THE *THOUGHT* THAT COUNTS! ⸨SLURP!⸩

PORK RINDS

SALT DOODLES

DONUTS

BREAKFAST TIME

GUMMY WADS

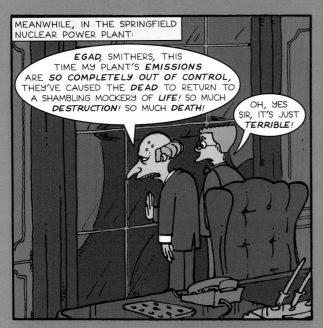

MEANWHILE, IN THE SPRINGFIELD NUCLEAR POWER PLANT:

EGAD, SMITHERS, THIS TIME MY PLANT'S **EMISSIONS** ARE **SO COMPLETELY OUT OF CONTROL**, THEY'VE CAUSED THE **DEAD** TO RETURN TO A SHAMBLING MOCKERY OF **LIFE**! SO MUCH **DESTRUCTION**! SO MUCH **DEATH**!

OH, YES SIR, IT'S JUST **TERRIBLE**!

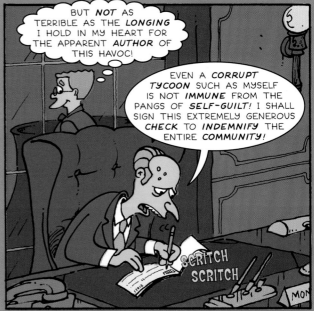

BUT **NOT** AS TERRIBLE AS THE **LONGING** I HOLD IN MY HEART FOR THE APPARENT **AUTHOR** OF THIS HAVOC!

EVEN A **CORRUPT TYCOON** SUCH AS MYSELF IS NOT **IMMUNE** FROM THE PANGS OF **SELF-GUILT**! I SHALL SIGN THIS EXTREMELY GENEROUS **CHECK** TO **INDEMNIFY** THE ENTIRE **COMMUNITY**!

SCRITCH SCRITCH

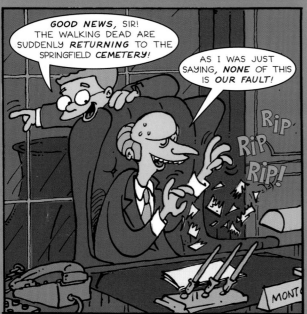

GOOD NEWS, SIR! THE WALKING DEAD ARE SUDDENLY **RETURNING** TO THE SPRINGFIELD **CEMETERY**!

AS I WAS JUST SAYING, **NONE** OF THIS IS **OUR FAULT**!

RIP RIP RIP RIP!

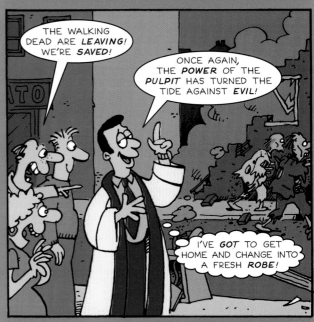

THE WALKING DEAD ARE **LEAVING**! WE'RE **SAVED**!

ONCE AGAIN, THE **POWER** OF THE **PULPIT** HAS TURNED THE TIDE AGAINST **EVIL**!

I'VE **GOT** TO GET HOME AND CHANGE INTO A FRESH **ROBE**!

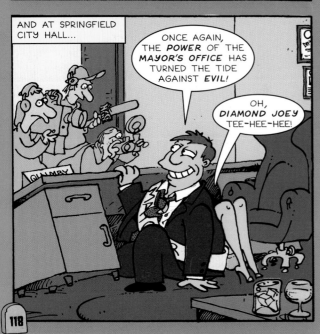

AND AT SPRINGFIELD CITY HALL...

ONCE AGAIN, THE **POWER** OF THE **MAYOR'S OFFICE** HAS TURNED THE TIDE AGAINST **EVIL**!

OH, **DIAMOND JOEY** TEE-HEE-HEE!

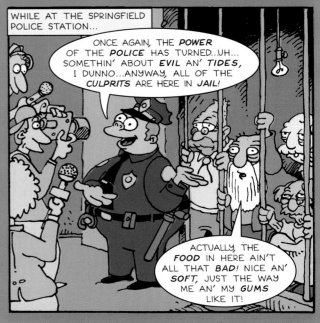

WHILE AT THE SPRINGFIELD POLICE STATION...

ONCE AGAIN, THE **POWER** OF THE **POLICE** HAS TURNED...UH... SOMETHIN' ABOUT **EVIL** AN' **TIDES**, I DUNNO...ANYWAY, ALL OF THE **CULPRITS** ARE HERE IN **JAIL**!

ACTUALLY, THE **FOOD** IN HERE AIN'T ALL THAT **BAD**! NICE AN' **SOFT**, JUST THE WAY ME AN' MY **GUMS** LIKE IT!

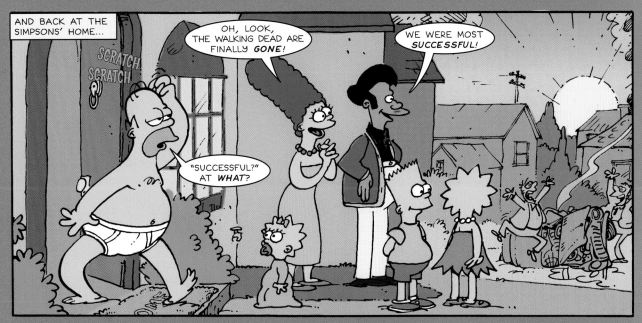

AND BACK AT THE SIMPSONS' HOME...

SCRATCH! SCRATCH!

OH, LOOK, THE WALKING DEAD ARE FINALLY *GONE!*

WE WERE MOST *SUCCESSFUL!*

"SUCCESSFUL?" AT *WHAT?*

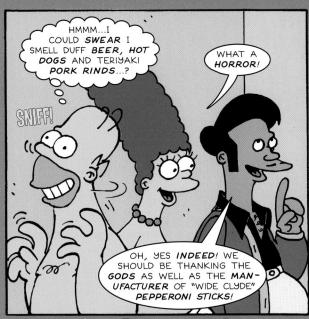

HMMM...I COULD *SWEAR* I SMELL DUFF *BEER, HOT DOGS* AND TERIYAKI *PORK RINDS...?*

SNIFF!

WHAT A *HORROR!*

OH, YES *INDEED!* WE SHOULD BE THANKING THE *GODS* AS WELL AS THE MAN-UFACTURER OF "WIDE CLYDE" PEPPERONI STICKS!

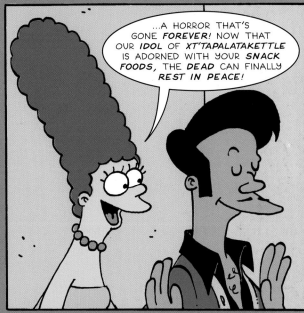

...A HORROR THAT'S GONE *FOREVER!* NOW THAT OUR *IDOL* OF XT'TAPALATAKETTLE IS ADORNED WITH YOUR *SNACK FOODS,* THE *DEAD* CAN FINALLY *REST IN PEACE!*

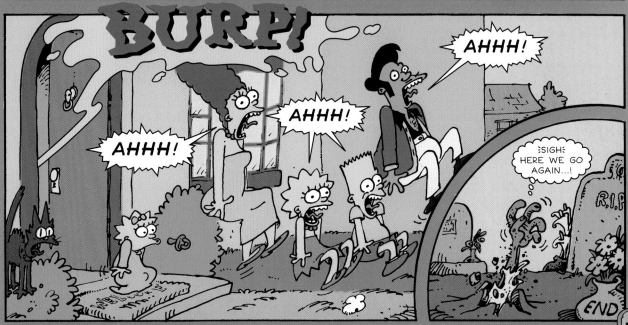

BURP!

AHHH!

AHHH!

AHHH!

≶SIGH≶ HERE WE GO AGAIN...!

R.I.P

END

119

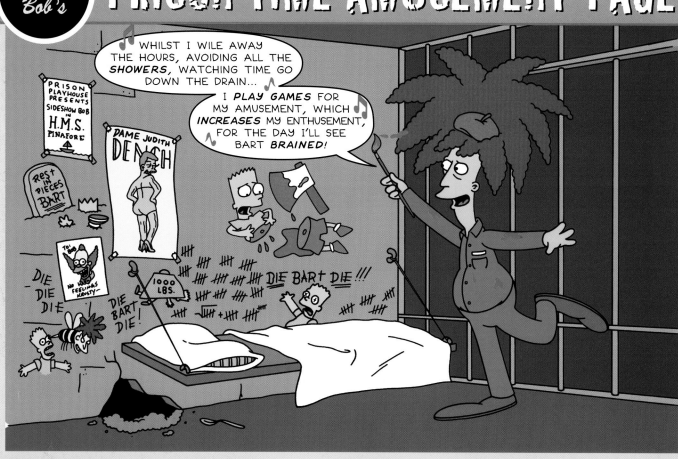

Match the Ivy League School With Its Team Mascot

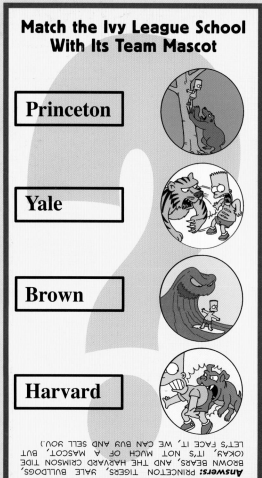

Princeton

Yale

Brown

Harvard

Answers: PRINCETON TIGERS, YALE BULLDOGS, BROWN BEARS, AND THE HARVARD CRIMSON TIDE (OKAY, IT'S NOT MUCH OF A MASCOT, BUT LET'S FACE IT, WE CAN BUY AND SELL YOU.)

STORY PROBLEM QUIZZLER!

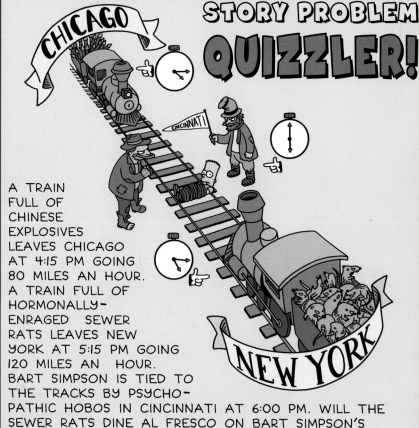

A TRAIN FULL OF CHINESE EXPLOSIVES LEAVES CHICAGO AT 4:15 PM GOING 80 MILES AN HOUR. A TRAIN FULL OF HORMONALLY-ENRAGED SEWER RATS LEAVES NEW YORK AT 5:15 PM GOING 120 MILES AN HOUR. BART SIMPSON IS TIED TO THE TRACKS BY PSYCHO-PATHIC HOBOS IN CINCINNATI AT 6:00 PM. WILL THE SEWER RATS DINE AL FRESCO ON BART SIMPSON'S PANCREAS BEFORE THE EXPLOSIVES BLAST BITS OF HIM TO EVERY CITY WITH AN NFL FRANCHISE?

Answer: THE JOY IS IN THE FINDING OUT.

Connect the Dots

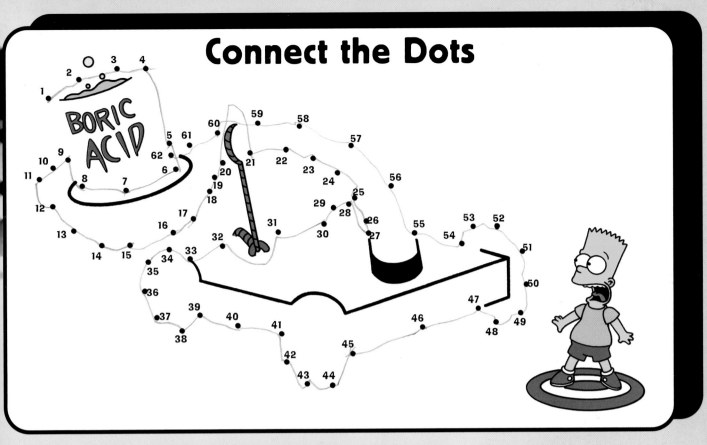

HELP BOB FIND HIS LITTLE CHUM!
(And don't forget to pick up a few important "friendship devices" along the way!)

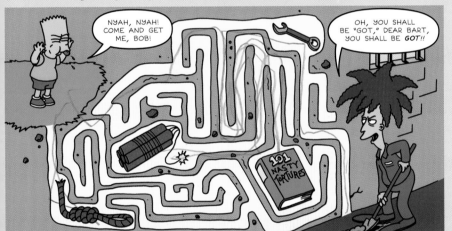

NYAH, NYAH! COME AND GET ME, BOB!

OH, YOU SHALL BE "GOT," DEAR BART, YOU SHALL BE *GOT*!!

101 NASTY TORTURES

FUN FACTS

DID YOU KNOW...

...I DON'T CARE ABOUT "FUN FACTS?"

What's Wrong With This Picture?

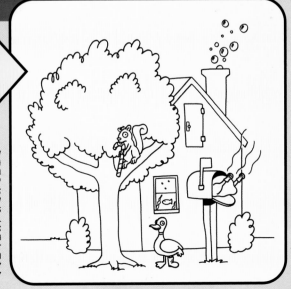

Answer: I'LL TELL YOU WHAT'S WRONG WITH THIS PICTURE! DESPITE ALL THE *ATROCITIES* BART SIMPSON HAS COMMITTED AGAINST ME, *I'M* THE ONE IN JAIL! I MEAN, REALLY, PEOPLE, WHAT KIND OF PLANET DO WE LIVE ON WHERE LITTLE JUICE BOX-SWILLING, MERRY-GO-FREAKS ARE ALLOWED TO *INCARCERATE* THEIR ELDERS! AND WHY? JUST FOR EXERCISING MY RIGHT TO BE AN *EVIL GENIUS!* DO YOU KNOW WHAT THE WORLD WOULD BE LIKE WITHOUT EVIL GENIUSES? MANITOBA! THE LOT OF YOU WOULD BE SITTING AROUND STARING AT THE ICEMAKER HOPING SOMETHING WOULD GIVE EXCITEMENT TO THE CORNFED MISERY BARGE YOU CALL A *LIFE*. WELL, I *WAS* THAT EXCITEMENT! BUT YOU WERE TOO GOOD FOR ME, OH, YES, YOU TURNED YOUR NOSES UP, TOSSED ME IN THIS PUTRESCENT *STINK HOLE* AND THREW AWAY THE KEY! BUT LIKE THE PHOENIX OF OLD I SHALL RISE AGAIN, RAINING DOWN UPON MY JAILERS A *HOST OF CATACLYSMS AND TERRORS* SO HORRIFYING EVERY MAN, WOMAN AND CHILD WILL SCREAM THE *SCREAM OF A MILLION UNHEARD SOULS!!!!* OH, AND THE DUCK IS WEARING A BOOT.

WANT A PLACE FOR A CLASSY BASH WHERE PARENTAL TROLLS CAN'T BARGE IN AND OLD THINGS UP?
JUST REMEMBER, "IF THE BRANCHES AIN'T BREAKIN', THE BOOTIES AIN'T SHAKIN'" IN...
BART SIMPSON'S ULTIMATE CREEPNIGHT TREE FORT FESTA-PALOOZA!
MEET A REAL LIVE OLD PERSON... IF YOU DARE!
PUMPKIN CARVING IS ALWAYS A TREAT!
CARVED!
NOW, LET ME SHOW YOU WHERE I PUT THE TALCUM POWDER...
BUT YOU HAVE TO BELIEVE ME, I KNOW THE OWNER!
YEAH, AND I'M TYNE DALY!
DIDN'T BRING A COSTUME? MR. BART WILL HAVE YOU STYLIN' AND PROFILIN'!
YOU TASTE LIKE MILKSHAKES!
FUN SURPRISE MAKEOUT ROOM!
MILHOUSE??!!
UH, OH...
Makeout Room
EGG CANNON!
ISN'T THIS YOUR MOM'S WEDDING DRESS?
EH. WHEN'S SHE EVER GONNA NEED IT?
CANDY ROOM!
CANDY ROOM REHAB!
I CAN SMELL THE FUTURE, AND IT IS CREAM-FILLED!
WHO WANTS TO WATCH "THE GHOST AND MRS. MUIR"?
I'D GIVE MY EYETOOTH FOR A SKITTLE!
YOU DON'T REALLY HAVE A PARTY WITHOUT AT LEAST ONE "FESTIVE" GUY!

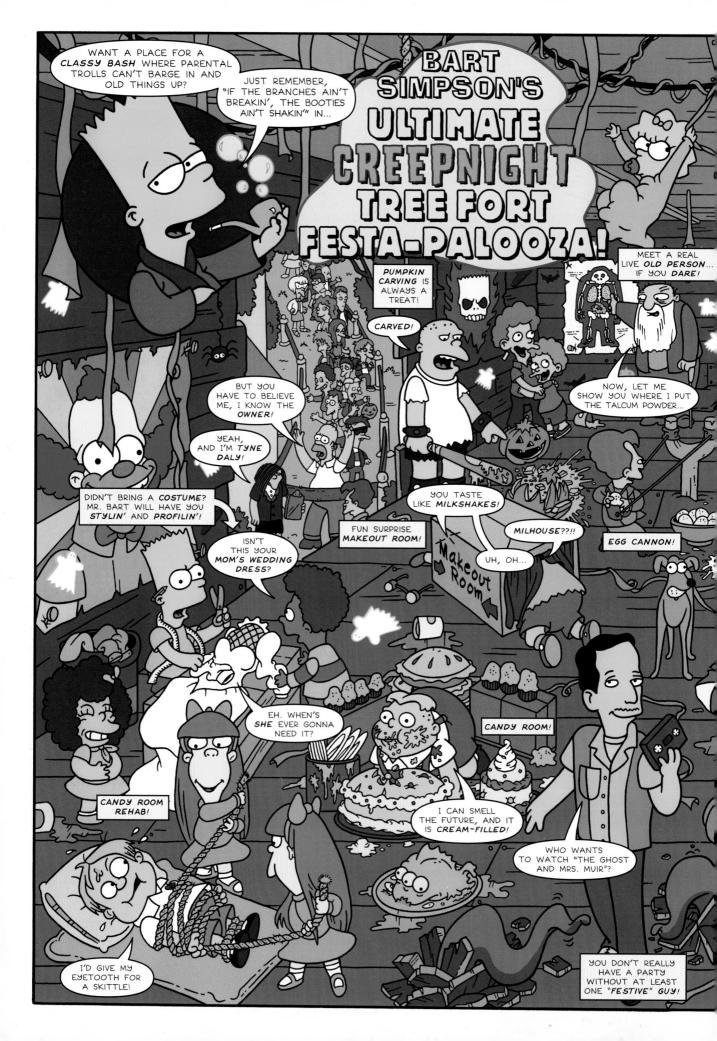

"...AND SHE'S BUY-UY-ING A STAIRWAY...TO HEAV-UH-HUHNNNNNNNN!"
LOOKING FOR THE BAND? THEY'RE IN AN ABANDONED ROOT CELLAR TWO MILES AWAY. TRUST ME, IT'S BETTER THAT WAY!
EVERYONE LOVES A PARTY CRASHER!
DON'T WORRY, LITTLE DUDETTE. I'M A FRIEND OF TITO'S.
WHO'S TITO?
EVERYONE KNOWS TITO!
REFRESHMENTS OF THE DAMNED!
DEATHCICLES!!! (FROZEN CHERRY KLOWN-AID)
SATAN'S DANDRUFF!!! (POWDERED CHERRY KLOWN-AID)
DEMON BLOOD!!! (CHERRY KLOWN-AID)
OSCAR
DUFF BEER
WITH A TREE FULL OF PARTY RATS, YOU MAY HAVE TO PAY OFF THE FIRE MARSHAL!
BILL
MATT
TERRY
7F20
YOU'RE THE FIRE MARSHAL?
I WEAR MANY HATS.
AND THE SUN SETS ON ANOTHER ROOTS ROCKIN', COPS-CALLIN', SPOOKNIGHT BART-TACULAR. BUT DON'T WORRY, I'LL LET HOMER IN. IT'S ALMOST TIME TO CLEAN UP!

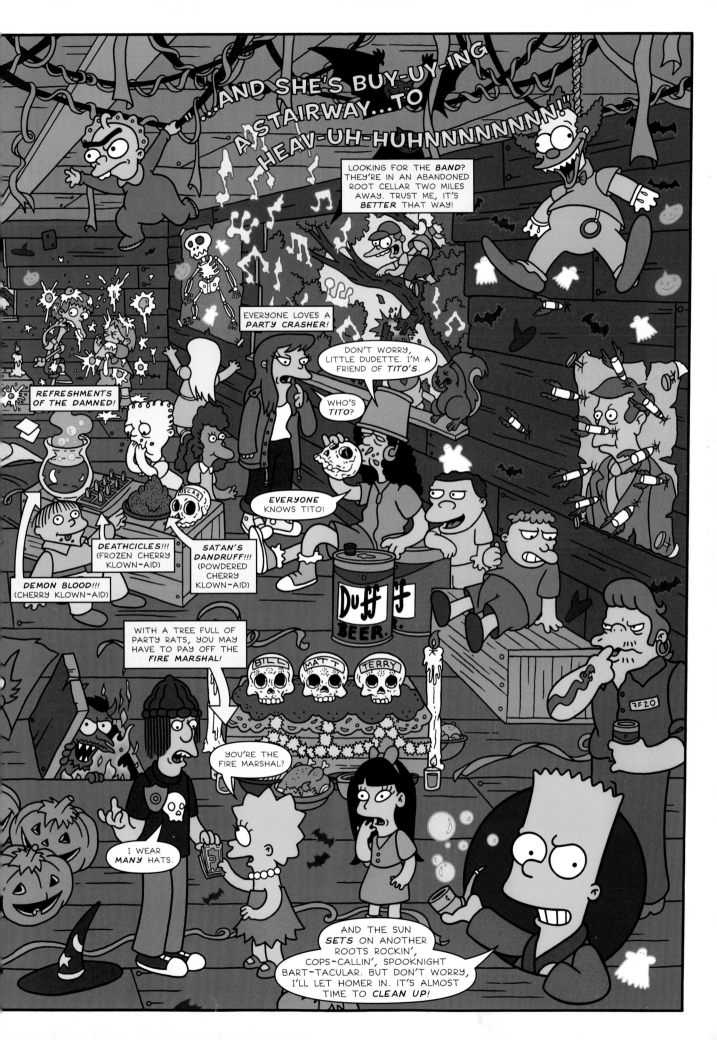

Do you like watching others feel crummy in the tummy?
Then watch Doctor Kang and Nurse Kodos in...

ERR

The extra "R" is a mistake!

The Critics Rave:

"So good, you will think you have had botched surgery, died and gone to heaven!"

— **Dr. C. Everett Koop, Former U.S. Surgeon General**

"I love the way Dr. Kang rescues humans before they become too spoiled for us to eat!"

— **Food Critic for the *Daily Rigelian***

Winner of over a million Semi-precious Awards, including:

"Highest-Paid Human Pretending to Have Trichinosis"
"Best Use of an Enema in a Drama or Variety Show"
"Most Episodes About Endangered Human Infants"
"Saddest Program Concerning Bunions"

Upcoming episodes include:

"What Is Wrong with My Human Infant?!"
"Look What Is Stuck in My Human Infant!"
and the soon to be award-winning
"The Postal Employee Is Eating My Human Infant!"

ERR will make you shed tears of interest.
As Dr. Kang says: "If you are not crying, you are not self-salting!"

DARK LISA

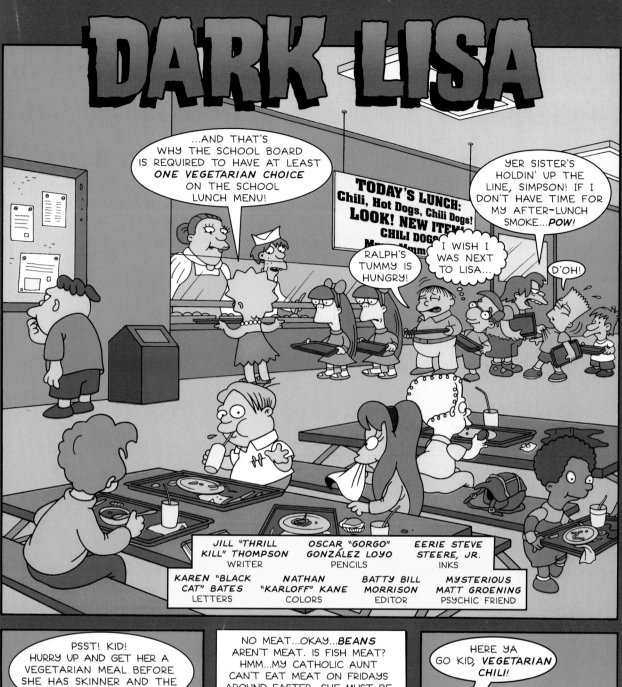

...AND THAT'S WHY THE SCHOOL BOARD IS REQUIRED TO HAVE AT LEAST *ONE VEGETARIAN CHOICE* ON THE SCHOOL LUNCH MENU!

TODAY'S LUNCH: Chili, Hot Dogs, Chili Dogs! **LOOK! NEW ITEM!** CHILI DOGS! Mmm...Mmm

RALPH'S TUMMY IS HUNGRY!

I WISH I WAS NEXT TO LISA...

YER SISTER'S HOLDIN' UP THE LINE, SIMPSON! IF I DON'T HAVE TIME FOR MY AFTER-LUNCH SMOKE...*POW!*

D'OH!

JILL "THRILL KILL" THOMPSON	OSCAR "GORGO" GONZÁLEZ LOYO	EERIE STEVE STEERE, JR.
WRITER	PENCILS	INKS

KAREN "BLACK CAT" BATES	NATHAN "KARLOFF" KANE	BATTY BILL MORRISON	MYSTERIOUS MATT GROENING
LETTERS	COLORS	EDITOR	PSYCHIC FRIEND

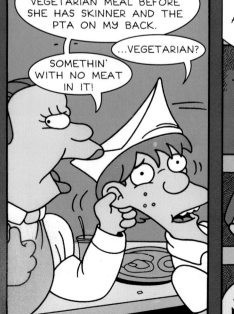

PSST! KID! HURRY UP AND GET HER A VEGETARIAN MEAL BEFORE SHE HAS SKINNER AND THE PTA ON MY BACK.

...VEGETARIAN?

SOMETHIN' WITH NO MEAT IN IT!

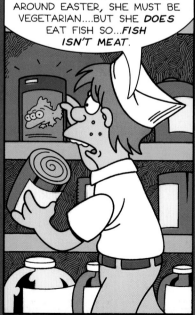

NO MEAT...OKAY...*BEANS* AREN'T MEAT. IS FISH MEAT? HMM...MY CATHOLIC AUNT CAN'T EAT MEAT ON FRIDAYS AROUND EASTER, SHE MUST BE VEGETARIAN....BUT SHE *DOES* EAT FISH SO...*FISH ISN'T MEAT.*

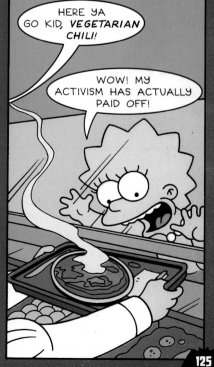

HERE YA GO KID, *VEGETARIAN CHILI!*

WOW! MY ACTIVISM HAS ACTUALLY PAID OFF!

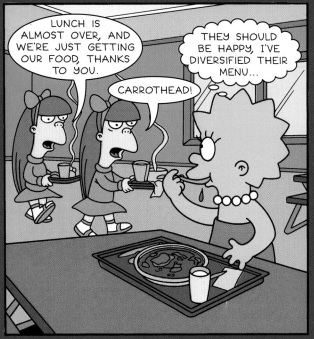

LUNCH IS ALMOST OVER, AND WE'RE JUST GETTING OUR FOOD, THANKS TO YOU.

CARROTHEAD!

THEY SHOULD BE HAPPY, I'VE DIVERSIFIED THEIR MENU...

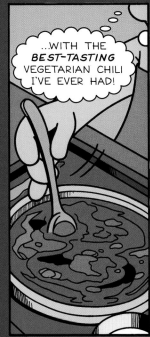

...WITH THE *BEST-TASTING* VEGETARIAN CHILI I'VE EVER HAD!

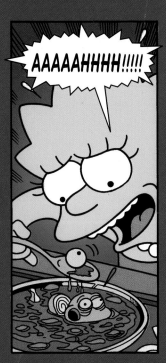

AAAAAHHHH!!!!!

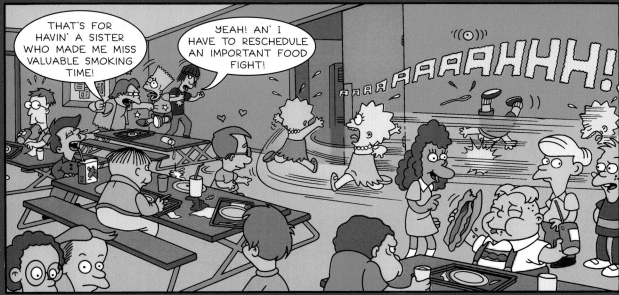

THAT'S FOR HAVIN' A SISTER WHO MADE ME MISS VALUABLE SMOKING TIME!

YEAH! AN' I HAVE TO RESCHEDULE AN IMPORTANT FOOD FIGHT!

AAAAAAAAHHHH!!

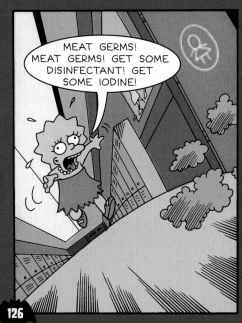

MEAT GERMS! MEAT GERMS! GET SOME DISINFECTANT! GET SOME IODINE!

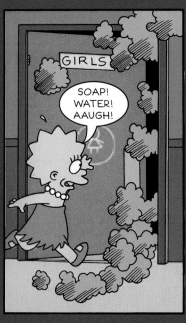

GIRLS

SOAP! WATER! AAUGH!

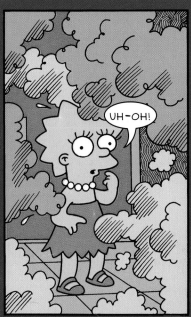

UH-OH!

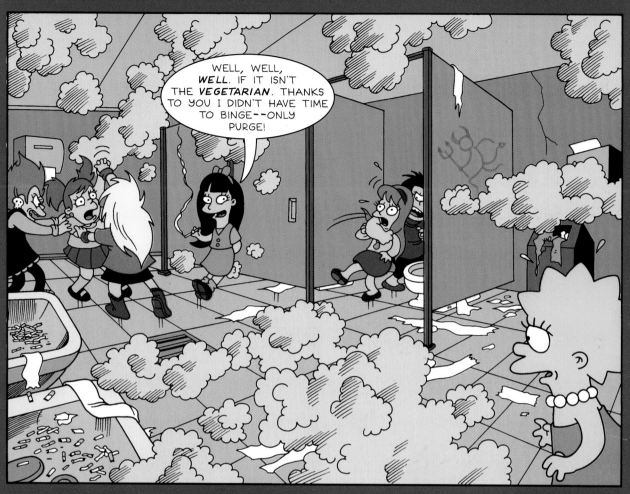

WELL, WELL, *WELL*. IF IT ISN'T THE *VEGETARIAN*. THANKS TO YOU I DIDN'T HAVE TIME TO BINGE--ONLY PURGE!

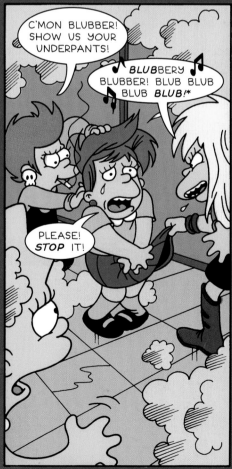

C'MON BLUBBER! SHOW US YOUR UNDERPANTS!

♪ *BLUB*BERY BLUBBER! BLUB BLUB BLUB *BLUB!**

PLEASE! *STOP* IT!

THIS IS CALLED A *SWIRLIE!* MAKE AN ANAGRAM OUT OF *THAT* SMARTY-PANTS!

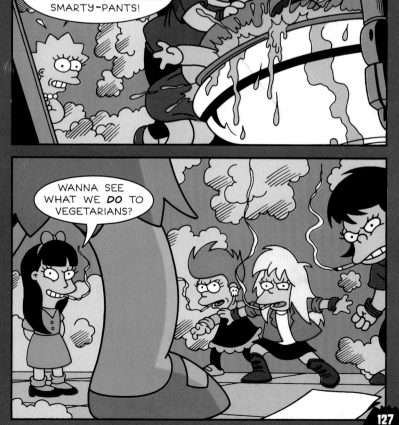

WANNA SEE WHAT WE *DO* TO VEGETARIANS?

*TO THE TUNE OF "BEAUTIFUL DREAMER"

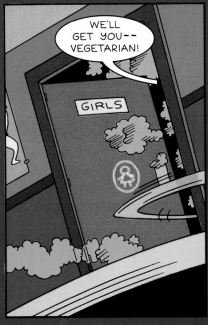

WE'LL GET YOU-- VEGETARIAN!

GIRLS

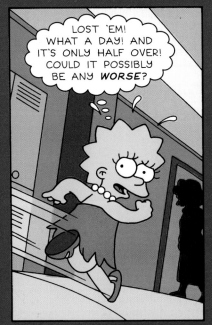

LOST 'EM! WHAT A DAY! AND IT'S ONLY HALF OVER! COULD IT POSSIBLY BE ANY WORSE?

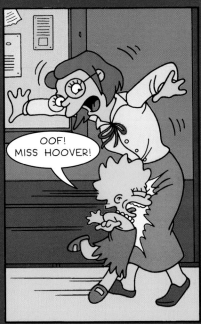

OOF! MISS HOOVER!

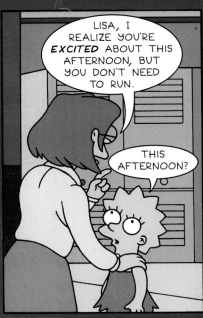

LISA, I REALIZE YOU'RE EXCITED ABOUT THIS AFTERNOON, BUT YOU DON'T NEED TO RUN.

THIS AFTERNOON?

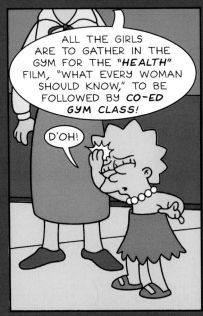

ALL THE GIRLS ARE TO GATHER IN THE GYM FOR THE "HEALTH" FILM, "WHAT EVERY WOMAN SHOULD KNOW," TO BE FOLLOWED BY CO-ED GYM CLASS!

D'OH!

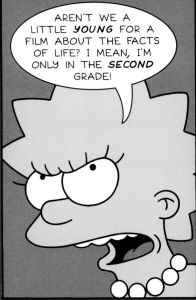

AREN'T WE A LITTLE YOUNG FOR A FILM ABOUT THE FACTS OF LIFE? I MEAN, I'M ONLY IN THE SECOND GRADE!

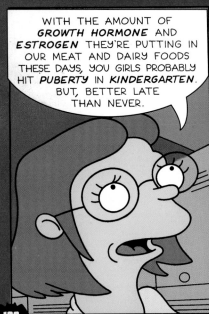

WITH THE AMOUNT OF GROWTH HORMONE AND ESTROGEN THEY'RE PUTTING IN OUR MEAT AND DAIRY FOODS THESE DAYS, YOU GIRLS PROBABLY HIT PUBERTY IN KINDERGARTEN. BUT, BETTER LATE THAN NEVER.

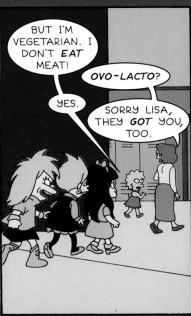

BUT I'M VEGETARIAN. I DON'T EAT MEAT!

OVO-LACTO?

YES.

SORRY LISA, THEY GOT YOU, TOO.

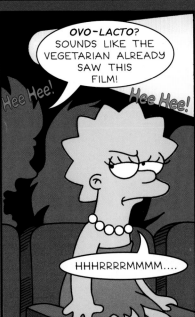

OVO-LACTO? SOUNDS LIKE THE VEGETARIAN ALREADY SAW THIS FILM!

Hee Hee!

Hee Hee!

HHHRRRRMMMM....

DON'T BLOW IT!
COME ON!
GET IT!
DROP IT!
BOP!
DORK!
MISS IT!
AWWWWWW!
AWWWWWW!
BOINK!
THAT'S FOR HAVIN' A WIMPY VEGETABLE-EATIN', CHILI-HATIN' SISTER!
THAT'S THE LAST STRAW, LISA! I'LL GET YOU FOR THIS....
LIMP LETTUCE ARMS!
CELERY HEAD!
SIGH
IT'S SUCH A RELIEF WHEN THAT HAPPENS TO SOMEONE ELSE, EH, FELLOWS?
NEIN! ITZ FUNNY!
IF I HAD POWERS LIKE RADIOACTIVE MAN, I'D SAVE YOU LISA...BUT, SORRY, I CAN'T RISK THE WEDGIE...
CHILDREN!
ALL RIGHT! BREAK IT UP! GET SHOWERED!

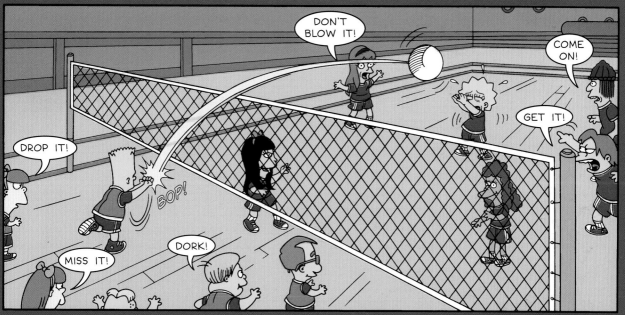

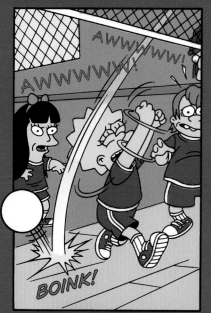

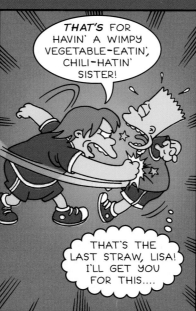

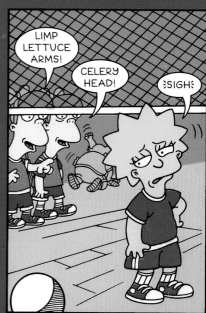

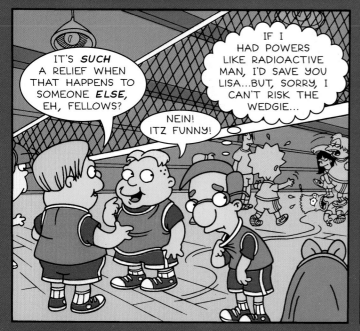

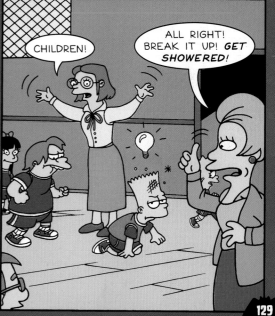

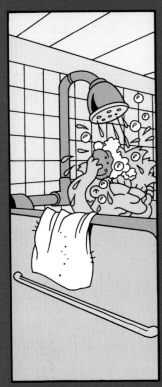

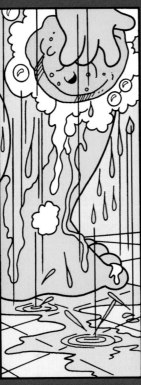

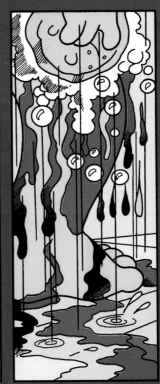

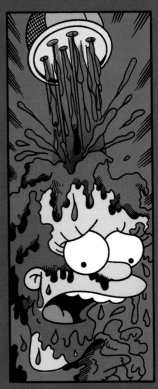

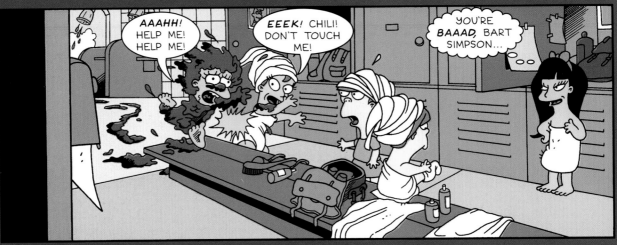

AAAHH! HELP ME! HELP ME!

EEEK! CHILI! DON'T TOUCH ME!

YOU'RE *BAAAD*, BART SIMPSON...

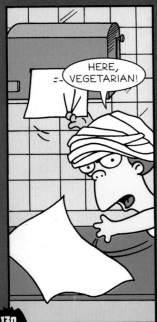

HERE, VEGETARIAN!

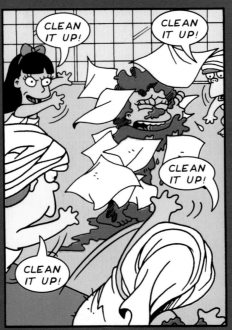

CLEAN IT UP!

CLEAN IT UP!

CLEAN IT UP!

CLEAN IT UP!

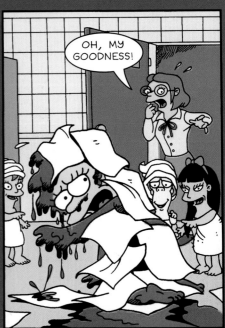

OH, MY GOODNESS!

BART, THIS IS A VERY SERIOUS OFFENSE--
SIR, THIS IS LISA SIMPSON, BART'S SISTER. YOU'VE ALREADY DEALT WITH HIM FOR HIS CHILI PRANK, REMEMBER?
AND WOULD YOU LIKE SOME OF YOUR "BART MEDICATION" BEFORE YOU SPEAK WITH SUPERINTENDENT CHALMERS?
UM... YES...OF COURSE...
I'M AFRAID IT'S REFORM SCHOOL FOR YOU, BART.
THAT'S LISA, MY NAME IS LISA! I'M A STRAIGHT "A" STUDENT!
YES, WHATEVER. IN ANY CASE, LISA. WE CAN'T HAVE YOU TRACKING PERFECTLY GOOD CHILI ALL OVER THE GIRLS' LOCKER ROOM.
I DIDN'T TRACK IT! IT WAS DUMPED ON ME!
DON'T YOU RAISE YOUR VOICE TO ME, BART.
MY NAME IS LISA!
SMASH!
CRASH!
WELL, SOMEONE'S HAD A TRYING DAY. WHY DON'T WE SEND YOU HOME EARLY...LISA.
TOUCHY!

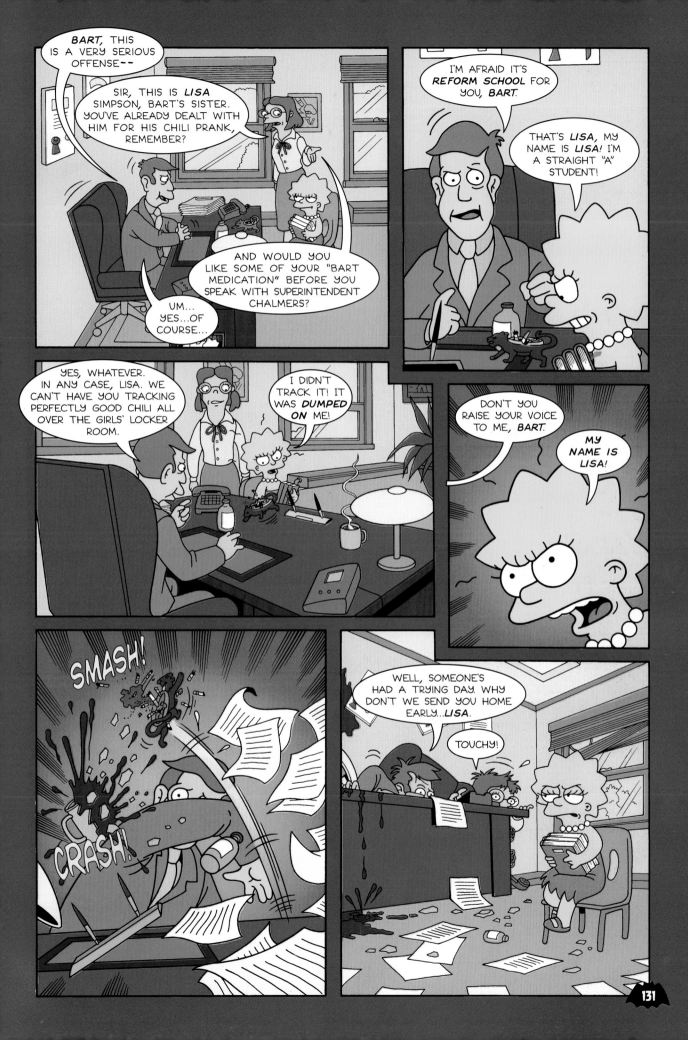

LISA VEGEMARITAN, LISA VEGEMARITAN!
HRRRRMMMM! THAT'S VEGE-TARIAN!
ALL I DID WAS THINK OF TEACHING RALPH A LESSON, AND HE HAD AN ACCIDENT...
COULD IT BE I'VE FOUND A WAY TO FOCUS MY THOUGHTS INTO PHYSICAL ACTIONS?
I'LL ASK MOM.
HURT ME, MY BIKE!
THE ANTS LOOK BIG FROM DOWN HERE!
HEY, WAIT! MOM, DAD! WHERE ARE YOU GOING?
DON'T WORRY, LISA! YOU'LL BE IN GOOD HANDS WHILE YOUR FOLKS ARE AWAY.
THEY'RE ON THEIR WAY TO TRY AND BARGAIN FOR BART'S RELEASE FROM REFORM-DIDDLY-ORM SCHOOL. AND SINCE THERE'S NO TELLING HOW LONG THAT'LL TAKE, YOU'LL BE STAYING WITH ME AT CHEZ FLANDERS! CAN'T HAVE YOU MISSING SCHOOL!
SCHOOL ISN'T MY FAVORITE PLACE RIGHT NOW, MR. FLANDERS.
SO I HEAR. THE SCHOOL CALLED ABOUT THAT WHOLE CHILI BUSINESS.
LOVE
I KNOW JUST THE THINGERINO TO END A DAY LIKE TODAY.

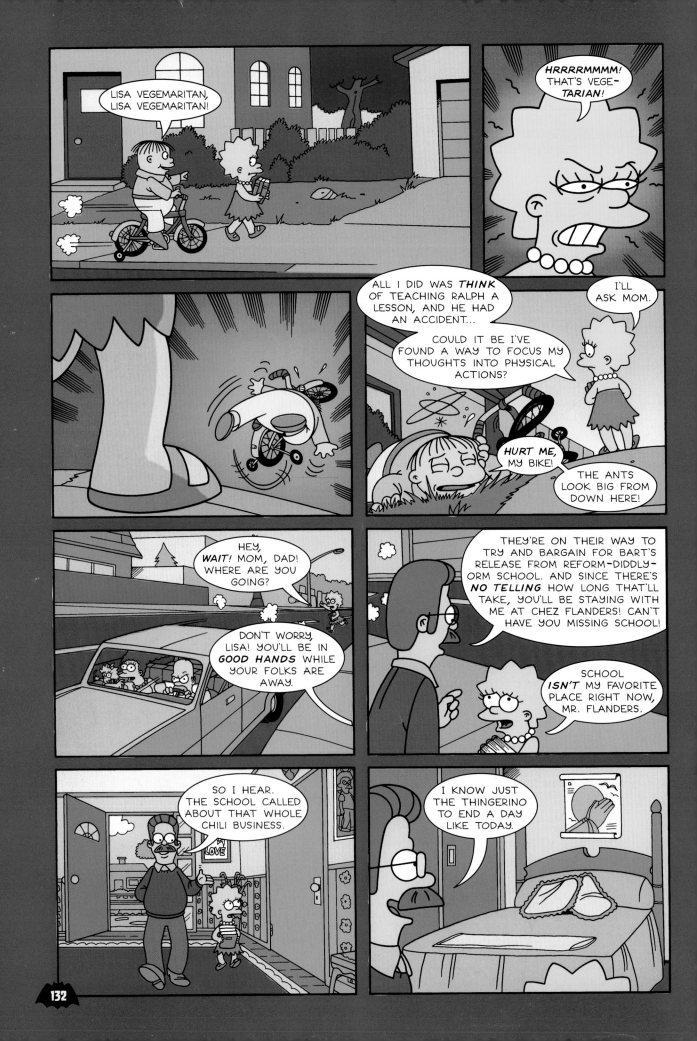

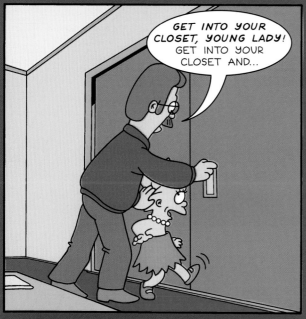

GET INTO YOUR CLOSET, YOUNG LADY! GET INTO YOUR CLOSET AND...

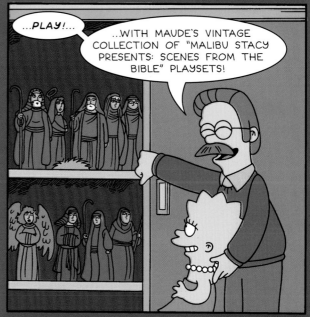

...PLAY!...

...WITH MAUDE'S VINTAGE COLLECTION OF "MALIBU STACY PRESENTS: SCENES FROM THE BIBLE" PLAYSETS!

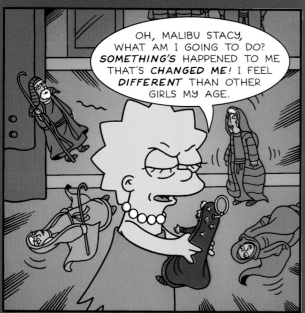

OH, MALIBU STACY, WHAT AM I GOING TO DO? SOMETHING'S HAPPENED TO ME THAT'S CHANGED ME! I FEEL DIFFERENT THAN OTHER GIRLS MY AGE.

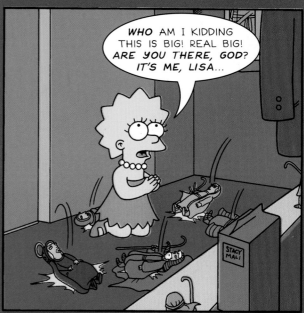

WHO AM I KIDDING THIS IS BIG! REAL BIG! ARE YOU THERE, GOD? IT'S ME, LISA...

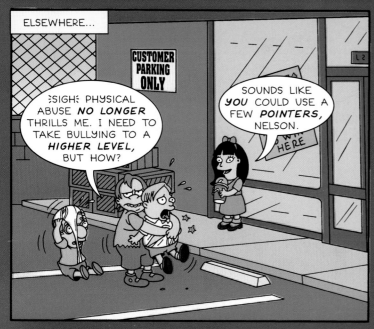

ELSEWHERE...

CUSTOMER PARKING ONLY

≤SIGH≥ PHYSICAL ABUSE NO LONGER THRILLS ME. I NEED TO TAKE BULLYING TO A HIGHER LEVEL, BUT HOW?

SOUNDS LIKE YOU COULD USE A FEW POINTERS, NELSON.

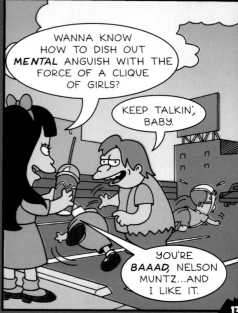

WANNA KNOW HOW TO DISH OUT MENTAL ANGUISH WITH THE FORCE OF A CLIQUE OF GIRLS?

KEEP TALKIN', BABY.

YOU'RE BAAAD, NELSON MUNTZ...AND I LIKE IT.

133

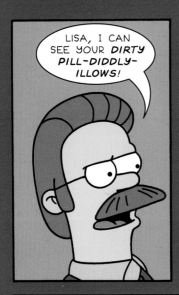

LISA, I CAN SEE YOUR *DIRTY PILL-DIDDLY-ILLOWS!*

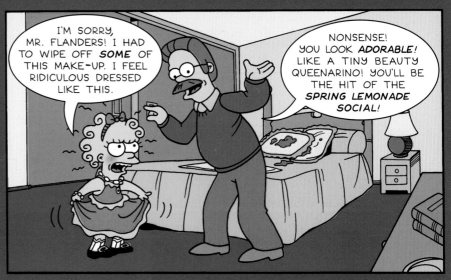

I'M SORRY, MR. FLANDERS! I HAD TO WIPE OFF *SOME* OF THIS MAKE-UP. I FEEL RIDICULOUS DRESSED LIKE THIS.

NONSENSE! YOU LOOK *ADORABLE!* LIKE A TINY BEAUTY QUEENARINO! YOU'LL BE THE HIT OF THE *SPRING LEMONADE SOCIAL!*

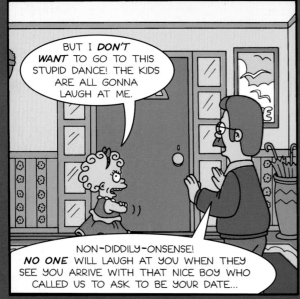

BUT I *DON'T WANT* TO GO TO THIS STUPID DANCE! THE KIDS ARE ALL GONNA LAUGH AT ME.

NON-DIDDILY-ONSENSE! *NO ONE* WILL LAUGH AT YOU WHEN THEY SEE YOU ARRIVE WITH THAT NICE BOY WHO CALLED US TO ASK TO BE YOUR DATE...

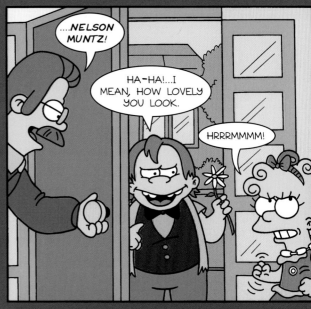

....NELSON MUNTZ!

HA-HA!...I MEAN, HOW LOVELY YOU LOOK.

HRRRMMMM!

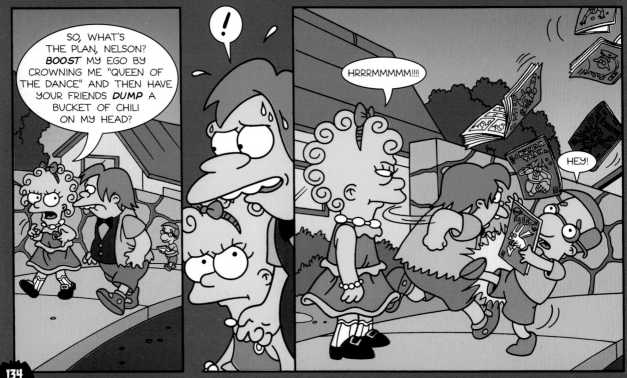

SO, WHAT'S THE PLAN, NELSON? *BOOST* MY EGO BY CROWNING ME "QUEEN OF THE DANCE" AND THEN HAVE YOUR FRIENDS *DUMP* A BUCKET OF CHILI ON MY HEAD?

!

HRRRMMMMM!!!!

HEY!

LET ME HELP YOU, MILHOUSE.
IF...IF I HAD SUPER POWERS LIKE THE HEROES IN MY COMICS, I'D TEACH THAT NELSON MUNTZ A LESSON FOR YA, LISA.
BUT I DO HAVE SUPER POWERS, MILHOUSE, AND THESE COMICS HAVE GIVEN ME AN EXCELLENT IDEA!
THE X-FRIENDS
PART 1 of 5
HAHAHAHAHA!
LISA! WAIT! YOU SHOULD READ THE REST OF THAT STORY.....
I'LL GIVE THEM ONE CHANCE TO APOLOGIZE...
SPRINGFIELD ELEMENTARY SCHOOL
GREAT ENTRANCE, "SHIRLEY DIMPLE." DON'T YOU KNOW EVERYONE CAN SEE YOUR UNDERPANTS?
SOCIAL SCHO DANCE
OKAY! THAT'S IT! THERE'S GONNA BE A CHANGE AROUND HERE. YOU WON'T BE PICKING ON THE WEAK, SCHOLARLY, OR CHUBBY ANYMORE!
LEMONADE SOCIAL SCHOOL DANCE
YAY!

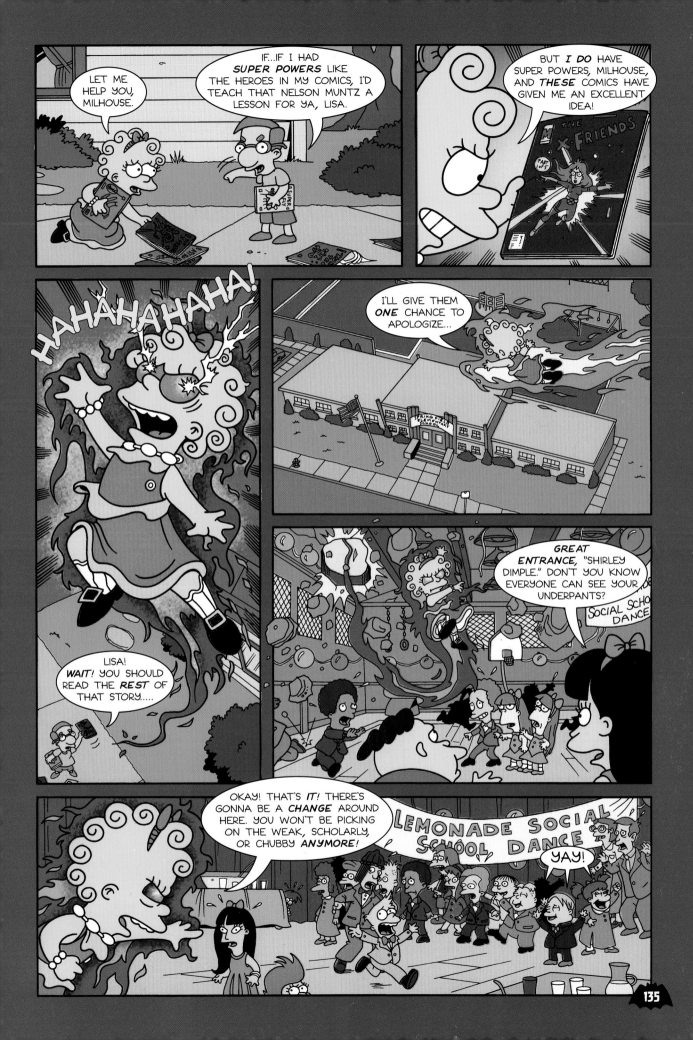

NOO! I DIDN'T CHOOSE THESE! MY MOM BUYS ALL MY CLOTHES... OH! GURK!
WE SEE LONDON, WE SEE FRANCE, WE SEE JESSICA'S UNDER-- URK!
HA HA HA HA
HAVE A TASTE OF YOUR OWN MEDICINE!
OHH! NOO! SPUTTER!
GLUB! GLUB! GLUB!
RUN YE WEE BAIRNS! AYE WAS THE GOAL TENDIN' CHAMPION ON ME FOOTBALL TE-EEEEEEEEE...
YEEEEEEE!

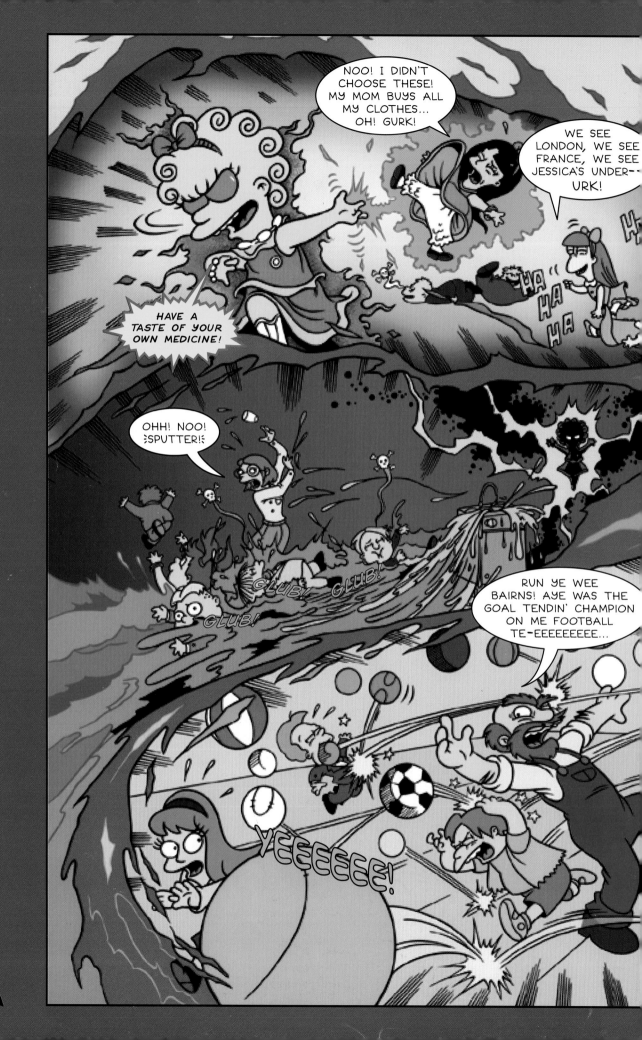

HA HA HA HA! HOW DOES IT FEEL YOU BULLIES? I SAID--HOW DOES IT FEEL?
OH, I CAN'T HEAR ANYTHING WITH ALL OF THIS POWER BUZZING IN MY EARS...I'D BETTER STOP FOR A MINUTE...

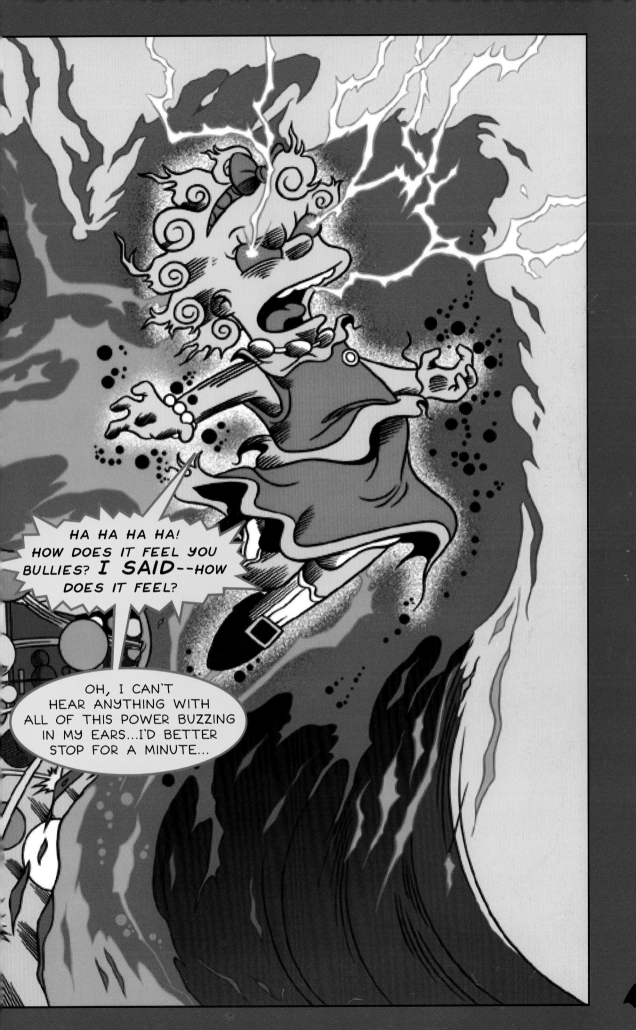

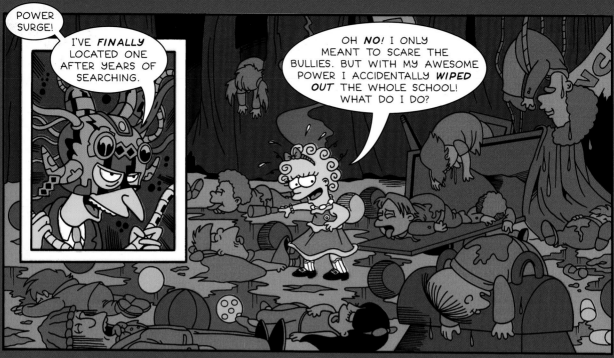

POWER SURGE!

I'VE *FINALLY* LOCATED ONE AFTER YEARS OF SEARCHING.

OH *NO!* I ONLY MEANT TO SCARE THE BULLIES. BUT WITH MY AWESOME POWER I ACCIDENTALLY *WIPED OUT* THE WHOLE SCHOOL! WHAT DO I DO?

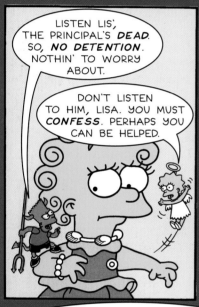

LISTEN LIS', THE PRINCIPAL'S *DEAD*. SO, *NO DETENTION*. NOTHIN' TO WORRY ABOUT.

DON'T LISTEN TO HIM, LISA. YOU MUST *CONFESS*. PERHAPS YOU CAN BE HELPED.

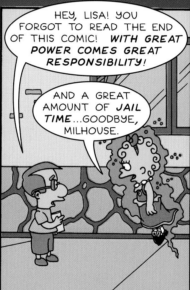

HEY, LISA! YOU FORGOT TO READ THE END OF THIS COMIC! *WITH GREAT POWER COMES GREAT RESPONSIBILITY!*

AND A GREAT AMOUNT OF *JAIL TIME*...GOODBYE, MILHOUSE.

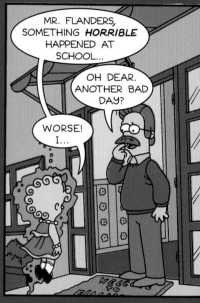

MR. FLANDERS, SOMETHING *HORRIBLE* HAPPENED AT SCHOOL...

OH DEAR. ANOTHER BAD DAY?

WORSE! I...

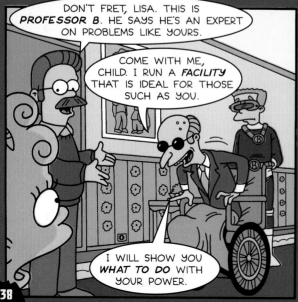

DON'T FRET, LISA. THIS IS *PROFESSOR B*. HE SAYS HE'S AN EXPERT ON PROBLEMS LIKE YOURS.

COME WITH ME, CHILD. I RUN A *FACILITY* THAT IS IDEAL FOR THOSE SUCH AS YOU.

I WILL SHOW YOU *WHAT TO DO* WITH YOUR POWER.

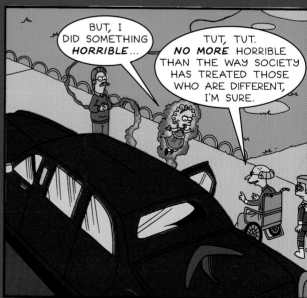

BUT, I DID SOMETHING *HORRIBLE*...

TUT, TUT. *NO MORE* HORRIBLE THAN THE WAY SOCIETY HAS TREATED THOSE WHO ARE DIFFERENT, I'M SURE.

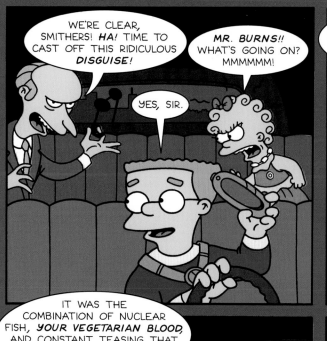

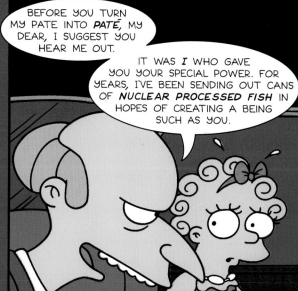

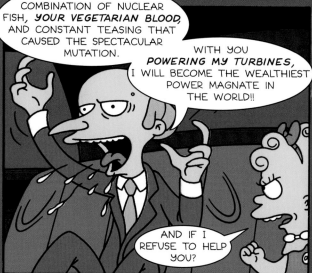

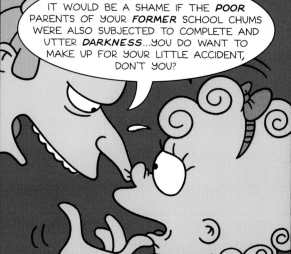

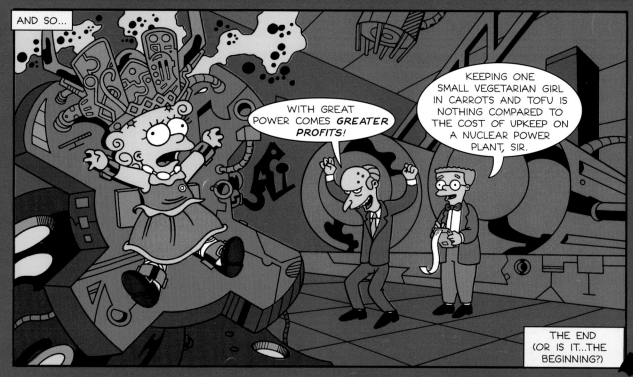

THE END
(OR IS IT...THE BEGINNING?)

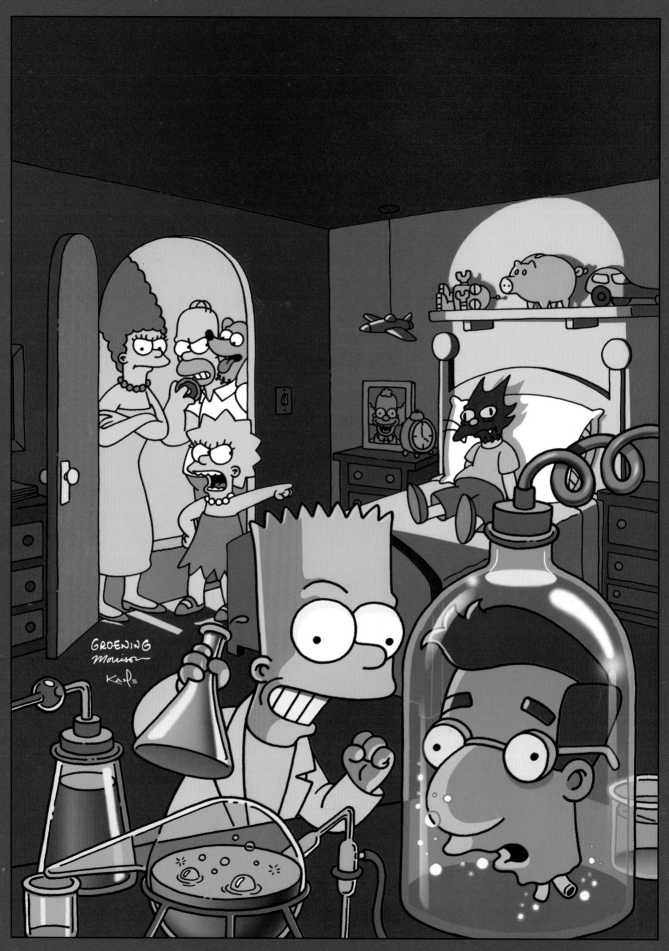

Cover Art to *Treehouse of Horror* #4

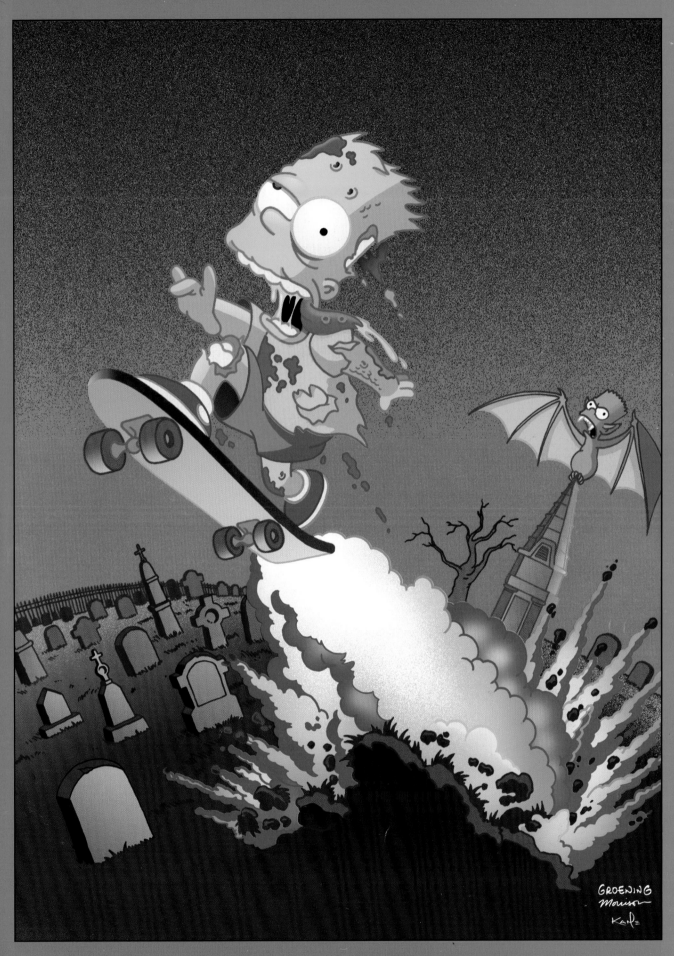

Cover Art to *Treehouse of Horror* #5

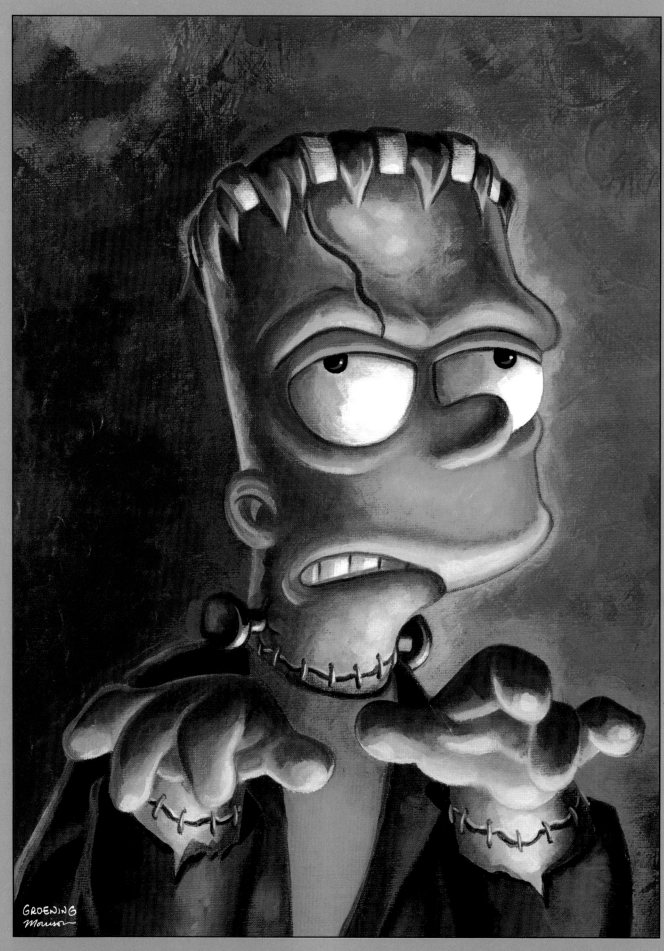

Cover Art to *Treehouse of Horror* #6

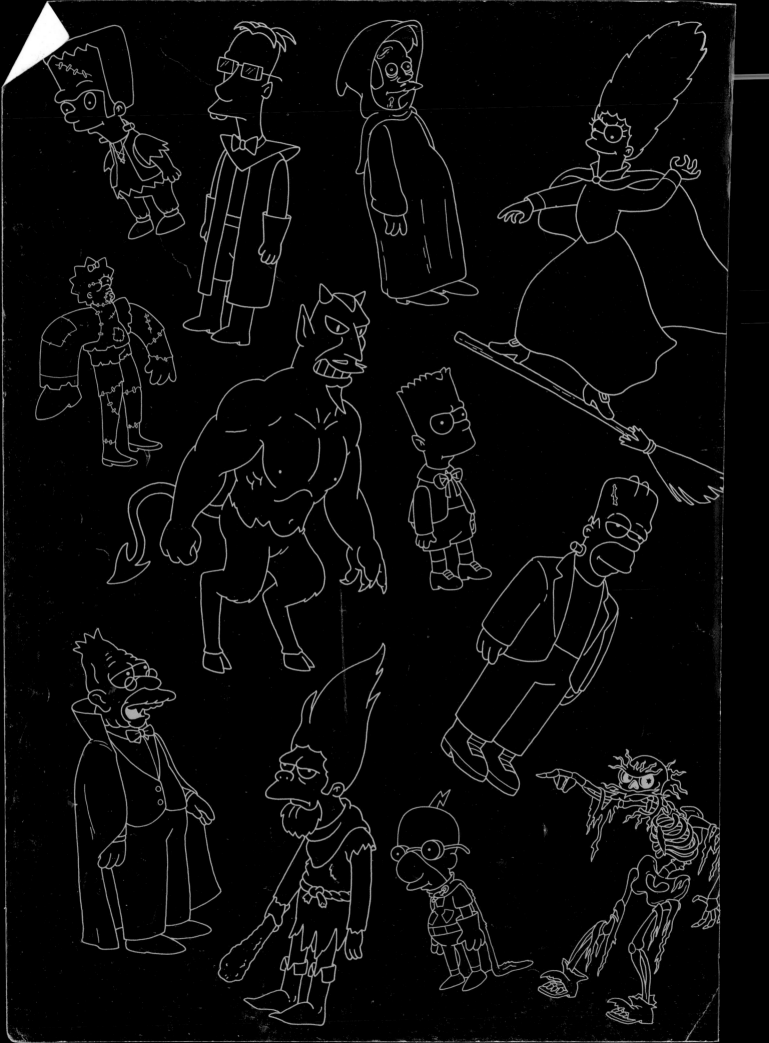